riding
the
continent

OTHER BOOKS BY
HAMILTON MACK LAING

Out with the Birds, 1913

Allan Brooks: Artist Naturalist, 1979

riding
the
continent

Hamilton Mack Laing

EDITED BY
Trevor Marc Hughes

RONSDALE PRESS

RONSDALE PRESS
3350 West 21st Avenue, Vancouver, B.C. Canada V6S 1G7
www.ronsdalepress.com

Typesetting: Julie Cochrane, in Caslon 11.5 pt on 15
Cover Design: Julie Cochrane
Cover Photo: "Laing pauses beside his Harley-Davidson." Courtesy Richard Mackie.
Paper: Ancient Forest Friendly Enviro 100 edition, 60 lb. Husky (FSC),
    100% post-consumer waste, totally chlorine-free and acid-free.

Ronsdale Press wishes to thank the following for their support of its publishing program: the Canada Council for the Arts, the Government of Canada, the British Columbia Arts Council, and the Province of British Columbia through the British Columbia Book Publishing Tax Credit program.

Library and Archives Canada Cataloguing in Publication

Laing, Hamilton M. (Hamilton Mack), 1883-1982, author
    Riding the continent / Hamilton Mack Laing; edited by Trevor Marc Hughes.

Foreword by Richard Mackie.
Afterword by the editor, Trevor Marc Hughes.
Issued in print and electronic formats.
ISBN 978-1-55380-556-4 (softcover)
ISBN 978-1-55380-557-1 (ebook) / ISBN 978-1-55380-558-8 (pdf)

    1. Laing, Hamilton M. (Hamilton Mack), 1883–1982—Travel—United States. 2. Motorcycle touring—United States. 3. Bird watching—United States. 4. United States—Description and travel. 5. Motorcyclists—Canada—Biography. 6. Naturalists—Canada—Biography. 7. Autobiographies. I. Hughes, Trevor Marc, 1972–, editor, writer of afterword. II. Mackie, Richard, 1957–, writer of foreword. III. Title.

E169.L35 2019   917.304'91   C2018-906381-5   C2018-906380-7

At Ronsdale Press we are committed to protecting the environment. To this end we are working with Canopy and printers to phase out our use of paper produced from ancient forests. This book is one step towards that goal.

Printed in Canada by Island Blue, Victoria, B.C.

to every lover of
the Winding Road

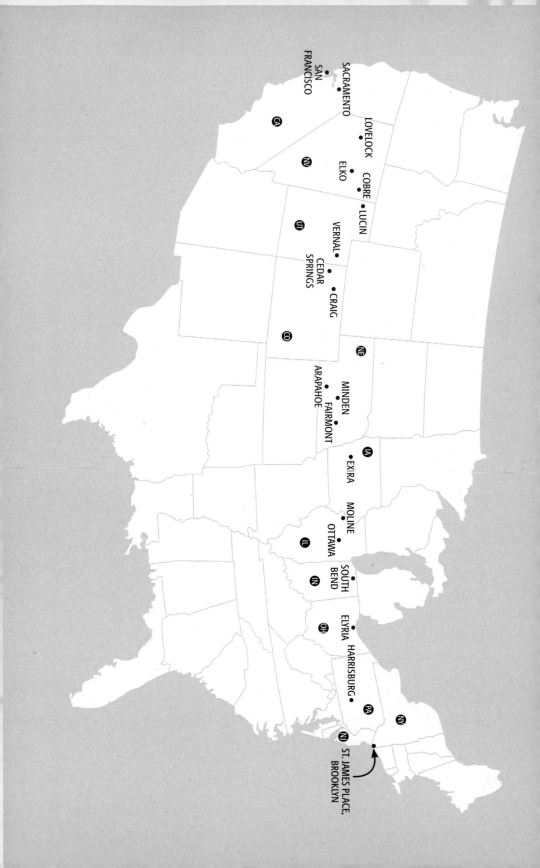

CONTENTS

FOREWORD

by Richard Mackie

IT IS A PLEASURE TO write the foreword to Mack Laing's *Riding the Continent*. It is also a pleasure to return to the subject of Laing and his motorcycle adventure. My first foray into the world of books and writing came with my biography of Laing, *Hamilton Mack Laing: Hunter-Naturalist*, published by Sono Nis Press in 1985, when I was twenty-seven. My biography of Laing was, and remains, the only survey of this remarkable naturalist's life, which spanned the century between 1883 and 1982. His career was so packed and varied that I could devote only two paragraphs to what was then his unpublished account of his motorcycle trip across the United States in 1915.

Laing used to say that he "should" have been born in Manitoba, where his older and younger siblings were born, but his parents (William Laing and Rachel Laing, née Mack) decided to visit the Mack family homestead in Hensall, Huron County, Ontario, over the winter of 1882–1883, where David Hamilton Mack Laing was born on February 6, 1883. It was a cause of considerable disappointment that he could not call himself a native Manitoban.

When he was a few months old, the Laings returned to their farm near Sainte-Anne-des-Chênes, 60 kilometres south of Winnipeg, where William — a Scot from Denny in Stirlingshire and a cousin, incidentally, of the Canadian politician Arthur Laing — had settled in 1872 in a tent walled with logs, banked with sod, and roofed with thatch. William named it Spring Bank farm, and the larger settlement of Clearsprings (today known as Clear Springs), just north of Steinbach, took its name from the three springs on the Laing farm.

Mack Laing's lifelong passions were set early at Spring Bank farm. His childhood revolved around a love of birds and his role as "official pest warden" or "game warden" of his parents' farm. He saw his first Wilson's phalaropes when he was three on a coulee at the edge of his family farm. Soon after, as "garden-warden," he trapped mice, pocket gophers, and Franklin's ground squirrels. He started using a rifle when he was eleven, shooting hawks that preyed on chickens and bringing home grouse, rabbits, and hares to his mother's kitchen.

Laing started school in 1888 when he was five and, after completing his schooling, he followed his older sister Jean into a teaching career. He entered the teacher training program at Winnipeg Collegiate Institute in 1898, aged fifteen, and graduated as a qualified teacher in October 1900, still only seventeen. He then taught at Glenora, Oak Lake, Boissevain, and Dunrea and was principal of the four-teacher school at Oak Lake from 1908 to 1911.

As a teacher, he excelled at everything he taught (except for mathematics), and he pursued his interests in the outdoors, birds, and hunting at all his teaching positions in rural Manitoba. Over the years from 1904 to 1905, he took a correspondence course from the National Press Association of the US and sold his first story, "The End of the Trail," to the *New-York Tribune* in March 1907, when he was twenty-four. The story was syndicated in the Associated Sunday magazines and proved, Laing said, that "It was more than I could earn teaching school. But I filed away the information on a shelf on my brain that I could write." A year before, in 1906, he had bought his first camera, a 4 x 5 plate glass Kodak, and he became, as he recalled, "a nature photographer."

"In 1910 I decided to change my lifestyle," he wrote, and true to his word, in June 1911, aged twenty-eight, he gave up his job as principal of Oakwood Intermediate School in order to enrol at the Pratt Institute in Brooklyn, New York. The idea and impetus came from Beverly Sharman, the mother of one of his students, Eddie Sharman, at Oak Lake.

At the Pratt, Mack found that his previous ventures in commercial writing, photography, and his deep appreciation of natural history and the Manitoba outdoors put him in good stead. Just before going to New York he had sold a story to Edward Cave, the editor of *Recreation* magazine. Soon after arriving in New York, he got to know Cave — a Canadian from Ontario — and also G.O. Shields, the former editor of *Recreation* and friend and mentor of the Manitoba naturalist and writer Ernest Thompson Seton.

Laing was soon selling articles illustrated with his own photos to both *Recreation* and *Outing* magazines, and also to a number of other American magazines, including *Field and Stream*, *Country Life in America*, and *Tall Timber*. He was regarded in New York as a Canadian nature writer. He recalled that he "earned a good deal more than pay my board." His stories were in such demand that in 1913, *Outing* published a compilation of articles on the birds of Manitoba as a book, *Out with the Birds*. A reviewer for the New York *Nation* called it "an uncommonly good book." He added, "Mr. Laing is evidently not one of those nature-students who finds it convenient to read their thoughts into the actions of animals they observe."

Laing later called his first years in New York (1911–1914) as "three of the most pleasant years of a long life." He described his time at the Pratt as "painting nudes by day and whacking a typewriter by night." The Pratt was proud of its practical, non-academic character, offering courses in everything from silversmithing to architecture. In one term alone, Mack took courses in commercial illustration, pictorial illustration, and life class.

In his New York summers, Mack returned to Manitoba and set up a camp at Oak Lake at a place he called Heart's Desire. He constructed a darkroom made of prairie sod in which to develop and print his glass plate negatives in the field. At Oak Lake he experimented with new camera techniques, wrote prolifically, and visited old friends from his years of teaching there, including the Sharmans. In the spring of 1914, he bought his first motorcycle, a 1914 Harley-Davidson, with the earnings from his outdoor articles: "In holidays I hied me away from the stifling city back to the Manitoban prairies and Oak Lake where, at my beloved Heart's Desire, I camped and spent my time with some new camera equipment making negatives of the interesting life of the marshes and wildlife generally, anything that would make an illustration of wildlife. For now I was a writer."

In the summer of 1914, Mack made his first major motorcycle expedition. He rode from New York to Manitoba as a "motorcycle-naturalist," a job description of his own invention. He also had professional reasons for returning — to apply for the job he expected as an art teacher at the Winnipeg Collegiate Institute. He made an appointment with the Provincial Superintendent of Schools, who broke it to him that, in the "filthy" pre-war depression, they were no longer hiring anyone.

Disheartened, he drove out to Oak Lake and spent the rest of the camping season there, pondering his future. He did not want to go back to rural school teaching and once again work his way up the teaching ladder to a principalship. Instead, just before the outbreak of war, in August 1914, he returned to New York for six months of postgraduate drawing and painting at the Pratt — all the while cranking out his fresh and lively illustrated stories for the New York outdoor magazines. A notable one from this last winter in New York (1914–1915) was "Gipsying on a Motorcycle: How a Greenhorn Rode from New York to Winnipeg and Enjoyed the Whole Way," published in *Outing* magazine in its summer 1915 issue and a fore-taste of things to come.

On completing his studies in 1915, Mack was in a quandary. Canada was now in the depths of war. Most of Laing's friends, con-temporaries, and former students would join up and some would die, including his best friend at the Pratt Institute, Newfoundlander Archie Ash, and his old pupil at Oak Lake, flying ace Eddie Sharman (Flight Commander John Edward Sharman, D.S.O., 1892–1917). But Laing did not yet feel he had to enlist. His parents lived in the United States, which would remain neutral until 1917, and so Laing recognized that he still had some elbow room. Moreover, he now knew that he was at a turning point in his life as to the direction he would take: art or writing:

> 1915 was a notable year in my life for another reason: I came to the Y in my way of life. Over the left branch was the sign *Art*. Over the right way there was a very different sign! *Natural History* — which really meant writing. It didn't need a judge of the Supreme Court to decide which branch I would take. Art, though I loved it, had let me down. The other branch had paid my board and tuition for the year [1914–15] and bought me another Harley-Davidson motorbike.

In the spring of 1915, he devised a very ambitious plan indeed, as the following pages show: to ride that Harley-Davidson across the United States from New York to San Francisco and then up to see his parents in Portland, Oregon, where they had retired a few years before to be near Laing's sister Nellie.

Laing would return to Canada in 1917 to join the Royal Flying Corps, later the Royal Air Force, but that is another chapter in his remarkable life — as are his expeditions through western and north-ern Canada between 1920 and 1940 as a natural history specialist with the Smithsonian Institution, the National Museum of Canada, the Dominion Parks Branch, and the Carnegie Museum, which form the basis of his contribution to science and to Canadian history. Along the way he would be naturalist on HMCS *Thiepval*'s trans-Pacific voyage to Kamchatka and Japan. He was also the naturalist on the Mt. Logan Expedition (1925), and in 1930 he worked at Jasper and Banff as the first Park Naturalist ever hired by the Dominion Parks Branch (now Parks Canada).

—◦◦◦—

I will hand you over now to Mack Laing himself, for the full and original story of his two-wheeled trip across the United States in 1915 on the unflappable "Barking Betsy."

A charcoal portrait of a young Hamilton Mack Laing, c. 1901.
(COURTESY: RICHARD MACKIE)

The Laing family in 1905 in Winnipeg, Manitoba.
Top row, left to right: Rachel Laing, Mrs. Rachel Laing, Mack Laing.
Bottom row, left to right: James Laing, William Laing, Jean Laing.
(COURTESY: RICHARD MACKIE)

Laing catches up on his studies at his parents' Clearsprings home, c. 1906.
(COURTESY: RICHARD MACKIE)

▲ Heart's Desire Camp, Oak
Lake, Manitoba, c. 1910.
Left to right: Jacob Norquay,
Mack Laing, Dr. Andrew
Alford. Here Laing spent
time developing his skills in
wildlife photography.
(COURTESY: RICHARD MACKIE)

◄ Mack Laing observing a
well-notched tree for
woodpeckers, c. 1910.
(COURTESY: RICHARD MACKIE)

Mack Laing's painting class at the Pratt Institute, Brooklyn,
New York, c. 1914 (Mack Laing seated at left).
(COURTESY: RICHARD MACKIE)

BIRD LIFE

▲ A unique use of the motorcycle
as birdwatching platform.
Ebor, Saskatchewan, 1914.
(COURTESY: RICHARD MACKIE)

◄ A sketch made by Mack Laing
between 1911 and 1915, possibly
in his commercial illustration
class at the Pratt Institute.
(COURTESY: RICHARD MACKIE)

riding
the
continent

Introduction

I AM ALMOST AFRAID to commit such an unpardonable sin. I know as well as any other man that we are notorious in our travels the world over for our ungodly haste; I know we are always in a hurry when we ought to stop and spend our time like gentlemen. Everything in the libraries is dead against me. During this six-weeks' perambulation on two wheels I once met a raw-boned farmer — and bone-headed I judged — who told me proudly that on six consecutive nights he had slept in a different political state. He was from New York State and he and his wife were touring in a light automobile. They were "seeing the country," they said. Be it understood now and forever that his viewpoint was not mine. He boasted of his speed; I am more or less ashamed of mine. But we cannot all travel slowly — on shoe-leather or with a donkey. We want to see a great deal in a short time; our intensive life demands it; and surely it is better even to just see it, than to never see it at all. The American who dies without having gazed at least once upon his mighty Rockies is to be pitied. Were it his last lingering gaze on earth, his soul must pass more easily at the sight.

For my apparent slight of the cities I humbly apologize. It is not that I love them less but rather that I love the country more. When summer clouds are in the sky I prefer to go out in the open and hobnob with old Mother Nature: "For whereso'er the highways tend, / Be sure there's nothing at the end," is good enough doctrine for me while I am on the winding highway. I dodged even Chicago by a few miles, because the Joy of the Road is not found in such places. There are many tourists — thousands now yearly take to the transcontinental trail — who en route fly from city to city taking in the movies, the musicals, the picture galleries at each stop. Theirs is a different interest. It pleases me better to see my Grant's Tomb and Statue of Liberty in a blue mountain in Pennsy, or a spire of the Rockies sculptured by the Almighty, to visit my Bronx Zoo and Smithsonian Museum in the woods and fields and plains, to see my paintings in the sunrises and sunsets of the wondrous desert West, and to hear my music in the dawn songs of the birds. If I have told too much about my birds it is only because they were my best friends of the long trail, and I cannot slight them.

If sometimes en route from coast to coast my appearance was unprepossessing, I can only beg pardon again. The Lincoln Highway was very dusty and on the plains the thunder-mills too often were very busy. Anyway, appearances often are deceiving, it is said. Though on the surface the two-wheeled little gas machine is the noisiest, least poetic and most impudent thing on the Road, I can only confess as did Pat, over his unprepossessing porker: he had to keep a pig and he liked that one. I have to travel and I move along the line of least resistance; the automobile is expensive and I prefer a motorcycle to a mule. It is quite as tractable, covers the ground infinitely faster and there is perhaps as much poetry in one as in the other.

And I travel because I cannot help it. The desire and hankering for the Road is stronger than my inhibition; the command — you may call it by what name you choose — is deep as my life-springs and will not be denied. I know that I am not alone with it. I have seen it in a thousand faces along my way: faces that yearned, but the great, in-human, devilish thing called Business had fastened an iron shackle on the owners' feet, and they stayed.

If I had not seen this yearning in my friends along the way, I would not attempt to voice this message, but I have seen it, and to my Brothers in the iron shoe, who long to go but cannot, I send my Joys of the Road.

Hamilton M. Laing
December 1915

Riding the Continent

THEY TRIED TO DISCOURAGE me, of course. They said that on such a long trip in such a short time I would shake my liver loose, that the sand fleas and mosquitoes would eat me, that if I travelled alone and slept out of doors "just anywhere," rattlesnakes would bite me and I would be held up and robbed, also that I would lose my way. They said many and divers other things of a chilly nature. It is always easier to use a dipper than to dig up facts and offer assistance, always easier to give advice on a subject about which we know nothing. As to the shaking and entomology, I could only plead a good constitution and offer the assurance that the things that were going to eat me up would encounter tough chewing.

As for the terrors of the night I assured my well-wishers that I had slept out in many and various places and never in the dark had seen anything worse looking than myself. I countered on the danger of robbery by an explanation of the merits of ABA cheques, good for face value only over my signature and added the clincher that no hand under heaven could forge mine. And as to losing my way, I had a road map, also a tongue in my head that was at least half Scotch. Such cold water, I knew, came from the well-springs of mere average human nature; in my heart I felt that the soul of every one of my comforters was gangrenous with longing. Some young lady classmates, I recall, were more honest and enthusiastic about it and asked if I would not take them too — on the carrier. Which tickled my vanity not a little.

Upon the question of motorcycle equipment I spent much time and study. To know what to leave in the ink pot is said to be the trick of writing; to know what to leave home is the critical test of the camper-out. Enough — but not too much — is the desideratum. In those three panniers had to be carried a light eating kit, a sleeping kit, a tarpaulin and groundsheet, a mending kit and shaving kit as well as the necessities in the way of extras for the machine and a big Kodak and its accessories. In my mind's eye I had made a meal by the road-side, and made my bed, torn my trousers and mended them, stopped punctures, whittled my beard and rehearsed mentally about a hundred other operations. I had gone further; I had made my bed on the floor and got into it — and said that it felt soft when it didn't — and I knew generally to almost the last ounce what ought to be included and what might be omitted.

We never realize how many things we use during the course of a day until we try some such elimination; nor quite realize how simple we can make life when we boil it down, reduce our life processes to primitive essentials. More than half the fun of an expedition or adventure consists of getting ready, in anticipation; anglers do more fishing at home than in brooks. So I did a deal of mental travelling without getting farther than the door. I had tried to follow the woods-man's rule which says: "Get together all the things you *think* you need; out of them pick the things that are absolutely necessary; then cut these things in two and take the half." My outfit weighed under forty pounds. It was arranged in three panniers: one of these was strapped upon the carrier behind the saddle; the other two hung at the sides.

▪▪▪▪▪▪ Meter 0

JUNE 23, 1915. The cock sparrow scolding his wife in the tall maple overhead seemed the only living thing on St. James Place, Brooklyn, when I adjusted the last pannier strap and stamped on the kick-starter. It was 4 a.m. Barking Betsy had been dragged out of her quarters in the garage half an hour previously. For it is well to start early, to make a good beginning. Especially it is well if one must face the traffic of Manhattan on a two-wheeled steed that is new and shiny, has a perverse tendency to wobble and is a bit shy of automobiles and trucks. The Bowery during busy hours is not a good place in which to practise two-wheeled locomotion. But the great city shorn of its streams and torrents of transport is a mild affair, a simplified edition. Hence, my early rising.

We were off. I say "we" for always I feel that the machine Betsy is more than an inanimate steed; rather a partner, a comrade of the Road, alive, and yet somehow, too, a part of me. I always address her in the feminine. In spite of her gruff voice she has very feminine traits. Anyway, it is more poetical to call her Betsy than Bill. If she had not been christened Betsy then it must have been some other sweet and euphonious female name. I confess it came near being Growling Gertrude.

I know she is alive because we often converse. True, I do most of the talking; and I have said it variously — sung to her by the hour on the smooth rolling roads, coaxed her and sympathized in the bad, petted her when she had a cough or a groan, whispered in her ear like a lover at times, and again cursed her roundly and at great length when she was perverse and wicked and threw me on my head. She surely partakes of the traits that are (said to be) feminine. No female ever was more constant yet more fickle. She can be smooth as silk one day and rough as howling Nick the very next. In spite of some of my friends, I insist on the fitness of her christening.

New York City never sleeps; it merely rests a little in the night and takes little of that. It dreams and dozes awhile, fitfully, open-eyed and is feverish to get going again in its terrible race in the dawn. Already there was a string of traffic on Manhattan Bridge, and though the fetid Bowery was quite deserted, the great markets beyond on the Hudson Riverside of the island, even this early, were hiving with truck wagons and a breakthrough toward the ferry was difficult. I had risen at 3 a.m. yet these men had far outdone me. It was a glimpse into that other half of the world's humanity about which most of us know so little — and care less. These men had toiled through the night: the drudges and owls of the human hive, toiling so that other men might eat on schedule.

The ferry churned and then hummed; the breeze was fresh on the mighty Hudson with its up- and down-stream vistas hidden as usual in the hazy distance. The Big City, with its roar that ceases neither by day nor night, fell behind, and I was glad to see it go. Jersey City and the Road lay ahead. The Road — a trail to be path-found, a clue to be unravelled across a vast continent: Coney Island on one end, the Golden Gate on the other, a picture gallery to be traversed, a motion film to be unreeled, a world of little experiences to be found — it was all in anticipation yet. And with most coveted things, anticipation is the sweeter part of the experience.

Jersey City was awake, roused, shaking itself after slumber like a great animal and settling into the harness for the day's grind. The spin across the green meadow flat beyond this city toward Newark was far more pleasant. These same verdant marsh flats were home to legions of those long-billed Jerseyites, so far-famed, so infamous, but they could not catch Betsy; and we turned into Newark and out again: the hill country, the Road lay ahead. On, on in the freshness of the morning. On toward the winding way, to the green hills and little mountains of Jersey and Pennsylvania.

"What is so rare as a day in June?" sang the poet, and I would like to add "on the Road." How sweet the scent of the fresh countryside of Jersey that now opened up before me: green land, little land, all cultivated spick and span with rural felicity in every changing scene. The air was laden with the early summer fragrance of this month of promises; the breath of green things was abroad. Somehow we must have a winter in order to feel the spring; and only city folks perhaps, by sharp contrast, can feel this smell lust of the country in its fullest. The elderberry was in white mounds of bloom by the roadsides; the red-headed woodpecker in dashing black and white and red flitted jerkily down the way; in spite of heavy rain during the night the running was good under tires; progress was a spin.

How long would such a road last, I asked myself. How similar to a road is our entire spin through life. We may see the path clearly enough to the next turn, but beyond it, only the future can reveal. As to what lies beyond the bend we can but guess. The same thought had often come to me at winter's dawn in the wood when, upon looking at a fresh deer's track, a voice seemed to whisper: "Somewhere on the end of this chain-track lies a big, five-point buck; follow it." Here in terms of the Road, I felt a similar whisper: "On the end of this road, far ahead, the waters of the Pacific are lapping; but you must follow long and unravel the clue."

Yet for a distance on this road toward Morristown, the traveller scarcely leaves the city behind. It is suburban territory mile after mile: residential, respectable, beautiful, cold, speaking of opulence. These lovely homes lie behind their trees and hedges to remind us that America has an aristocracy — if not an Order of the Garter, then an Order of the Stocking. Gold is the only open sesame to these quiet suburban retreats that are near the Great City yet out of earshot of its unceasing groaning. The oiled road from the hamlet of Maplewood to Morristown was fittingly smooth and kempt, for the road must always fit its surroundings, and to travel here was to sit and see and dream to the contented hum of the motor.

The Delaware Water Gap famous in the East for its scenic beauty lay off to the right but Schooley's Mountain was directly ahead. Betsy took this little "mountain" with a growl in her throat; but up on its slope I had to halt to hear the birds. For a field sparrow there was bubbling over with song, a towhee was trilling his inexpressibly sweet, sad strain, kingbirds were noisy and warblers were lisping from every hand. In the lovely shaded glen on the down slope I had to halt again. An ovenbird here was breaking the solemn silence of the deeper woods. For at no time or place does the symphony of the birds in the morning or evening sound so sweet as it does when I have just thrust from my ears the din of the sweating city. I could not hurry here. It is good to spend time sometimes as though it were made to be wasted.

There was a delightful little, clear-running river that wound through the countryside, and I halted on the bridge. In fact it is very hard to cross one of these rural bridges without halting halfway to pay my respects. Instead of thundering over with a furtive glance to right and left, it is much more companionable and gentlemanly to halt and dismount and lean over the railing, to look down into the clear liquid in a vain eye-search for the trout that are elsewhere, to watch the dragonflies skimming and the barn swallows daring zigzag as they catch insect dinners for the nestful of young in the mud nest up on the unpainted barn yonder. There was also evidence of a phoebe nest under this bridge to provide wonder food. I always feel better-hearted after I have hung by my mid-section on the railing for a time and pondered the clear water. Such a stream is better than a sermon — most sermons anyway.

As I ruminated thus, waiting to see if the kingfisher on the dry elm-tip downstream would not make his strike, the jingling sound of a mower out of gear came close and a farmer driving a fine grey and bay bumped upon the bridge. Good old-fashioned sound! Good old sight that stirs deeply! No such reminiscent sound or sight of boyhood days may be had at any price on Broadway. I asked:

"Hey! What is the name of this stream?"
And he said: "Whoa! This is the Musconetcong River!"
"Musky — what? Spell it?"
"M-u-s-c-o-n-e-t-c-o-n-g"

He was a big-chested chap, what is called a product of the soil, rural rusticity in every line of him, and he spelled deliberately as though I had challenged his ability. He said more too. One can say a great deal sometimes without uttering it. What he said but did not utter was: "Where do you come from, Brother, that you don't know the Musconetcong River: and where did you go to school that you can't spell it?" So I said: "Thanks. I never heard of it before. I live on the Assiniboine."

And he remained silent. "When in doubt, hold your tongue" may be a good enough motto, but it does not always serve. He would have been equally enlightened had I said that I lived on the Skyhomish.

I was rather cutting across country here and not following the main highway of the state marked as preferable on my road map. Easton, Allentown, Kutztown and Reading lay in my path and at the latter town I was to meet the state highway running toward the capital of the new state (Harrisburg).

It was a pleasant even loveable land to traverse. It was rural: that farming country of the East that is like no other; it is established, settled. There are no new fields or new fences or new buildings. They all seem to belong to a second or a third generation; to a Westerner, they give a feeling of middle age, stability, tight-fisted opulence. There is little of the rush and run of the West. Here where the harvest comes in early, it comes gradually and in patches. One man is cutting wheat while another is making clover hay and a third is cultivating. Everything is easy and well ordered; no one seems in a hurry.

It was a rolling green land of hill and hollow, with a little woods: a timber remnant, a trace to remind the retrospective visitor that pioneering here in other days meant chopping farms from the grasp of the forest. The decaying split-rail fences that remained stood like the last guard of the Days of Old. A land without waste: black and white cattle grazed upon close-cropped pastures; fields were tilled to the fences; small orchards flanked the farm buildings.

Also it was a land of birds. After crossing the Delaware into the new state at Easton, I sped out into the country again and lunched by the roadside. Sandwiches out of doors have an added tang that does not come from the mustard, when these good old birds — everybody's birds — of the countryside are at hand to sing. There were meadowlarks in the field piping jubilantly and two or three vesper sparrows that even now at noontide were singing as though in competition. Kingbirds chattered and some grackles went by and, best of all, the bobwhite sang from a field of green waving grain. I say "sang," for to me, Bob is more truly a song bird than a game bird. Perhaps this is because I never have hunted him — and never shall — but I like him better as a voice in the dawn chorus of summer than I could as a shot-riddled trophy in my game pocket in autumn, or as a browned, savoury morsel on toast at breakfast time. To me, his song is worth more than his gravy and dressing.

The first meal in camp or the first on a gipsying expedition always is doubly pleasing. This first eating under the sky while the birds sing always seems to hold more romance than the subsequent ones do. It is the dash of the unusual, the thing that in our mundane ways we are seeking daily in every field of living. It was good here to squat upon the grass and to eat and eat. That northwesterly breeze, cool after the rain, that all day had been rambling over these green knolls and fields, had carried with it an appetite.

And then it was good also to stretch out at full length and lie and just listen to the sweet voices of the country, to watch the grey and white cloud-rafts floating over — they had never floated so over the Big City — to whistle to Bobwhite, and generally tell the whole busy world to go to Kingdom Come. It is a good thing for a man's soul to be able to feel that way once in a year at least. While I was eating, an old couple on their way to town passed in a buggy. The old chap gave me a smile and nod that said plainly "I would like to be with you!" His better half, true to her nature, was much more interested in what I had to eat.

But the lure of the unending road is a call that will not be denied. On! On! Forward! is the spirit of the prompting. Which in its way is both good and evil; the call of it is the fascination that makes the game worthwhile, but it is more fitting for the rover to run easily and observingly rather than to tear through the country as though the police were on his trail. The ungodly haste of the average road-running tourist is a most unwarrantable thing. Better far for him to take it easy and spend his time like a relaxed gentleman. In which respect, be it understood, I wish my precept to be followed, rather than my example.

The noon bells and whistles of Allentown were noisy as I passed through the place and then skimmed off for Kutztown. Soon I met mud and some of the romance of the Road went out of it. I have been in Kutztown but twice, but each time I met a muddy fate; perhaps I have been unlucky. Betsy abhors mud; in it she is as sprightly on her feet as the proverbial pig on glare ice. But Nature in making out my original credit sheet, gave me a good pair of legs, even if nothing much else, and so we came through it by and by and at Reading met the main highway that connects Philadelphia and Harrisburg.

We take to the Road for experiences and we get them. Riders on two wheels have more of them, I think, and get them in shorter compass than drivers of four wheels do. But on this thirty odd miles of highway that ran out of the Capitol, there was one experience that I think every Brother of the Road would wish to avoid.

I may be all wrong about this. But a toll-road with gates and bars that can be dropped like a portcullis to break your neck for you if you are in a hurry, and a decrepit old woman or a fat and improvident old male of the species to take a three-cent fare every several miles always gives me the feeling that I have been seized by the collar, yanked out of the free institutions of America and dropped *kerplunk* somewhere in the Middle Ages.

I take mean pleasure in telling these hold-up folk, though I know they are not to blame, that they are a set of humbugs and public nuisances. It is not so much the rankle of being mulcted a cent a mile or so for the privilege of travelling a road that is not as good as many others; it is the unholy stopping and starting; the sudden breaking of our pleasant road dreams. Local folk may grow accustomed to the usage — it is said that eels grow accustomed to being skinned — but for myself, a toll-road in America is out of its place and its century. The best consolation I could offer myself here was that there were nearly four thousand miles ahead of me without another traffic obstruction of the sort.

Otherwise the late afternoon running was like the rest of the long day: a chapter of pleasure filled with that fresh keen fullness of heart that is inspired by a road that may be run carefree and untrammelled in spirit. There were no time schedules on my road map. I was feeling what a friend and lover of a two-wheeled steed once wrote to me. Letters often are eloquent for the reason that their authors did not try to write anything but to tell something.

This letter is heart-told; and because S. in speaking his heart probably told the story better than I can, I shall plagiarize him. "But who can find anything greater or more enticing than the winding road ahead, the valleys stretched out in rolling green waves dotted here and there with white houses and the spire of some little church showing; with the sun bright overhead, the wind in your face and the feeling inside of you that says: 'All's right with the world.'"

It is well for the road gipsy to begin early to cast his eye about him for a night roost. As a matter of course he always passes a number of excellent sites and is all too apt at dark to find himself in the straits of the proverbial old maid of thirty-five — the species is said to be extinct but I doubt it — and have to accept perforce a most mediocre bivouac spot, knowing sorrowfully that a dozen better spots were looked upon but coldly.

After a day on the Road I abhor night quarters within doors and so had no stomach for a camp in a Harrisburg hostelry. I have a delicate nose and after a day in the sweet air of the countryside such quarters always smell of tobacco smoke and second-hand breathings and other things. So when the sun got low I picked my campsite. It was high time, for I had been nearly fifteen hours on the Road; the meter said that I had travelled 176 miles — horrible, sacrilegious haste!

Some ten miles out of the city, a green country lane between old-fashioned rail fences turned off at right angles to the pike. A big weeping willow stood within the field and reached its drooping arms over the fence. At the sight I knew my fate, but I went on to the first

First night's camp in a green lane in Pennsylvania. (COURTESY: BCA J-01408)

farmhouse, borrowed a wash and clean-up at the well, and then returned. First camp on the long trail — what a satisfaction to strip off cap and gloves, leggings and sweater, spread the poncho and blanket and then, after pegging the tarpaulin, to sit down and write the diary to the accompaniment of the vesper sparrows singing as only these feathered little saints do in the gloaming. Not all of us can hunt big game in Hindustan, but most of us may have our little adventures and pleasures of the Road. And to be able to venture out merely to sleep under the stars and see the moon is worthwhile. But perhaps only those who know the heart hunger that comes to some natures in the City, know how really worthwhile it is.

My last waking thought, I think, was of Frat [Mack's brother, Jim]. Somewhere in North Dakota he too was making a gipsy bivouac and I wondered if the big plains mosquitoes were at this moment boring holes in him. For within a day or two he also had taken to the Road. His course from Winnipeg lay due south on the Meridian Road; out in Nebraska our trails were planned to intersect and we were to join forces. Slumber did not claim me for a time; one cannot convert city retiring hours into such early-to-bed habit all at once; and also I was feeling a trifle lonely.

▪▪▪▪▪▪ Meter 197

JUNE 24. A song sparrow is a pleasant alarm clock. When I wakened, bright daylight was abroad and one of these loveable sparrow chaps was in the big willow almost over my head, while from the fields and the nearby woods and copses came the dawn song of the birds of Pennsy. Blessings upon the man who leaves a tree or two along his fences, or plants them to harbour the feathered musicians that have so largely been robbed of their timber birthright. A thrasher voice came from the distance, meadowlarks and vesper sparrows fluted and sang in the fields and robin matins came from everywhere, while strangely enough a Canada goose honked vehemently not far away, a captive or domesticated bird I judged. Pleasant comrades of the morning these, as I straightened the kinks out of myself — the ground always is a trifle insistent for the first night or two — and set to packing my panniers. A cheery good morning from the birds is a day well begun.

The dawn was fair as birth of a summer day could be, and the hours that followed were in keeping. It was clear and cool with drifting clouds of wondrous size and colour — one of those days in which the sky makes a landscape composition wherever the traveller turns his eye over the countryside. The sky is perhaps about eight-tenths of most pictures and there are certain days made delightful to the appreciative eye on account of this. The earth partakes of the nature of the heavens; the day is full of colour delight. Such is a day for the roadrunner where a hundred new scenes meet his eye every changing hour. Because I was too busy and engrossed to try to write anything original, I put in the diary that it was a day for the gods, and I meant it.

I breakfasted hugely in the city, then chased away for Carlisle and Chambersburg. The hill country was not far ahead; the thought loaned wings to the fleeing Betsy, and she ate those level pikes at a shocking pace. Even the great bridge across the mighty Susquehanna, where the view was splendid and the cool breeze invited me to linger, had not the necessary seductiveness to halt us long. The run to Carlisle was in a southwesterly direction in a level country, and we paralleled the distant foothills of the blue Appalachians.

A town or city, like a person, makes a certain impression on us even though we make but a pleased-to-meet-you road acquaintance. Carlisle, like many other centres of this sturdy old state, appealed to me as a snug, comfortable, complete place — a town taking on a few of the grown-up airs of the city. Such towns seem neither going ahead or back; they fulfill their excuse for being by supplying the wants of the surrounding country. Everything seems well ordered. Though I know nothing of interior decoration, I can fancy the same style of curtains and the same style of furniture holding the fort in many homes as they did fifty years ago, and I fancy the kind of sermon I would hear if I halted here on Sunday forenoon and attended service.

The Western towns in their newness are different. Westerners themselves are also new; and being one of them, there was not enough sawing and hammering and road-making here for me. The Western town and townsman is always doing something, going somewhere. He may be only dreaming — of that only Western realty that is heavily mortgaged: the future. Or merely talking bombast and super-heated air, or generally going to ruin; but in any case he is full of bustle; he dreams big and talks big and goes to the devil even with enthusiasm. Carlisle is typically an eastern town.

It is easy to be misunderstood; I shall try to express the difference in other terms. On a former pilgrimage in the state, my motor developed sudden trouble and refused to carry me. I was luckily in a little town at the time so I pushed across the street to the garage, stated my case, and the repair angel, standing at the moment with a screw driver in hand said:

"Start her up."

I did so. He listened a moment, laid the tool upon the cylinder to connect plug and cylinder, front and rear, and then said:

"Missing on the front; clean your plug."

My mechanical ability was equal to it, and in a moment both cylinders were purring evenly, and as I locked the tool box I called out to him half jokingly:

"Thanks, what's the damage?"

He thought a moment and then came back in dead seriousness with:

"Oh — ten cents."

It was worth it. It was worth more, but such a thing could not happen west of the Mississippi. The Westerner would say "Forget it!" or wink inwardly to himself, take out and put back the intake valve (cleaning the dirty plug casually during the operation), spend fifteen minutes and charge a dollar. Each to his way of it. Exacting eye-for-eye honesty may be a very commendable thing; so may be a certain small amount of the Westerner's enterprise.

I passed through Carlisle early and took a roadside luncheon well down toward Chambersburg. It is characteristic of the freedom of the Road that one may make his meal indoors or out. Oh, the joy of being fancy-free over even such a prosaic thing as filling a stomach! There are those who complain of the chance-met meals that must be picked up in travelling, but I am not one of them. I can enjoy any sort of a meal if I am but hungry enough.

Variety is the spice of life here as elsewhere, and I ate under a locust tree that stood above the sod by the roadside. I found it a most enjoyable place to eat too; I was not alone and my company was not of the sort that may be bought at Delmonico's. I watched two or three buzzards circling over the fields, listened to the ever-present vesper sparrows nearby, while overhead in my locust, a field sparrow every few moments sang his lovely, clearly-whistled strain.

It was here that I made note in my diary that the roadside tree of Pennsy is the locust and the typical bird is the red-headed woodpecker. A pair of these noisy and confiding creatures had a home in the top of the telephone pole almost above me. Like the flicker, this

Mack Laing working on his Harley-Davidson underneath the locust trees of Pennsylvania. (COURTESY: BCA J-01410)

beautiful woodpecker has adapted himself to the ways of man and now finds in the telegraph and telephone poles a substitute for the dead stubs of the forest. I took delight in watching this gaudy pair feeding their young. They were a part of my meal as well as the sandwiches and cake.

I repeat that the roadside tree here is the locust; and in travelling, if we are not merely whiz-fiends, every tree species, even every tree has its story for us. That is, if we are susceptible or impressionable to Nature's wayside tales. To me the locusts are civilized and companionable; one is like another, as are most domestic things. They are comely and thrifty and prosperous like the country in which they live. The elm, I always feel, is stately and dignified, a fellow of some importance; the gnarled oak is a knight; the poplar is a guilty, nervous chattering gossip; the flowering catalpa is a half-pretty, last-rose-of-summer sort of a flirt. I cannot imagine a locust growing far out of earshot of Chanticleer's clarion. Once today I halted to photograph a locust-fringed road by a farmhouse; but though I captured the trees all right I could not get the songs of the orchard orioles that sang so clearly and jubilantly in the whispering branches.

The mountains were close now. A spur of the Blue Ridge had hovered on the north for an hour. It was intensely blue — so blue that it was purple — a mountain strangely well named. But the road aimed southwesterly and did not cut the mountain. Not till Chambersburg had been passed did we enter the hill country. And oh the loveliness of this land of blue hills and green valleys, the former wooded and wild enough, the latter, for the most part cultivated. A certain peculiar charm hovers over this land of little mountains. Every scene is full of comeliness. It is civilized and domestic when compared to the grandeur of the snow peaks of the Rockies, but it has a beautiful soul that we can all appreciate and enjoy. It is kindly and loveable. It is typical of the East and contrasts most sharply with the gaudy painted lands of the desert West. I have seen a beautiful woman without a soul; such oftentimes is the bright desert. But the hill country of Pennsy is the antithesis of this, quite the opposite sort of scenery. In terms of womankind: a comely little maiden with heaven in her manner, and I am almost sure, a country girl.

Hill-climbing began for Betsy in earnest at Cove Mountain where the road swings from the valley, enters the heavy woods and coils about the mountain side. It was quite a new world here in the cool shadows and silences of the forest. I love my Road even where it is bad, but such a one as this kindles things in me that I can never get into the notebook.

Many times I halted, not to take photos, but to stand and gaze out through the trees on some blue vista, or just to listen and to sit down on a green log and *feel* it all. To hurry over these mountain roads as some motorists do is rank sacrilege against the god of the out of doors. The fresh breath of the shady woods was upon the still air.

"Surely," says Robert Louis Stevenson, "of all smells in the world, the smell of many trees is the sweetest and most fortifying." Especially so the breath of the deciduous trees of these lowly mountains, for all of these ridges are under 2,000 feet. The higher altitudes of more ambitious mountains up where only the conifers find footing have their sharp, tangy pungency of balsam to nip the nose and fill us with high desires, but the scent of these green woods is different; it is sweet and more tender and languorous.

I have said that the woods were silent, but it was that sweet hush that is broken only by the voices of the birds. These were the lovers of still places remote from mankind. The mourning dove was there to dust on the road and to coo from perch unseen; the blue jay to cry "Stop thief!" — the only discordant note abroad; the towhee whistled "Sweet bird sin-n-n-n-g!" in that solemnly ecstatic way that towhees have in places remote and apart; a pewee called now and again; a robin that had chosen the forest rather than the farm orchard for his summer home sang of good cheer; and an ovenbird set the trees listening for the last note of his "Teacher-teacher-teacher" song. But when the saintly wood thrush sang — ah then was a stopping well justified and repaid. The wood thrush singing out of sight truly is an angel in the forest. And pity the man who cannot once or twice a year at least get into his ear and heart a little of the wild birds' songs, even such as the birds of the green woods of Pennsylvania.

But no transcontinental pilgrimage could be complete without its rattlesnake adventure, and I might as well get it over. My friends had said that the rattlers would get me, and I expected to be assaulted by these snakes in due time, but scarcely so soon. While I expected rattlers to share my bed in the Colorado desert, I had not thought of them as liable to dispute my right of way in the hills of Pennsy.

But as I rounded a turn on a stiff up-grade, a patch of sunlight lit the roadway ahead, and on it, stretched at full length, lay a big snake. I swung a trifle to the left to avoid it, but instantly I noted the figure of a man standing in the shadow of the maples beyond the creature, and guessing a dead snake, I swung back to go over it. I did not succeed for the reason that the double swerve was too much for me in such short length and because the dead reptile very adroitly yanked back the leading foot of himself out of the way of my tires. As I passed I noted that the end of his tail carried a ridgy nubbin that was erect and trembling and I am almost sure that even above the growl of the motor I heard that same tail tip singing a wicked little tune. As quickly as I knew how, I stopped, dismounted and ran back.

My friend under the tree was a young chap of twenty-odd from McConnelsburg. He carried his coat on his arm displaying a starched shirt, brand new suspenders and the most Ethiopian collar that ever, I think, went for a walk. And from the manner in which he admonished me to keep away from the snake I knew right well why he had spent a goodly part of a lovely summer day standing under a tree by the roadside. I was greatly surprised that Sir Rattler had not reached cover; he was in no hurry whatever, but his apathy was soon explained. He had just had a meal, a real full meal, and he objected to undue exercise. He would fight if he had to, he said, with many a "Bizzzz!" and a wicked lunge with his fangs showing, but he clearly preferred to sleep in the sun.

I crushed him under my heel. I know it was cruel of me and I ought to have poked him from the path, but my thirst for natural science got the better of me — my heart the better of my head, and many a better man has fallen thus — so I dissected him and held a post-mortem. I wanted to see the thing he had dined upon, though to tell the truth, when I began I did not feel certain whether the operation was to be gastric or Caesarean. However, it proved the former; the wretch had swallowed a full-grown gray squirrel! Bolted him head first, tail and all. Oh, to have seen this woods tragedy from the first, cruel though it must have appeared.

When I set out again I had a nine-ringed rattle in my shirt pocket, but I went off with the feeling that I think every hunter experiences after the game is down and bled and the chase and excitement over. Disappointment. Soon I had other things in hand, for I had come out on the top of the ridge. The road swings out of the woods upon a bald top from which a fair view of the surrounding country may be obtained. Here in mid-afternoon I halted again to play with my Kodak — and learned incidentally that my tripod, like Gilpin's bottles, was somewhere on the road behind — and to fill my eyes with the hazy blue vistas and my lungs with sweet air, to watch the southerly-drifting cloud plumes of which no two have been alike since the world began, to listen to the birds and to be restful or even indolent for a spell. For though if any one should even hint that I am lazy, I would burn with desire to have his life's blood, yet I confess it, I can waste a little time thus now and again and feel the better for it.

Here, an automobile laden with travellers whizzed past me; they did not stop upon the mountain top and I felt that they missed much. I doubt they saw the blue landscape or the solemn clouds or heard the wood thrush sing. Doubtless, though, they enjoyed the "whizzing."

McConnelsburg, the next station on the road map, lay far below in the green and blue valley, a little dotted town spread out like a portion of an aerial war map. Soon I set off down the winding mountain way. These roads had many safety signs: "Blow your horn," "Sharp curve ahead" and they were there for a purpose. The eternal vigilance that must be exercised by the traveller tends to rob him of the enjoyment of many things, but straight mountain roads are impossible and the pleasure of guiding the nicely balanced two-wheeler around such swinging curves has all the exhilaration of sweeping about on a pair of skates on a frozen stream.

I spent an hour in the little town on a still hunt for a tripod and then, with the commissary restocked, I set sail again. Toward sundown I had crossed the third range of hills (the Cove, the Tussey and Evitts ridges), and later when the shadows grew long, some five miles from Bedford in a fertile valley, I turned my steed into a fence corner below the friendly locusts. I had not hurried through the day, yet the telltale meter said Barking Betsy had made 126 miles. The thought that the flat lands were lying ahead and that I was wasting the mountains sent a pang through me, but such is the way of a man and a motor. I knew I would do the same on the morrow.

There were new bird neighbours here. As I squatted on the sod and ate with the outdoors relish of a wolf, a bluebird warbled evening song from the telephone wire, a chipping sparrow buzzed as though to interrupt a robin carol, and cedar waxwings whispered gently among the locust tops. The last minutes of afterglow light were devoted to the diary and then in the words of the beautiful little song: I had come to the end of a perfect day and there was nothing for me but the tiny friendship fire and my thoughts. But just at dusk a lad of thirteen or fourteen astride a rangy farm horse came along. He eyed my outfit and then said "Whoa!" and to me:

"Do you intend to stay there all night?"

I assured him that I did. In fact I think I implied in my tone that if he intended to the contrary he must needs requisition the services of his dad and the hired man and perhaps some of his neighbours. He seemed a little taken back but he said:

"Well I wouldn't. Do you see that telephone pole? There was a fellow killed there a couple of months ago — riding same machine as yours! That dent there was made by his lamp when he struck. We picked him up stone dead. Better come up to the house!"

The pole was only a few feet distant; I could see the deep dent in the wood. It was evident he told the truth. But I could only assure him that I had cast off shingled roofs for a season and that I felt sure that I could sleep in spite of the fact that I was on tragic ground. I did go up to the farmhouse with him, however, but an hour later when I said good night and started for my roost, I knew that the best team of horses on his father's farm could not have been bribe sufficient to induce this well-meaning lad to exchange night quarters with me. Superstition, the belief in the uncanny, dies hard in us. There are various ways and degrees of it; many of us are carrying a rabbit's foot somewhere about us.

As I returned down the road in the moonlight a voice drifted to me from afar. It was a whippoorwill, America's best-loved night-singing bird, fluting off in the distance toward the hazy mountain that was faintly visible to southward across the dim valley. Another voice took up the strain: "Whip-poor-will! Whip-poor-will!" then another and another till it became a scattering chorus of voices — voices from near and distinct, but not too distinct — and others from so far that they drifted home like echoes. Nearly a dozen seemed within earshot at once. There is magic and mystery in such a symphony of the night! As I rolled in the grey blanket and listened in the silence, the moonlit world became a fairy place unfit for the thrall of the slumber chains that grosser Nature fastens upon a man.

▪▪▪▪▪▪ Meter 323

JUNE 25. I was awakened by the dawn chorus of the birds: the June matin chorus, and with the birds, June is the month of wooing and winning, love and marriage and song. It is verily "the high tide of the year." Friends that I had not suspected during the previous evening, now burst out rapturously at sun-peeping: an alarm clock more sweet and pleasing than the most tinkly-belled product the clockmaker ever invented. A bluebird warbled in fine fettle; a wren bubbled and boiled over and rippled with a dozen songs to the minute; a goldfinch let go goodly snatches of his rollicking melody and paused only for breath. The tiny least flycatcher came near and called "Pet-it! Pet-it!" and his cousin the kingbird chattered saucily and sang a snatch of a wild strange effort that is only heard by dawn-risers. A killdeer shouted a "Hurrah!" from the pasture; a chippy sparrow buzzed as though content to be with the noisemakers even if he could not hold up his end with the musicians; Downy, the little woodpecker, drummed his noise contribution from a dry limb; and a Maryland yellow-throat, unseen but plainly heard, called aloud his "Wichity-wichity!" song from the wet hollow below the hill. There was no late slumber here by the rail fence below the locusts! I was on my way early.

There was wonderful running on these hill roads. The only jolts I noted were in the towns, but a native smoothed away the enigma by remarking that the town had to pave its own street while the state took a hand at the road. These rolling up-hill and down-dale spins were the cream of road travel. I have heard teamsters maintain stoutly that draught horses make better time over hilly roads than over level. Having an equine streak somewhere in her composition, Betsy was on her mettle and swept over the land at a rousing clip. At eight o'clock she chugged up a long, curving slope in the woods and came out upon a brow of the mountain. It was a spot that more than any other on this route compelled attention and a long stop. A signboard at hand said that here was the finest view between Pittsburgh and Philadelphia, and it was easy to believe.

Standing by the curving stone wall that trims the road, the beholder may stand and look far across the hill country of this beautiful old state. Tall trees frame the view on either hand, the mountain drops off roughly below the wall, a map of farmlands lies spread out in the distance for miles — cut off on the far horizon by hill and hill and over-cuttings in hazy blue. He sees the land as the wild goose far aloft sees it on his journeys. And even as I stood and gazed, there was a wild croak overhead and three ravens swung from the wood and winged out and down over the blue valley. I felt that I would have given empires to have been able to ride upon the back of one of these black rascals and be borne out over such a scene.

Then came an auto party to share it, and soon a Brother of the

Road leading a bicycle; I had passed him on his toiling upward way a few minutes earlier. What a mixer of men is the road, what a disdainer of ceremony and the fixities of life. In five minutes we were all acquainted and sharing sandwiches and cake and fruit. My new friend of the "push bike," as the English call it, was also headed for the far Golden Gate. He had left Boston in May. He was sweating profusely when he reached the pinnacle. The others were going to New York, and though there were no formal introductions, of course we soon knew one another.

Had I met these men on Broadway a day gone, no second glances would have been exchanged, had I accosted these ladies thus freely, who were now feeding me cake, doubtless they would have called a policeman. Here we could throw away the little stickling, starched things of life and meet the man himself. It can be done so even with propriety on the Road.

Brother H.N. Baker and I exchanged stories of the road; mine were easily told; but when I am on the trail, I like best to listen to other men anyway. I complimented him on his healthy stand of alfalfa, and enquired about the brand of hair tonic he represented. He asked me if I carried a mirror, and if so to use it myself. When I produced my tiny little reflector it was to find that though my facial crop was about a week behind his, I was quite as much an oddity; for, having ridden a few hours hatless, my forehead was now red and swelled. I had a head like a gigantic puff-ball.

The popularity of this spot on the road was told by the number of film-pack tabs and roll-film cases and lead papers and sandwich wrappings that could be seen without much decided effort. When, oh when will our tourist travellers learn to hide their unsightly rubbish and leavings and go and come and not leave a trail behind like a paper chase or the slime track of a migrant army of slugs! As H.N. Baker and I said our farewells an auto with two in it came down the turn and stopped. It carried not a single banner but it told all about itself otherwise. It had an air about it that cannot be mistaken. It had come from the town of Matrimony and was following the first few miles of the new-found trail of Married Life. It was a honeymoon car.

"Time for us to be going!" said H.N. Baker, and from the glimpse of the bride that I stole as I tore by, I hope that the newcomer had the lovely spot all to himself for at least an hour.

On to Stowestown perched on the hillside, to Ligonier, to Youngstown. A lovely country, a perfect road of hard surface, a land where skimming on two wheels becomes a joy second only to flying, a rolling, sweeping rollicking country where two sweeps, one down, one up, leave a mile behind — such was the way of this Pittsburgh pike. The miles were left in the rear as the swallow leaves them when the southerly wind blows and he sweeps northward toward his summer home. When Greensburg had been passed, I was filled with a twinge of sorrow, for I knew that the mountain roads of lovely Pennsy were to become memories, the sort we cherish of sweet and comely things. The last touch of the Alleghenies, the farewell came at Turtle Creek, and then I came into the city of steel kings, smoke and some other things.

After the carefree running and daydreaming of the open road, the congestion of traffic at 4 p.m. was disconcerting; it was almost terrifying. I did not see Pittsburgh on this trip and I am making no apologies. The Road beyond was calling. For when the fields are green and the birds singing and winding roads are beckoning, such a city is a cruel place. I can meet neither man nor Nature there. Men are not themselves there, and Nature is not at all. When I got out of that tangle of seething traffic, and upon the bridge leading over the Allegheny into the suburb of the same name, Betsy herself gave a delighted bark and I had to keep an eye on the speedometer.

Then the weatherman took a hand. Great black storm clouds rolled out of the northwest; every few moments thunder bellowed angrily. Winds came rushing, bringing dust and smoke. In my poor judgment things direful seemed portending, though at the time I was not sure that it was not merely an unusual stirring of the local atmosphere. But the rule on the Road is: go on while the going is good, and so I chugged along, hoping that when the storm broke it might cut across behind me. But it did nothing of the sort; it broke upon my head. It smote me as I was leaving the suburbs of Allegheny, and struck quick and hard. It was with difficulty that I got halted and pulled my tarpaulin out before the deluge was upon me.

I was luckily caught upon an asphalt street; so I sat in the saddle with my mobile roof overhead and watched the torrents rush below my footboards. How it pelted down! In those dirty streams below my feet I saw the story of the flood and creation and other things geographical and mythological. But I was comfortable enough; I even had a bite to eat.

To enjoy the humanity side of the situation, I had but to raise the side of the tarp. For out on the spattering, splashing pavement wet folks went by; a very great number of them were as wet as drowning kittens, and as happy. They were making wry faces as the big drops beat them; but every one of them took time to be more or less interested in the chap by the curb who carried his roof on his back like a snail. I invited some of them to come on in out of the rain.

It ceased more slowly than it began and the sun by and by made half-hearted attempts, but I told myself that I was in no hurry — although to wait inactive is one of the hardest trials of the road-lover. As I oiled up and tinkered, I had a visitor. He had the ample and well-rounded front, the ruddy face and heavy features, the grey hair and the tongue of the Teuton in his sixties; and in the hour of our acquaintance he told me much of himself and asked nothing in return. He had fought through the Franco-Prussian War, then come to America, raised a family, gained a competence and now had nothing to do and, in consequence, was unhappy. Poor old man! I realized soon that he was amusing himself by talking to me — as the unkind Frenchman said of the cat that purred against him. But I led him on. It seems well for the unhappy heart to unburden itself if only to a stranger, to find a staff however frail to lean upon.

He invited me to drink with him and I was a trifle sorry that I had to decline. Yet I could not help wondering that if this hardy old Prussian, forty years democratized — though I suspect that democracy had never got under his skin — had known that across the water my friends were in deadly grips with his friends, whether I would have been offered that glass of beer. As for the war (1915) — "Pooph! Yes, the Fatherland would win it."

Every road day has its adventure and an hour after I took up the thread of my travel again I had mine. I missed a signboard that I ought to have seen (I discovered this later), and followed a road that was abominably muddy, came down a winding hillside that was far worse, and presently stalled. Four or five times I had to dig out the mud from my clogged rear wheel: Pennsy clay, heavy, adhesive and vile. Then I came around a little turn and shouts and warning hands from a road-making gang stopped me. The boss, an oldish man, came out and berated me as though it were part of his duty. I would have to go back; did I not see the sign: ROAD CLOSED back at —? Had I no eyes in my head?"

Alas no.

There is something perverse in my composition that causes me, when a man tells me that I cannot do so and so, to want tremendously to try it. It most probably is the Scotch streak in me. I said that I would try to get through somehow. Then I got it hard and heavy! Did I not see all that fresh-laid concrete? Cross that and — well I have forgotten the particulars that were to befall me; in the aggregate it sounded a little worse than crucifixion. I would have to go back, and the sooner the better. But I couldn't. To climb up that sticky mess was impossible; it had taxed me to get down! I was surely conscious of a great deal of sympathy in the dusky faces of the labourers; fellow feeling can show through a man's skin regardless of its colour. But that cold taskmaster had no more heart in him than his concrete mixer had. He was as dry of the milk of human kindness as a wild, male Siberian tiger.

When the whistle blew, the men quit work and straggled up the miry hill, most of them walking the curbstone which already had been laid. Old Stonyheart, after idling around with the foreman and plainly itching to see the last of me and to get off to his supper, asked me what I was waiting for. I told him I was waiting for the mud to dry; whereupon, after another warning about his precious concrete, he too went up the hill.

I would have ridden or pushed along the stone curb but for the fact that bricks and other material were piled upon it at both sides. I had either to cross the forbidden ground or go back, and I could not go back. I thought I could see some semblance of concern on the face of the foreman, and turning to him I abjured him in the name of his maker to tell me if he knew how I might get over that fresh-laid concrete. He said that in ten minutes he would be gone, then I could lay boards upon it and push across. But he was not enthusiastic about it. Then suddenly he changed and said to go ahead, and he would give me a hand. He did, but I saw clearly that there was something on his mind. The boss, I surmised, and felt guilty.

At last! But a few minutes later when I had put that detestable mud a quarter of a mile behind me, I realized what the matter with Mr. Foreman was. A new barrier lay across the way. Two of them: great square timbers to remove which must have taken the united efforts of the entire gang. The road tumbled off to the railway below; the steep, wooded hillside rose above; I was wedged tighter than before. I spent half an hour here beating around like a weasel in a cage. Despair had almost claimed me when a friend came down from a little house in the wood on the hillside. There was a place back two hundred yards, he said, where wagons sometimes crossed the railway tracks. Perhaps I could also.

Back I went and found it: the hole in the wall. There were four sets of parallel rails to this road (main line to Chicago) only one had a plank crossing; to push Betsy across these rails at right angles meant that I must have help. But help is usually at hand when we stand really in need; my friend volunteered to carry a plank for me. This last precaution was most necessary, for trains thundered over these tracks every few minutes. The thought of being caught with a plank on the rails!

So Betsy with the brake tight was skidded on her head down the steep bank, pushed across the first track, the second, the third, the fourth, ridden up to the return crossing beyond the barrier and driven at the hill. She tore into that ascent of clinkers and cinders and gravel like a barking fury, lost ground, stalled, started backwards, cramped and fell on her side. Her hind wheel was over the rail; when I tried to get her off she seemed to have taken root. She was bedded in the gravel and weighed a ton. The rumble of a train somewhere did not help me much, but the odds were with me three to one and it came on another track.

Then three or four young fellows who had been spectators at a little distance changed their role to that of participants and together we heaved the befuddled Betsy up that unstable footing and upon the new concrete roadway. I was through. But before riding off, I regis-tered my vow that in future I would read *all* the signs on the road — even the chewing tobacco and gum, the lard and bacon, soap and perfumery and the thousand other things that so painfully smite the eyeball and harrow the soul of the road traveller. So farewell, old Mr. Stonyheart. And if you found any shoe-tracks, size seven and one half, in your concrete, they were probably mine. Those boards were unconscionably narrow.

The woods were dripping, the earth sodden, the hillsides trickling brown streamlets; a night out held scant attraction in that too-civilized land, and so when I came into Sewickley I prepared for an indoors bivouac. As I was leaving the garage after a short chat with the proprietor, the latter asked me where I was going and when I told him I was headed for So and So's hotel, he said: "Go upstairs here if you wish. There is a room and everything. We used to keep a night man; you are welcome if you want to use it."

I could not quite learn whether he was sorry for the hotel that must accommodate me or sorry for me, but I took him at his word. It is safe to try almost anything once, and this time I read my man correctly. The accommodation lacked nothing. The diary was entered up by electric light, and as memory ran back over the events of the preced-ing twelve hours, the days seemed a week in length. How far, far back now seemed the dawn song in the locust trees, the Road Brother with the alfalfa beard, the two lovebirds in the touring car, and those lovely blue hills and little mountains, which now were all left behind. Even the more recent old Stonyheart, his mud and his concrete, seemed safely behind, a joke mellowing with distance as wine with age. But such is the way of the spinning Road where bivouacs are a hundred miles or more apart.

▪▪▪▪▪▪ Meter 433

JUNE 26. The unholy dawn song of the alarm clock called my somewhat weary body back to realities and I set out at once. Nothing short of the apprehension that it was not raining in North Dakota and that Frat might be beating me all hollow could have set me in motion so early (4:30 a.m.) on such a soggy morning. The air was steamy, the sky half clear; the farther I went the harder the rain seemed to have fallen. The roads were of brick or stone or I should have been halted at once. As it was, when we splashed into the outskirts of Beaver Falls, Betsy was very muddy and so was I.

At a pile of construction materials by the way, I halted to enquire directions and passed a few words with the watchman. When he learned that I was heading for breakfast he said: "Want a fine place to eat? Well, listen to me; I'll tell you where to go. I eat there — best place in town. Nothing swell, you know, but good stuff."

Such a place sounded enticing to a chap in my then physical condition, external and internal, and so I took his directions, thanked him and wished him luck. It was impossible to miss the place and once in, I lacked the moral courage to seize my cap and come out. It was during that breakfast that I formulated a new road rule. An old one had stood for some time: "When in doubt, ask two men — ask three if possible." Now it was changed to: "Never believe *one* man about anything." I have happily forgotten the culinary details of that breakfast. But I do remember with intense clearness that several of my feeding comrades tossed or spat their quids under the table before they began, and they ate their porridge last.

I had lost my appetite long before I was satisfied. Doubtless it is beneficial to us now and again to partake of chop suey in Chinatown, to break doughy bannock with an Indian or to twirl vermicular, boiled macaroni with an unwashed section-gang and to learn by so doing a little of that other half of the world about which ordinarily we care so little. But the experience is not always a treasured one.

The sun now broke through and a fresh air presaged a fair day. But shortly after we said farewell to Pennsylvania and chugged over the state line, we encountered a hog-back earth road that was as untrustworthy as a greased pig and Betsy grew frivolous and evinced a desire to skate. After two close calls to muddy disaster we ended in the ditch, right side up by the grace of heaven, but satisfied. So I stood the machine on her stand, propped her safely, and went to spend an hour with a farmer and his son who were staking out a new building site by the road.

It was not a bad place to stop here out in the green fields with the woods just dimly near enough to hear a thrasher sing. While we discussed the chestnut trees — my new friend had not yet heard of the blight that had swept this noble tree from the land east of the mountains — I took auditory stock of my bird friends about the place. The song sparrows and vespers were busy with their matins, and blue-birds warbled from the telephone wires, but best of all a red-headed woodpecker family lived in the pole and the old birds were almost constantly in sight.

What a loveable companionable bird of the Road is this wood-pecker. What dashes and flirts of colour he shows ahead, what welcome he bobs from the poles and fences. How common, how noisy, how satisfied with himself and with man is he. How easily he has adapted himself to civilization. The pioneers cleared away his timber and robbed him of nest sites and drumming stubs, but man had to spread his news, the bird had to have a home, so today the red-head, like the flicker, is a tenant of the open country where timber never grew. The pickets, posts and poles of the fences and news carriers are his refuge. He is a noisy fellow but not boisterous, and he is an early riser and hard worker. I have found it poor scout-craft to camp near a telephone pole without first ascertaining if there is a hole near the top. If old Red-head has a home there, no sleep may be had nearby later than the earliest summer approach of dawn.

There was a wood beckoning from somewhat less than a mile ahead, and by and by after some wild gyrations across the back of the rounding road, we made the edge of it. I was almost glad that I could go no farther. An old-fashioned zigzag rail fence — there are few of the kind left now — lay on my right enclosing a grain field, a wooded ravine was ahead, and to the left a farm premises hidden in the wood, from sight but not from sound. The valley was full of singing birds. Every scene impresses itself upon us in some way, stirs a mood in us, and this spot I felt was farther removed from cities than any I had yet fallen upon by the way.

Every snake fence is an invitation to any man who has a trace of the boy left in him, and soon I was seated in the sun upon the topmost rail and busy with my notebook. The season of bloom was tardier here. The elderberry clumps along the roadside were quite short and stunted, almost pygmies by comparison with the big, broad-frocked, ten-foot mounds of bloom of the roads of Jersey and eastern Pennsylvania. An apple tree, unkempt and neglected, standing in the oat field back of my perch, showed still a trace of bloom. Close by the road were tangles of wild raspberry bushes holding out big promise of fruit, but I had come too early. Two locusts, still ever-present comrades of the roadside, stood nearby whispering in the morning airs, and the valley held a company of staunch old oaks.

Presently I left my perch, went down into the hollow, sat on a stone below an oak and listened. It was a bird valley, one of those rare rendezvous spots of the summer that hold the hearts of many species and make rare hours for the bird students who happen to stumble into such feathered sanctuaries. Water babbled laughingly and chattered in the trough of the ravine and song sparrows in the willow there sang in relay. Two nuthatches, rather uncommon summer friends, were noisy in the oaks and raising great to-do; blue jays were shouting

"Thief!" and the crows, their partners in nest-robbing villainy, called over the treetops.

Still, these were the harsh-voiced coarse-mannered ones, the commonality; there were also artists at hand. A towhee's sweet voice came often from the woods, a catbird sang at great length, and selfish thrasher tuned his liquid instrument, tried a measure or two and suddenly quit. A robin sang that homely, homey old song that bespeaks a brooding mate and contentment. At the wood's edge, a chippy sparrow buzzed at regular intervals while a vesper sparrow and meadowlark replied from beyond the oat-field.

Songsters indeed, yet when a solemn strain from a wood thrush floated out of the ravine shadows, it seemed that all the rest paused in deference to listen. I know I have said this before, but the man who knows not the song of the wood thrush has a corner of his soul unbroken and untilled. And as though to add the touch of the ridiculous, the juxtaposing of the sublime and the foolish that is said to be the essence of the joke, three rascally roosters at the farmyard, in the too-near distance, insisted on shoving their insistent and defiant obstreperations into the bird symphony.

When I had skimmed the cream of the possibilities of this little dale — and I knew that not many such bird valleys lay ahead on my westerly trail — I mounted again and slid down the winding wood road. Near noon on the way toward Petersburg, I halted again for a spell. It was not that we were beaten but we needed a rest. The road now lay through a hilly, rolling sweetly rural land. The hills were drying rapidly in the bright sun and were easily rideable, but the hollows almost without exception were under water: a hodgepodge of mud and soupy liquid left behind by the wagons and a few autos that had preceded us. There was no way of avoiding those hollows; they were a necessary part of that road and Betsy and I became so disreputable to the eye that respectability would not have walked on the same side of the street with us. This game of cross-purposes with the unstable roads was wearying and the sight of this deserted farm place with a well and a big, open-ended machine shed seemed an invitation to stop and go prowling.

A splash at the well was a good beginning. There is a sort of primitive pleasure about washing out of doors with unlimited water to slop about in, and here, in contrast with being covered in dried mud, the feeling of cleanliness after bathing felt tenfold gratifying. For our whole lives are matters of contrasts. We cannot appreciate the spring until we have endured the winter; a coloured sunset is thrice lovely when it follows a grey day; we cannot rightly appreciate being clean until we have been really dirty. And we were dirty.

Then I took out the tonsorial kit — the seat of the old mower made a first-rate barber's chair — and killed twenty minutes to good purpose. I doctored my magnificent sunburn, posted the diary, watched a phoebe that had a nest on a beam, listened to the orioles and the locusts outside, and then fell to musing upon the deserted house. I had built up a fascinating rustic romance over it and was in the third chapter when the story went to pieces because my hero became so entangled over two women that his case was utterly beyond my redemption, and so I quit the mower seat and went outside.

I was looking down the road to the nearby hollow where several little pigs that had strayed from home were wallowing coolly in a glorious mire, when I glanced up into the branches of a big tree close at hand. Pomona be praised! Not fifty feet distant from the building stood a great cherry tree. Within a few days it had been laden with fruit, and even now only the most accessible of the limbs had been stripped. What was more, a long ladder stood ready. I looked twice at the cherries, I confess, and three or four times at the ladder, once up and down the road and then made a run for it. The limbs were so large that I straddled out far from the trunk; the farther out they grew, the better were the cherries.

We cannot buy such a cherry feast. It is possible to buy fresh-picked fruit as fine to the palate, but we miss the setting: the whispering leaves, the sunlit vistas out over the fields, the song of the orioles, the adventure of it. And though I cannot see exactly why, I know that cherries gathered so have an extra flavour that may not be tasted when I go in to the farmhouse and buy or inveigle permission to help myself. I have tried both ways.

But the sunlit road has a voice that stirs wanderlustings and soon I was off again, riding the hills and catamaraning through the detestable hollows. At the next stop, an entry in the logbook stated that in all probability I was possessed of the dirtiest pair of shoes and leggings in Ohio. But I can claim some excuse, for to sit down by the roadside and wait for the mud to dry is one of the slowest jobs I have ever tried. Then by and by I came to Petersburg and a good stone road. Most of the mud had now dried and fallen off in the breeze stirred up by Betsy. Progress was speedy and of course uneventful, for I rode now on the flat lands. The rolling swells of the Appalachian highland were no more.

It is an old saying that one cannot have his apple and eat it. Nor can one enjoy the cream of the Road on the flat, uninteresting lands. For the privilege of running easy and fast on level pikes, a price must be paid. That price is a dearth of adventure. The diary holds but little in remembrance of this stretch of country. Youngstown fell behind in mid-afternoon; then the road went out toward Niles and turned toward Ravenna. I think I fell asleep, or at least turned into that sort of open-eyed automaton that drives machinery when control becomes habit and second nature. However that may be, I know for a fact that I wakened roughly up on the side of a bank with Betsy mostly on the top of me. All of a sudden we had encountered a little stretch of sandy, fluffy road, and Betsy had skidded entirely out of the wheel-track. Variety to be sure!

In the suburbs of Cleveland two motorcyclists overtook me, looked my outfit over, and decided that I was going somewhere and might need some help. Fraternalism of the right sort truly. They guided me through the intricacies of this far-scattered city, started me on the right road toward Elyria, said "Goodbye! You're welcome!" and roared away again. A few miles from Elyria I recognized my campsite below a fine tree near a farmhouse. But when I asked permission, the owner insisted that such a spot was no place for a man to sleep. He urged that I take the barn loft. The building he indicated was really a garage, two automobiles having displaced its former occupants. But there was hay in the loft, a door at each end stood open wide, and the place had an air of invitation. So I accepted, and I commend the judgement and hospitality of the owner.

When the telltale little meter registered its mileage for the day it showed that between this night roost and the last lay 151 miles. A continent was slipping away beneath my tires.

▪▪▪▪▪▪ Meter 584

JUNE 27. My watch said 5 a.m. and the sun was hazy and low across the fields when I turned out of the farm gate, but later in the day I discovered that I was gaining on Sol and in reality I had set out at 4 a.m. Bobwhite was calling from a grain field and a meadowlark was in tune. The air was so chill that I shivered even in my heavy sweater. The road was a cold one, for a rough and jolting road means warmth, a smooth and speedy one the reverse. I passed through two or three towns before the occupants had quit their beds.

It was a land for a speed fiend: level almost as a floor, traversed by excellent thoroughfares of brick or stone or "dirt." A "stone" road here means macadam; a "dirt" one means a grade of natural earth. The fields lay mile on mile, cut by the fences and margins, and with trees plentifully yet scatteringly planted to relieve the monotony. A small woodlot here or there still told of days of another generation, and one zigzag fence of rails stood by the roadside with a last-leaf-on-the-tree aspect to remind one that this smiling, sun-warmed land of comfortable farmsteads had seen other and harder days. It was a wonderful land to travel in.

The birds by the wayside are always a part of each day. The commonest here was the vesper sparrow that sang everywhere in the fields and dusted on the road and darted off showing the white feather. The mourning dove, too, was often routed from his bath of road dust and sent clap-clapping off, a dusty meteor, toward the woods. Quail often sang from the fields and on one occasion when I stopped in a little town for road directions, Bob's voice came clear and strong from the field margin a few yards from the back doors of the townsfolk. Bob is one of those birds that would adopt us if we would allow him. The red-headed woodpecker still bobbed his greetings from the telephone poles; and more than once I noted phoebe about a bridge where I knew that if I tarried I could find a nest.

These tree remnants that stand guard over the flat, fertile lands are most suggestive to the traveller. The locusts now had given away a good deal to others. There were elms and broad-leafed maples and oaks, a few locusts and many catalpas. The latter were in bloom. There was one that I met beside the country road in the morning so lovely that I was compelled to halt, put away my steed, and sit down to enjoy the bloom-filled sight.

The tree had a good many summers behind it, stood fully forty feet, was quite symmetrically formed, conical or rather spheroidal in shape, and from the top of its heavy foliage to the lowest green mass it was atwinkle with bloom. A few of the thousands of these blossoms had fallen and lay in the shade like a flurry of vagrant April snow-flakes. And how great and broad-skirted and full-bellied do these tree beings grow on the rich flat lands where they may stand and develop without the competition of their fellows. No shouldering of their comrades here, no fighting to the death for air, no race skyward to achieve the sunlight. Instead they grow strong-rooted, sturdy and shapely and, if we try, we may read a lesson for ourselves, perhaps from the trees.

Toward noon the road skirted a bend in a little stream that chat-tered over a stony bed through a pasture and I stopped and went down. There is no bathroom like the out-of-doors. To have a splash in the stream and a good rub, and then to loll about in the sun attired in the brand of regimentals that old Adam is said to have worn, may be a juvenile, boyish sort of pleasure, but it banishes road weariness and induces a good frame of mind. One is apt to grow sour and rabid from too constant riding in the sun.

It was on these level roads that I first took to singing as I ran. A vile habit no doubt from the standpoint of the folks who lived along the way and had perforce to listen, but was a pleasing pastime of a sort to me. A case akin to the chap who smokes bad cigars: a pleasure only to the perpetrator. And a sorry duet doubtless we made of it: Betsy's bass growl and my half-cracked tenor; and I am reminded of a passage from the essay "Walking Tours." "A little farther on," says Stevenson, "and it is like as not he will begin to sing. And well for him, supposing him to be no great master in that art, if he stumbles across no stolid peasant at a corner; for on such an occasion I scarcely know which is the more troubled, or whether it is worse to suffer the confusion of your troubadour, or the unfeigned alarm of your clown."

I met no "stolid peasants" in Ohio, but I met farmer folk and many others in autos, and I sang the hats off their heads. A man singing on the march would have been bad enough, but singing on a barking motorcycle! I read their astonishment and alarm in their faces. They felt sure there were screws loose in my upper works. But I knew that they could not catch Betsy, and so I banged away in song and pounded out a mileage.

All day my road led westerly almost straight for Chicago. Oberlin, Norwalk and Bellevue came and passed early in the day. Clyde and Freemont and Woodville followed. At the latter town, because cities and I now had so little in common, I took the westerly road for Bowling Green and Napoleon, leaving Toledo slighted off to the northward. Bryan and Edgerton were passed late in the afternoon, and then I crossed another state line, said adieu to Ohio, greetings to fair Indiana and sped on through Waterloo and Kendallville. A few miles beyond the latter centre, just as the sun was dipping, I stopped by the roadside. A great rough-barked rugged maple stood by the fence in a quiet spot; green sod lay all about its feet, and as I was road weary, I fell in love with the spot at the first glimpse. Indeed it was high time to quit; the meter said that I had travelled during the day 213 miles.

It was a perfect summer evening in the country: the country being rural Indiana. In the long twilight as I lolled on the poncho and stretched my tired limbs, a tree toad in the branches overhead sang his mystic vibrant trill, and from the topmost leaf pinnacle of the maple a field sparrow poured out his fine song upon the sleepy air. It was good to be gipsying — even alone.

■■■■■■ Meter 797

JUNE 28. The "Growff!" of a passing dog returning homeward after a night of skylarking wakened me at dawn. Sleep now was impossible, and for a few minutes I lay and listened to the birds — an orchestra of no mean pretension. I appreciated it the more as I knew that it could not last many more mornings. The air was brimful of whistle and song. Wrens were spilling over with ecstasy; bluebirds were warbling; vesper sparrows breathing up spiritual hymns from every field at hand. Old Red-Head, the ever-present, was hammering and shouting about a pole not far away, and he even had the audacity to flip over to my tree, select a dry limb near the top and rattle out a tattoo that certainly would have wakened me had I been sleeping. From the wood over in the pasture, crows were calling and a family of the black young scalawags were very noisy. Breakfast was evidently not forthcoming to their fancy, and as usual with them, they were raising an unholy din about it.

A blue jay there added his unharmonious yell and I judged from his tone and remarks that he had discovered an owl and was speaking his mind without reserve as he always does upon making such a discovery. More pleasant, however, was the voice of the red-eyed vireo, and as he tuned his throat with the first notes of his sermon — he has been well called the preacher — his forceful exclamations and interrogations in melody drifted across the opening, faintly yet distinctly.

Up and away: the early morning is the time to ride. The world then seems fresh, reborn. Before the sun has dried the air, it is laden with the moist outbreathings of the night: the breath of living green things. The hollows, the hillsides, the woods, the fields each then give off a different aroma. Oh, to have a nose with the keenness of the bird dog's or bee's to catch and identify and interpret the scents of the countryside! Yet even with my blunted olfactory, such as it is, I can always catch the breath of clover or of timothy, or new-cut or cocked hay or ripening grain or the scent of cattle that chew cud or of the hot milk that sings in the pail before the quick strokes of the milkers. Truly the morning is the time for a good nose. What is more: Betsy herself always pulls more willingly in the cool of the early day.

Ligonier and Elkhart slipped behind; a river or two (the St. Joseph and Elkhart) made a little diversion in these flat lands, and toward noon I came to a big farmhouse flanked by a wide cherry orchard. I saw red masses of beaming fruit and two women and a man busy picking, and suddenly I developed an uncertainty over my route and I went in to enquire. Of course they told me to help myself at those burdened trees, but the cherries proved rather a fraud and delusion. Those Early Richmonds were better to the eye than the palate, and though I started in with the will to consume about a bushel, I fell far short of it. Although that tart fruit juice was wine without headiness, it at least banished road dust and all tiredness, and when we popped off again upon good gravel roads it was with a new perspective upon life, and Indiana cherries.

Roads of hard gravel of themselves induce a complacent and satisfied frame of mind in the man who runs on tires. These were mostly good roads, well hammered down, solid. Such roads have a song that they sing below rubber tires. The latter grip them firmly; the wheel touches the earth at few points; it runs on secure footing, on spiked shoes. There were some stretches of loose gravel encountered too, but I shall hurry over even the recollection. Such a thoroughfare in language of the Road is "skiddy." A skidding two-wheeled machine may be expressed in terms of skating. The motorcycle is balanced on two points and so is a skater, and the slithering (to use a Scotism) gas cart, with its wheels at sixes and sevens in the loose gravel, produces in the rider the same sense of insecurity that is felt in the skater when suddenly he finds both feet in the air at once.

Such a bit of loose road is as two-faced as an elder of the church. It is far worse: it is friend one minute and a downright foe the next, and events happen with the startling celerity of a Russian revolution. But worse even than pockets of loose gravel in an otherwise good road, was the long stretch of broken stones we encountered on the way leading into La Porte. A road construction-gang was at work there; such men are angels, I know, but they are wondrously disguised.

It was hot toward noon, really dry, summery inland heat, and I realized that I was within the corn belt. At noon I rested and lunched below two big black walnut trees. By comparison with the hot blast rising from the sun-baked road, the shadows were cool. It was a fine place to spend an hour, to be an irresponsible idler and not feel constrained to make apologies to anybody — to stretch out on the sod, to look off across the rounding green land of corn field and comfort, and to listen to the irrepressible vesper sparrows and the squeak and ripple of a warbling vireo in the branches overhead. Also to cause a tremendous concern and worry in the farm dog that lived a hundred yards up the road. He simply could not make out my species at all. Dogs are quite a large part of a journey. I always feel that I know the sort of people who live in a countryside by the behaviour of the dogs along the way.

In a garage in the city of South Bend where I stopped to annex some road information, I met a German doctor. At least I put him down as that, for his professional, pointed beard, his well-preserved hands, his exaggerated waistband and his patronizing way all spelled scientific sawbones to me, and so doctor he must be, and German to boot. He detached himself from a little group of three or four to whom he seemed to be expounding something, and with great seriousness and precision told me the way to reach La Porte. Such directions were notable in that they were repeated, the last detail driven gently but firmly through my brain-pan.

As I rode off down the street I could not do other than wonder over this touch of Teutonic efficiency that had come to me so unexpectedly. All directions are not so explicit. Too often they are somewhat after the tenor of: "Oh, go out west a ways and you'll see the road; you can't miss it." Now my Teuton had said: "You wish to go to La Porte? Yes, listen and I will tell you. You are now on such and such

Street. You go north two blocks, or two and one-half to be exact for you are now in the middle of the block. You turn west, that is to your left, and go three blocks. You cross the railway track, etc."

In short there is something in being born here or there after all and having certain things engraved in you while young; and when a Brother of the Road is in the Valley of Doubt, I commend to him the German doctor. But if he were in need of a meal or a gratuitous night's lodging and had to choose between the true-blue son of Uncle Sam who gives such abominable directions, and this mathematically precise Teuton, who in my somewhat impressionistic diary was recorded as "very direct, very impressive, very big-bellied and full of beer and importance," I know to which port I should advise him to steer his bark. But of course nothing short of the thumb-screw could induce me to tell.

The land here seemed less interesting to me, or it may have been that my taste for the Road was becoming blunted through repletion, the edge of appetite dulled by fullness at this feast of wanderlust. All things cloy on our palates in time. Certain it is I was now running on the flat lands; there were no vistas of rolling hills, and imagination easily fell to dozing. I chugged on to Valparaiso, and with nothing to awaken me quite so much as a wild twirl from a sandy rut followed by a short journey in the ditch, I came in the evening after a short spin over an excellent pike, to Dyer and halted for the night in the grain fields beyond the little town. This was an indiscreet move, and I had not more than half unpacked when I realized that I must break camp at once. I was on the plains now; night sites henceforth must be picked with some discernment.

Oh the miscreant mosquito! When will a man arrive with the scientific cunning to banish the wretch from earth! Skeeterless nights would be the open sesame to unimaginable delights for out-of-doors folks. What perfect heavens could we not find in the wild woods of America were it not for this accursed tribe. And how well I knew that tribe of the plains! Knew the song, the very smell of them.

They were not the light-weights of the far-famed Jersey City environs, but the bigger Amazons of the prairie. They came in regiments and battalions, wave on wave of assault. They fought me and fought each other for possession of the choice parts of me, and with curses in my heart I hastily packed and retreated to town. There I surrendered to the heroics of the indoors, but long before I had become wrapped in the dull comatosity of a hot and stuffy room — about as pleasant now by contrast as the gas chamber at the city dog pound — I had decided that henceforth I would pick my night roost earlier and fight it to the death with Culex.

▪▪▪▪▪▪ Meter 940

JUNE 29. It was with something of the alacrity and sprightliness of a half-chloroformed cat that I got out of my quarters in the morning, and none too early either. But the cool air and a good road made amends. Heaviness was thrown off; the early zephyrs are freshness itself. I came into Joliet in time, and with appetite for a good breakfast. I had left another state behind me. On the way out of the city that they said had the biggest penitentiary in the United States, I noted that I was passing the local agency handling the breed of machines to which Betsy claimed kindred and so I stopped and went in. There is a very pronounced fraternalism of gas machines. Many times on the Road I have noted it. A thousand miles from home a passing stranger gives me a wave and smile or hurrah simply because I happen to ride the same brand of machinery he does.

A man seems to get attached to the mechanical clique in which he gyrates and to feel that all others are without the pale. It is very foolish perhaps, but it is very human and quite as deep-seated and deep-rooted as most men's patriotism, so called. I mean the feeling in most of us that our own native land is the best on earth and its quarrel always in the right. But this mechanical feeling is very kindly and fraternal; it is a veritable secret society without pass-words or insignia. When I am in trouble on the Road the man who slows down or stops and shouts "Want any help?" is all too certainly riding a relative of grey Betsy. When a rider of a red X or a blue Y shouts that, he dares not smile. I scent irony and sarcasm on the instant and would throw "No, thanks!" at him were I downright stuck.

So Mr. F.N.B. of Betsy's agency took me in his arms, a stranger in a far land. He seized upon my steed and in five minutes did more things, the fine points and niceties, than most mechanics could do in an hour, made her hum like a fiddle and vibrate with eagerness for the Road again. When he was through with her, he advised me that if I wished the best road toward Davenport, to leave the highway and follow his directions. In a few minutes he sketched an impromptu map — he knew every yard of the country within forty miles — and explained every detail. When I said farewell, he begged that I would drop him a card reporting progress, and he said that I could not forget his address, for he lived in the city with the most rogues in America.

We were now heading for Morris and Ottawa to join the main pike from Chicago to Davenport. My westerly road from Valparaiso to Dyer and Joliet had been calculated to cut out Chicago, and this metropolis of the Middle West now lay safely off to the northward and to the rear. For the line of chimneys and bristling architecture under a smoke cloud on the fair horizon has little appeal to the road-lover, at least to me while I have given myself, body and soul, for better or worse to the joys of the country. Indeed the prospect of threading its seething human wilderness always gives me a mental chill. The Road is somewhat like the old definition of the line: there is nothing much at either end; it is pretty much all between. However I follow the highway because I must. Had Betsy wings, I should much prefer to take cross country for it and sweep over the valleys like a harrier hawk.

Now we were upon the prairies of Illinois: a flat land of corn and grain, of earth roads in good condition, of farm groves that had been planted by the pioneers — a fat and fertile and substantial land. Box elders and cottonwoods were the tree friends of the Road with a weeping willow here or there shading full-bellied stock in a green pasture: trees big of girth, quick in growth, short lived, as are those who get all the good things of life in a hurry or too abundantly. Sweet clover, rank and tall, stood in forests by the roadside and the breezes were fragrant and heavy with the scent of it. A red-headed wood-pecker or two still clung to the prairie way and vesper sparrows still sang from the green fields, but now the kingbird was becoming very common, and Dickcissel's voice sounded in my ears so constantly as to become half monotonous. His shrill song was very audible even above the purring of the engine. More than once during the day I heard old Bobwhite whistling cheerily.

The roads whether of earth or macadam were excellent and all day we spun westward. A good stiff thirty miles was often possible in long stretches, yet they were not all alike and I fell to sermonizing them for jotting later in the diary. I had much material: the Road that seems friendly and enticing, but is actually rough and forbidding, that appears inviting, but is two-faced and full of sharp little jolts and meanness in spite of careful steering — that is the reverse: a bluffer, far better than its countenance portends. And there are others that are bad consistently, brazenly, and do not care to hide it. Others that have a fair face but sudden treacherous little spots. Others that have been made badly in the beginning and can never be good, unless replaced.

And some others, goody-goody that were made properly, reared strictly in a Puritanical jacket and never had chance to be bad, like virtue untried in the fire. But I love them all. Thus sometimes on the flat lands when interest flags a trifle, I turn my eye inward and preach a sermon to myself, a sermon built of the stones of the road. This is at least a pastime, and if it does me no good, like the doctor's homeo-pathic pill, it does little harm.

Morris and Ottawa and Princetown fell behind. At Ottawa — and how would Canadians wonder to hear their capital city pronounced Ottaway! — I met with my first mail. Yes, Frat was coming, so his postcards said, coming down the Meridian Road. He had had a blow-out, met miles and miles of Red River mud, poor fellow! Had broken his chain, waded and pushed and slept overnight in a cemetery, but he was coming. He was emphatic about this; he was coming awhooping. He would reach our trysting place (600 miles ahead of me) about as soon as I could, if the weatherman would only have a heart. But "if" though small indeed in print, is of tremendous size when it has any-thing to do with the weather.

Some distance out in the fields beyond Mineral I made camp, and I picked the site with an eye to Culex. These long-billed miscreants, letters of out-of-doors blood, love the low and damp spots, the herb-age and grassy cover and hate the wind and the smell of smoke. So when I came to a bare pasture lot with only a stunted thorn hedge along the fence and a row of huge cottonwoods forming a right angle in the corner, I halted to make a new trial of it. But I soon had occa-sion to move. By a freak of chance I had landed close beside a brown thrasher's nest in the thorny hedge, and the old lady gave me to understand, with rumpled plumage and angry yellow eye, that I must be off with me or have my nose tweaked. She said that I was an inter-loper, a good-for-nothing tramp, and a lot of other things.

So I went to the gate, entered, and took up post about fifty or sixty yards within the bare-cropped field. Experience in other wars with Culex came in handy. I placed Betsy fairly across the wind, spread the tarpaulin on the down-wind side — foolish in most cases, but a war measure here — then just to leeward, I built a smudge fire to make the foe sniff and sneeze and to drive all the lurking outposts from their cover. At turning-in-time, I squirted several shots of gasoline into the ground beside me and with the rustle of the huge cotton-woods in my ears, in a few minutes I was winnowed by the night zephyrs off across the border of Shadowland.

The trick of it is based on the fact that the mosquito has a nose keen as a fox and hunts up wind; also on his liking for a sheltered spot out of the breeze. The smudge fire drives him from nearby footing down wind and throws him off the scent. If he should come up when the fire dies low, the tarpaulin leaning to leeward outwits him. He buzzes about in the shelter of the sloping roof and is slow to come over the top. Were it sloped as a wind-break (upwind) he would promptly take refuge under it, take possession of it, hang on the roof between assaults upon his victim and generally turn a slumber roost into a savage siege.

Also, he has no stomach for gasoline; the smell of it dulls the edge of his blood-craving. The object of squirting it into the ground rather than upon the blanket is that in the ground it evaporates more slowly. It must be admitted, however, that on a windy night, such position for the tarpaulin is impossible, and also that if Culex is at his worst, no such lay-out will secure slumber. A tent properly screened then is the only recourse, and if it is lacking the camper must retire before superior odds to indoors defences.

The straight row of giant cottonwoods that ran from the road along the pasture fence up toward the farm buildings in the distance impressed me more than anything else about my campsite. They would have been accounted huge trees even if met in a forest, and here on the prairie they took on magnificent proportions. Their rough trunks were nearly three feet in diameter; they were very tall and stout and altogether gigantic. Plainly they must have been forty or fifty years of age. Doubtless they were planted by the hand of the first owner of this prairie homestead — memory more kindly and fitting to the memory of a plainsland pioneer than any granite mnemonic in the neglected cemetery of countryside could be.

Indeed what more loving labour could be found for the hand of a child than that each here should plant a tree or two and grow up with it and add a touch of arboreal beauty and majesty to these flat and naked lands. I can even speak from experience, for in my extreme youth I planted a tree seed, the little winged samara of the box elder, and today that seedling had so outstripped me that I might be hanged handily enough on its lower limbs. If I live to be ancient I can imagine my future satisfaction in going back to greet this tree-child of mine that has weathered the same suns and moons and seasons years and decades that I have, and that will doubtless be my best reminder after I am harvested.

▪▪▪▪▪▪ Meter 1089

JUNE 30. Early to bed means early rising in primitive conditions, like the habit of the fowls of the air and beasts of the field. So I was spinning again at 5 a.m. The road was excellent. I passed early through Geneseo and soon came to the ferry across the Rock River. A stream here in these flat lands has a personality quite its own. The rank box elders and elms and huge, elm-like willows that lined the muddy banks, full of birdlife now and once shelter for the game animals of the plain, told a story that was rather new.

Heretofore I had seen no such stream on my thousand-mile trail. I realized that now I was in the alluvial mud lands of the great and mighty Father of Waters. In pioneer days, such timber-fringed streams threaded through the leagues of green prairie with often not a tree clump in the miles between.

On the way in toward Moline, I encountered the first sand road. Sand to a motorcyclist is a tangible nightmare; it is as bad as mud. He never knows whether or not he can really ride until he has made an assault upon such an unstable medium. Two wheels have little anchoring quality: they skid drunkenly; the machine and rider get off balance at every slew and tack, and his good legs must get down as outriggers and save the day. It is a gruelling sort of exercise; it is the test of a rider. But in the cool of the day, Betsy was on her mettle.

On account of its capillarity, sand is then most compact and moist and most rideable. And in second gear we flailed through it to the tune of Betsy's growl and the shrill encouragement of Dickcissel from the telephone wire. There was some satisfaction in noting that other two-wheelers had gone before me recently and left trails that showed much the same exactness and precision of direction that one sees in the trail of a hungry ground mole.

At Moline a brother rider picked me up and led me at a furious pace to Davenport. He was a road-burner; I was not. But as he had volunteered to pilot me out of the next city I tried to keep him in sight. He could not understand why I could wish to stop on the long bridge and take off my dusty cap in silent homage to the great Mississippi, the Father of Waters. To him I think this huge aorta of a vast continent was doubtless at its best but a muddy old river. For, with most of us, familiarity and contempt are two little sisters walking hand in hand.

But as for myself I always experience a strange stirring in me when I meet some historical feature such as this river, something that has been much told about in books and much pictured from these in my mind. The reality never quite fits into place. I find myself saying: "Can this really be?" But a heartless policeman told me to move along, and so with a jumble of bits of history in my head, of Marquette and Jolliete, of La Salle and certain Spanish adventurers, I hustled across into the city and a new state. Verily, whole states were whirling by me even as landmarks on the shore pay farewell to a down-stream boatman.

Beyond Davenport my first four or five hours of Iowan riding were not as pleasant as could have been wished. I was not in the land of earth roads. Most of the soil was clay but in spots we hit sandy pockets where spills were avoided once or twice by a winker. The clay had been very wet within two days and still was rough and rutted. It must be said of such roads that, like the weather, "when they're good they're very good, and when they're bad they're horrid." I was in the mud lands but there was nothing I could do, save steam ahead easily and hope that no more storms were lying in wait for me. Alas!

Yet I had come to a delightful land. In this stretch of southern Iowa I was pleased to greet again samples of far and pleasant Pennsylvania: rolling, gently hilly country of fertility, field after field leading off to the blue horizon. But there were no little mountains, no blue valleys, no fruit trees to speak of and not the general atmosphere. Instead, there were acres of young corn waving, and acres of half-grown grain rippling in shadowy folds as waves chase one another on the sea. There was tree greenery enough, but most of it was about the opulent farm buildings. It needed but a sniff of the nostril near each farmstead to glean the tale of corn and hogs and fat stock. A farmer atop a great load of yellow cobs in a huge double-decked wagon box clinched it. I was in the land of corn.

New life, too, greeted me by the way. Wherever there was cover in the valleys, cottontail rabbits, big and little, popped out on the road to race me for a few yards and pop in again. Several striped ground squirrels (spermophiles) sat up at attention to pat their bellies and flick their tails at me saucily as I sped by. The old friends too were more numerous than they had been in Illinois. Red-head came back again, quail whistled at every stop, bluebirds and orioles were in song in the trees about the buildings. But if the box elder was the typical tree, the Dickcissel now was the typical bird. With the enthusiasm of a real musician and the persistence of an amorous cricket, he shrilled away jubilantly in every mile.

It was somewhere near here that I met my first real meadowlark, that is the Western species. He sang from a telephone pole almost overhead, and his rich tremendous fluting sent a thrill through me that can only be stirred by some birds and by the divine touches in the musical masters. Association as well as melody in this case, for the Western meadowlark is the bird of my boyhood. And to one raised within sound of this chap, the eastern species, with his weak little penny whistle, never seems quite a meadowlark at all. The Westerner is a singer of wondrous talent; there seems no end to his variety. From coast to coast no songster rivals him in repertoire, and not only has each bird a long list of tunes but different birds vary very considerably. He is ever springing a new surprise in song; in short he is the best-loved bird of the plains.

The day sped by all too rapidly. Such is the fickleness of the heart of a road-rover that sometimes I fancied I had seen no fairer country-side anywhere on my trail. A case of the last love perhaps, or it may be that the plainsman like the sailor never quite loses his taste for the open, the freedom and sense of farness that can be felt only on the prairie or on the water. The joy of the Road is its changeability; it is the love of the new. In a different relation, I realize that such fickle-ness of heart would not do at all, but for myself while I am on the spinning highway, give me the sun overhead, the breeze in my face, a bird to sing to me stronger than Betsy's purr and a new scene to love at every mile.

At sunset I dipped into a little wooded hollow in the bottom of which ran a companionable stream, and I could go no farther. On the left, inside the wire fence was a pasture with campsites to please an epicure, but I could find no gate to enter and had to content myself with a site on the other side of the road where a big elm shaded a clear and level spot at its feet. Here with the sleepy chatter of an early-to-bed bird or two in my ear and the pleasant laughter and murmuring of the water just below me, and with the "cricking" of a wood frog for good measure, I lay down in the silence of the dusk. And tuned as my ear had been all day to the rush of air, the growling of the motor and the vibration of machinery, the dusk now was tenfold quiet. Culex did not come and I knew instinctively that his hosts were not abroad in this land. How lucky I felt to be able to enjoy sleeping out in such a silent dell that was full of fairy fireflies, rather than have to hunt an indoors roost in stuffy quarters.

"Biz-z-z-z!"

I had one foot on the borderland of waking and the other across into the dusky realm of oblivion, and I came back with a start that paralyzed me. Nothing short of a rattler could have let loose that wicked "Biz-z-z!" and he was under my tarp! The vile prophecies of my stay-at-homes had been fulfilled; the rattlesnakes had come to bed with me. I cannot vouch that my hair stood on end or that my blood froze, for my hirsute thatch was badly tangled and the night was warm, but I do know that I reacted in most of the orthodox ways that a man does when he is scared almost stiff.

"Biz-z-z-z!"

The wretch was beside me. I ought to have known better than be such a fool, I reproached myself. What was to be done? Make a dash head-first or feet-first or cover my head, stay put and sleep with the beggar? I discarded the first: I was not a torpedo; and I felt the villain could execute his deadly work on my nethers while I was making exit. Yes, I had read that the rattler was largely a myth, that he was not nearly so deadly as popularly supposed, that he was a gentleman and always gave fair warning; but after all that I drew the line at sleeping with him. What was he bizzing about anyway? Third warning now. Was it armed neutrality, watchful waiting or declaration of war?

"Biz–z–z–z!"

It suddenly came to me that the sound was originating above the level of my head and towards my feet. Was he on the tarp roof or standing on his tail — one of those diamond-back leviathans I had seen in the Bronx Zoo? At the thought, I contracted another chill, as the newspapers say. Then something flashed in my mind, and reaching out cannily — heretofore I had not dared move a muscle — I found the little flashlight and shot it straight in the direction of the foe. "Darkness there and nothing more." Then I discovered him. A small beetle was on the roof of the tarp. He was sharpening his wings or his beak or doing some other mechanical job that beetles do, and the process made the rasping resonance that had scared me. Perhaps like the cricket, he was wing-fiddling an impromptu serenade to his lady love, or he may have been a King's jester of the Coleops. But whatever the meaning of his work or play, I vengefully cut it short, and feeling a bit foolish snuggled down and went to sleep.

▪▪▪▪▪▪ Meter 1248

JULY 1. I wakened to the songs of birds; it seemed that I was almost back again in the green valley lands of the East. This little glen of the firefly — I did not learn its local name — was alive with song and noise. Every bird with a tune or a call in him was letting it go with might and main. Pewee was crying his mournful "Pee-wee-er!" and a phoebe scolded near the cement bridge in a meaningful way. A thrasher was throwing out his belated love song, though perhaps he was reviving new passion for the task of raising a second family. He was the musician of the morning; by comparison all the others were but noisemakers. For mourning doves were cooing; crows and the flicker and red-headed woodpecker were shouting each in his fashion; wrens and goldfinches were chattering and rippling.

And while I packed my panniers, a downy woodpecker and a black-billed cuckoo, no less, came over into my tree, the former to "Brrrr!" with his bill upon a dry limb, the latter, to peer at me from the lowest branches and to cluck and make that strange knocking, wooden noise of his that can be heard only at the closest quarters. Even a chickadee was heard calling from across the road; he most of all was a surprise here.

I was off again at 5 a.m. Rising with the birds had become almost a habit now. The road was dry and good, the morning was fair; the countryside wore a smile in every vista. Grinnell and Newton came and fell away and the country became, if anything, more pleasing. In the vicinity of Colfax I decided that it pleased me most; it was more steeply rolling and with fairer fields and greener, wooded valleys, and I put it down so in the diary. During this forenoon my cup of road joys was brimming. There was not a care in the world.

It was glorious running, for in spite of what old-fashioned books say, all the poetry of locomotion is not found in "the green turf beneath my feet, a winding road before me, and a three hour's march to dinner" of Hazlitt; nor is it all found in the heaving, striving sailing craft or the stealthy gliding bark of the Indian, nor in the saddle. A mint of it may be found by straddling the purring, whirring, barking, growling engine of an impudent little gas cart and whirling off toward a new horizon under a summer sky.

Toward noon I came to Four-mile Creek near the outskirts of Des Moines, took the habitual lingering eyes right and eyes left as I slowed down upon the bridge, and then I shut off and applied the brake. These woods of black walnut and butternut, ash, maple, elm, box elder with mounds of elderberry and other shrubbery simply called for a visit, and anyway a bath was overdue. As I was inveigling a change of clean under-clothing from a badly rumpled kit on the top pannier, a young chap of twenty came along and without any prelimi-naries made himself acquainted. Bill R. was the right sort. When he noted my intentions he invited me to come down to the swimming hole, and I was delighted. A short quarter of a mile walk along a path, in that lovely old wooded pasture under the trees that seemed to stand as the Almighty had left them, brought us to the bend in the "crick" and the "swimmin' hole."

It was occupied. A dozen or more boys, arrayed in the costume in which boys enter this good old world of fun and tears, had absolute possession, and were at the game that all of us who have been real boys have played in those days that once gone can never return. It was the typical "swimmin' hole" to a turn — too small for a man yet too deep on the diving side under the abrupt bank for a youngster. So I tried to play the old game, to throw off a couple of decades and in make-believe feel like a juvenile again. I think I succeeded fairly well, although I had a notion that I was probably spoiling the fishing for the "bare-foot boy with cheek of tan" who, quite by himself, was pulling out wriggly mud-cats from a hole a little distance below. But then mud-cats prefer muddy water, and for all I know, the goodly quantity of road dust that went down stream may have been a factor in sending Sonny home happy with a full string of whiskery pouts upon his willow.

Shortly after leaving Des Moines my troubles began. Heavy rainfall had preceded me by but a matter of hours, and though Iowan clay dries wondrously fast under the summer sun, it was not yet all dry. In addition, the roads in some stretches were badly cut and rutted. Progress was painfully rough and difficult, and Betsy called for middle gear again and again. But in comparison this was easy to what was to come. At about mid-afternoon she suddenly turned sick. She coughed and grunted. She became weak as a cat and called for low gear on the first real hill — and even then stalled.

With a final cough and spit she fainted away outright on the hillside, so after heaving her to the side of the road I placed her on her stand and set to work to make a gigantic bluff at playing doctor. A doctor of machinery is a vastly different thing from a doctor of medicine. It is all very well for your saw-bones to wear the There's-nothing-much-wrong-with-you smile, to pretend he knows when he doesn't, to fall back on the old maxim that says: "When in doubt, look wondrous wise and work on his bowels." Such treatment has saved many a man's life, but it will not work at all when you are sitting by the roadside trying to diagnose a gas engine. Mental suggestion is of no avail whatever; indirect treatment will not help. Even prayer is a waste of time, for the mechanic must put his finger on the sore spot and heal it or he has failed absolutely.

I was no mechanic. Out came the manual that I carried in the pannier and I ran through the list of "Mechanical Troubles." Betsy had them all! And yet she had none of them. The push-rods were not too loose, the lifter-pins were correct, the valves were working; there was nothing tangible amiss with her lungs, although I knew that a carburetor was one of those simple-complicated things that was perhaps beyond me. There was a kick in her magneto that lifted my cap. I tried to look as wise as forty long-eared owls or four hundred Solomons, but she would listen to none of it.

Evening was drawing around, a storm was brewing to westward, and I understood these prairie storms fairly well. It was plain that I must make my steed travel to help or camp on the hillside. So we tackled the road again. She ran stronger when cold and made a mile or two only to be halted by a grading gang in the bottom of a sharp, deep gully. When I arrived, an automobile was just finding solid footing after being hauled out of the mire. Half a dozen willing hands seized upon Betsy stem and stern and half lifted, half shoved her over the bad hole. Easy enough, but I wanted to meet that foreman. I felt sure somehow that he knew more of the *materia medica* of gas machinery than I did. It was a flash of inspiration, a "hunch" — any port in a storm.

We seldom give our "hunches" credit enough; if they lead us out of difficulty we imagine vainly that it was our superior wisdom that guided. I want to record full recognition for this "hunch" of mine. Mr. O. listened to Betsy's distressful wheezing and popping and then told me to try to make the first farmhouse on the left side of the road; he lived there and as it was nearly quitting time he would be along shortly. As I was leaving, one of the hands told me quietly that if Mr. O. could not find what ailed her, no one in Guthrie County could. As I toiled up the long slope I blessed my own foresight and then suddenly recollected that it had been merely a "hunch" — a blind stroke of blessed luck.

After fifteen minutes of diagnosis when he arrived, Mr. O. suggested bad gasoline. Where had I last filled my tank? Better drain it out and try her on new fuel; he would draw some from his car. At which I recollected that the last supply had all been put in the right-hand compartment; my reserve tank held other gasoline. And in five minutes, Betsy was barking with a vengeance in her good old way and signifying power and speed and a readiness to climb anything short of the pyramid of Cheops! But to give her good measure he brought out the kerosene can and gave her a vile dose, a vengeful carbon purge intended to make her think twice before feeling bad again, or a pre-remedial thrashing of the small boy who would need it in the future some time anyway. But most of all, we were working on the second half of the adage of the mystified saw-bones.

My good angel and now host offered me indoor quarters, the orchard or the barn for a campsite, and I chose the orchard. And with the hooting of a screech owl in my ears I fell asleep. At midnight, however, I regretted my choice, for a tremendous cannonading to westward and much fierce lightning cutting the black sky warned me to retire to the timothy hay in the barn. Fickle blustering summer storm! It roared and blasted and then passed harmlessly to southward leaving only a fresh wind to rustle the trees and fan me on my couch in the feed passage. But someone off there got it, I knew. I realized fully that now I was in the region of electric storms: the short, sudden and fierce bombardments of the summer prairies.

▪▪▪▪▪▪ Meter 1394

JULY 2. I was astir early but so were the farmhands, and I was not allowed to get away without a substantial breakfast. Blessed indeed is the man who shows genuine kindness to a stranger, to one he has never seen nor will ever see again. We meet much apparent benevolence in life, which, if we dissect it, proves to be largely someone's self interest, but the kindness of this man had no strings to it. We do not meet much of it on say, Fifth Ave., but I find that oftentimes it crops up by the road in less pretentious places. So after a "Goodbye!" and

"Good luck! Drop a card!" I shot out through the wooden gate and with a voluminous wake of kerosene smoke trailing in the rear, we made for Omaha.

The previous day's mileage had been 146, yet though it was less than a hundred miles to Omaha my mind insisted on rehearsing that storm of the midnight. While I hate pessimism I prefer to play fairly safe with my hopes. The rainbow in the morning might do for the sailor; I had had my warning in the night. I felt that there was either a hard day or a rest ahead of me.

Yet the early running was good and I came into Exira without hindrance. Here I overtook three other riders, two of them Frisco bound and we joined forces. Friend T. and H. had ridden from Milwaukee, Wisconsin. Friend G., a student at the University of Chicago, was riding home to southern Oklahoma. I recognized that our diversified quartet would at least stir up some companionable fun, so stepped into the procession. Here for a surety was a fraternity of a machine; we all rode the same brand and swore by it in concert. Yet the first question my friends from Lager-town asked me was: had I had any trouble? And followed the sorry tale of the performance of their motors. When T. cranked his steed, there followed a popping and banging, a veritable Battle of the Somme, compared with which Betsy's noisy protestation of yesterday had been but a hymn tune. We had all filled at the same station.

A few miles beyond Exira we ran into the path of the night storm. First one and then the other acquired a pair of very muddy feet. Finally we tobogganed down the side of a deep ravine and halted on the wooden bridge in the bottom. No one had the temerity to try the ascent. Stalled! We must wait till the sun did its work.

Waiting for mud to dry is an interminable occupation. It is said that no pot ever boiled while the cook's eye was upon it, and I am fully convinced that if a motorist sat down at the side of a rain-pool on the highway and waited for its disappearance, he would take it out in waiting. He might camp there, begin in the spring and hold his job, but his pool would lie and blink at him, mirror the summer clouds and turn brown and oily as each pair of wheels disturbed it. But it would hold out till the very autumn. Yet I know that if he left it for a day, it would be gone upon his return.

Since there was not a vestige of woods at hand where I might follow my hobbies, we had to confine our perambulations to the bridge: to sit upon the railing, watch the northwest prairie breeze chasing shadows across the fields, and listen to two or three red-winged blackbirds that, having nests in the tall grass in the wet hollow, came over to sit upon the telephone wire and make much ado over us. A long-winded Dickcissel came to the same perch and shrilled away without pause either for breath or refreshment. Were Dick a real musician, he would be worth millions to these highways.

We killed time as best we might; I even got out the shaving kit and while T. obligingly held the little mirror, I harvested a crop that was already overripe, to the mighty interest and amusement of an old rustic couple who came along in a buggy and went away with a "We're-at-the-circus" smile. We killed time, murdered it foully, assassinated it. But that brown pool ahead grew not a whit less; the hillside appeared no drier. Then about eleven o'clock I began to sing a song and broke up the meeting. Before I had reached the second verse, T. was tearing furiously up the hill and G. and H. were cranking hurriedly. I followed happily.

We made a few miles and then our procession jammed again in the bottom of another deep ravine. But at the farmhouse nearby, we secured some valuable information: there was a better road by a roundabout way, and it needed no second ballot to decide our course. So we turned aside. The new way was in a stiffly hilly country of heavy clay, but if this was the better of the two, the other must have been shocking indeed. Still, we managed to keep travelling. T., a devil-may-care rider, set the pace and it was a reckless one.

When we came out upon more level running where only the dips of the road were rutted and rough, we travelled fast and took the bad spots on the fly. Which is not the safest way. Not a line, not a day dream found its way into the diary during the entire afternoon. At the end of the day's journey I recorded the following: "Heavy going until finally we got through to better roads; reached Omaha after riding for four hours like devils." And that was all there was to it.

Then we lined up at a lunch counter. It is simply grand at times to be nobody and to be able to eat at one of these "short order" filling stations, to take perch on a stool of repentance with an iron foot-railing, and feed without frills among men who do not look askance at muddy shoes and respectable road dust. I am well aware that too many things taste alike here, but providing the plates and cutlery are reasonably clean and the service fair, I hold it a pleasing experience.

For if I transport my road samples — it is impossible to shake them all loose — into a dining room of better quality I feel too out of place to enjoy my meal. The linen is too clean, the waitress is too immaculate and I know that the ladies across the aisle are praying fervently that I will not shake myself unduly. I do not feel easy, and by the time I pay my bill, my chop or steak is on the highway leading straight to Indigestion. But at the eating counter where I rub elbows with a locomotive fireman, a teamster and a hod-carrier, I have no such trepidation. We discuss the weather and the war without any formalities. Life is considerably simplified; there is a Fraternity of Dirt, a socialism, a better democracy.

▪▪▪▪▪▪ Meter 1489

JULY 3. It rained heavily in the night and again in the morning. The roads ahead were declared impassable for motorcycles, and so we accepted city life perforce with the best grace we could. At noon we parted: T. and H. were to take the road north of the Platte; G. and I were to follow the southern way. Although most of the wise men of the city garages and some bespattered auto tourists coming in from westward declared emphatically that we could not make it, yet such is the lust of the Road that we could stand inaction no longer and shortly after noon set out for Lincoln.

The first few miles of road out toward Millard were hard-surfaced, but so fierce had been downpours of recent date that much mud had been washed across the top in places — the most treacherous footing that I can imagine — and Brother G. having but a single-speed machine and thus at disadvantage, twice went down with his steed like a discomfited knight. Progress was necessarily slow and canny. When we had made a few miles we met another westerly thunderstorm. There seemed an unending supply of electrical material in that direction, and it quickly developed into a case for the tarpaulin. Standing the machines side by side we stretched out our roof and then sat on the foot-boards beside the warm engines, and waited till the shower had passed.

It rained but lightly upon us, but the storm that worked south of us wore a villainous, black and greenish face, and I felt truly thankful that it had veered away. It spelled hailstones to me, and a balloon-silk roof, while waterproof enough, seemed a trifle on the thin side when used as a bomb-proof shelter against the Olympian shrapnel that all too often I knew is lashed down by Jupiter's guns concealed in those black-visage clouds of the plains.

I noted that not even the cannonading of the approaching storm, the fear of a deadly pelting of ice, or the dash of cold rain that fell, could in any measure dampen my Dickcissel's song. He sat upon the telephone wire as usual, and sang with no other pause than his short intermissions between trills. When the pause was longer, it was because he was busy shaking the water from his coat. Before I left, I noticed Madam Dick dart from somewhere down into the forest of sweet clover by the roadside. Aha! A clue. And a nest is easy when that is given. The pair had built upon the swaying stems of this sweet-breathed follower of the road. The nest held two beautiful bluish eggs of Madam's own laying and two spurious speckled impositions of the cowbird; and I wondered, as I always do, why she did not throw the foistings overboard.

It was not good camping-out weather. In fact, old-timers now assured us that we were entering a section of country that was experiencing the wettest spring and summer since '98. We were glad to get our mud-smeared steeds into Millard and to hunt up quarters. Plainly, we were stalled for a time.

Quite as plainly, killing the hours and doing it mercifully must be our occupation until those roads improved vastly. So we set about it grimly. A round of the garages brought more horror stories of what lay to westward — always westward. A circuit of the town brought little relief. The pre-Fourth celebration that was banging away rather damply lasted perhaps an hour (next day being Sunday, the Great and Glorious had to be antedated). Anyway I never could see the philosophy of throwing rings for a knife when I could buy a better one at less cost in the hardware. A pioneer with tales of the wondrous flocks of geese watering in the Platte in early days made me prick up my ears for a short time, but we had little else in common, and more and more I realized that my antidote to ennui rested not in Millard, but in my new friend G.

G. was a Kansan. Though his present home was in Oklahoma, most of his twenty-four years had been spent in the former state, and he was a repository of the chronicles of early days there. His father had been a pioneer, fought Indians and bad men and stock rustlers and helped hang them, fought for his first claim, survived cyclones, grasshoppers, drought and other things, and now was sufficiently well to do to help G. through college; he had even told the boy that as long as he wished to study he would help him, even till he (G.) was grey-headed. Thus my friend had hopes of a post-graduate course in Europe after the war.

G. I think was a worthy chip, a knotty one. The casual way in which he recounted the lore of early days — he could remember a little of the last dying spasms of the wild doings before law and order got the upper hand — was indeed artistic and wonderful, and though most of his own physical battling had taken place on the football field and baseball diamond, it was plain that the blood had lost nothing. He was not a boaster and I had much judicious angling in drawing him forth. An athlete with muscles that had grown in the harvest-field as well as in the gymnasium, he had been in much rough play and had had his arms or legs broken at three different times.

He had been through "one real good fight" with a husky mill hand who had abused his dad. He won it by a close margin, he said. Pater's years could not combat the youth of his detractor; but the young chip could, and when Pater said, "You go ahead and lick him and I'll pay your fine!" why G. naturally went ahead. And Pater paid. G.'s first two initials were E.Z. and he said that his friends dubbed him "Easy," but I fancy that the mill-hand did not find him anything of the sort. He had a breezy, easy way with him and somehow, though I know not why, I nicknamed him "Texas." He had what is commonly called a personality. I had made the common mistake at first of not being able to see deeper than road dust, sun tan and whiskers. Now I was charmed with him. But when he laughingly owned that he was going to transport his present tall crop of ruddy facial pubescence all the way down to northern Oklahoma in order to show "the best little girl in the world" what he looked like at his very worst, then I loved him.

JULY 4. It rained steadily a good part of the night and when we sallied out early it was to find the roads in the consistency of clay porridge. Being somewhat given over to pessimism, I asked Texas how he relished the prospect of a week or so in our present urban retreat, but he laughed and said that he would be in Lahoma, Oklahoma, by then and intended to try the road by about mid-afternoon. At which I learned that optimism, while an admirable quality at any time, is an asset especially valuable when you are waiting on roads of clay to dry, during the palmy height of the "wettest season since '98."

And at 2 p.m. we did try it. There was not much dry road, but most of it was toughening and only the holes were soupy. These we avoided when we could. Indeed it had been a marvel to me that clay could dry so quickly even under a summer sun and prairie wind. But progress was so provokingly slow and so painfully rough that my go-lucky chum advised me to button the flaps of my pockets and hang on tight to the fillings in my teeth, if I had any. Being blessed with a mouthful of solid bone and ivory I had to heed only the first injunction. When he caught me in a tough spot saying something to my steed unworthy of Sir Galahad, he admonished me. There was no use swearing, he said; it was a useless habit. He was right. One simply could not swear properly in the midst of those hummocks, and there was no purpose in it after I got out. I envied Texas. He had no bad habits, though I think he said that he drank a glass of beer once, which doubtless was outside the state bounds of Kansas.

Our way was grooved and gouged by the tires of autos that had preceded us, and their erratic trails could scarcely have been due to conviviality on the part of the drivers. None but sobriety itself in the third generation could have got through at all. Just before we started down toward the valley of the Platte we encountered one of these cars abandoned by the roadside. It was of a make extremely well known, popular, and seldom stuck, but this one was vanquished. It had skidded from the rounding grade and stopped in the ditch. The two outer wheels were half buried and the body dragged on the black mire. It had been abandoned but stood in no danger of being stolen.

When we tackled the grade across the level lands of the Platte valley, we met more four-wheelers in the toils of trouble. Near a little culvert, quite a dozen east-bound cars formed a blocked procession. The first was down in the ruts so that its body dragged and the drive-wheels spun impotently and it took some shovelling and a deal of yeo-heaving from many hands before it got out to better footing. Then No. 2 tried it, and after we had watched several others win their way through, we led and pushed our own steeds (two to a machine) along the comb between the ruts, and then went on again.

The river was very high and brown and turbid, with mud bars visible only here and there. As we stopped to get acquainted with this great tributary I was struck by the destructive forces playing in it: the wearing and tearing, the hungry devouring of its hurrying current. Millions of tons of the finest alluvial soil in America were going by here daily bound for the Mississippi and the Gulf. Whole farms formed a continuous procession of waste.

When I came to consider it, I knew that I was standing in one of

Texas had never tried camping out but thought he could stand it.
(COURTESY: BCA J-01404)

the greatest gardens of fertility in the whole world, perhaps the great-est. Once they had been the prairies, "the unshorn fields, boundless and beautiful," but they were not so now. For days I had ridden in fertility and I recalled the road cuttings that showed bottomless depth of alluvial, clayey, soil substance — soil that meant bread and meat for millions — and automobiles for the owners.

We crossed upon the long bridge, which was of the toll species, and found better roads at once, passed two or three small towns, and toward sunset were down near the capital city. Texas was no camper-out, but was enthusiastic about trying it, and in consequence I was able to assume quite the airs of a veteran. I picked a site upon grassy sod under a huge rustling cottonwood. We were out on a plain so flat for miles around that the whole world seemed to be spread out like a circular map. The groundsheet and the blanket were ample enough for two, and as my comrade would not accept my air-pillow, I showed him how to conceal a sheaf of daisies under the poncho to secure the same effect.

There was a magnificent plainsland sunset as Sol dipped to the circular rim of the prairie; the night promised fair and cool, and there was scarcely air enough to set the nervous cottonwood whispering. No mosquitoes came to us, although I had half expected them. The alfalfa field and the grass had a pleasant green fragrance, and when we turned in, Texas said that he was going to be able to stand it all right.

JULY 5. There were spots of fair road in the morning and we hurried where we could. Texas had assured me even in the worst spots of yes-terday, that during a normal season these same rutted roads allowed the very cream of motoring, and now I was half inclined to believe him. Yet here every little stream in its box elders and cottonwoods was thick with soil, eating and cutting and hurrying. The ditches often stood lipping and echoed with the orchestra of the prairie frogs. Once or twice I heard a rail tittering in the grassy edge of a grain field where rails ought not to have been. But in spite of the season I felt the long trail was winding by, more slowly but still moving.

I met some new friends this morning. In the little stream cuttings stood many clumps of elderberry in bloom. Companionable road friend that girdles a continent! There had been gaps in its ranks for a few days and I was happy to greet its white bloom-clusters again. Dickcissel still held his perch by the way, and Red-head, as staunch a road friend as the elderberry, also flashed from pole to pole, though I felt that he was rather out of order on these almost treeless plains. But the commonest bird of the way now was kingbird; he was constantly darting up from a roadside perch to spear his prey over the road and then dart down again.

The singer of these lands, however, was the western meadowlark, and his flutings at morning and evening awakened many a pleasant memory of the plains. And once as we halted on a little bridge above a coffee-and-cream rivulet in a diminutive ravine that held a few clumps of greenery, another old friend lifted his voice: a wood thrush no less several times quite close at hand sang his elfin strains — a voice from the East, a gentle reminder of the loveliness of my road as it had been in the wooded valley of the far Appalachians. It was truly a farewell, for we were now on the very limit of this thrush's summer range and we would hear him no more.

We had breakfast in the beautiful little city of Lincoln, Nebraska, having been in the new state since crossing the river at Omaha, a city deservedly associated in the mind of the stranger with grape juice, peerless oratory, and a certain brand of pacifism, and then we headed for Fairmont. This town was to bring both greetings and farewells. Here Texas must turn south toward his Oklahoma destination while Frat, I hoped, would be waiting for me. What he had been doing since he camped among the departed in North Dakota was a dark mystery, as no word had greeted me at Newton, Iowa, my second and last point of communication. I was full of expectancy and concern and doubt. If the "wettest since '98" had reached the valley of the Red River of the North, I knew that he was not in Fairmont.

Toward noon I encountered something that more than mud roads or meadowlarks convinced me that I was in the West. The running was so much better that we spun along rapidly, and once I spun where I should not have. A little wet patch on the road scarce bigger than a tabletop was deemed too insignificant to be worth dodging, although Texas who was leading deemed it so, and I picked myself up from the side of the grade where Betsy prone on her side had dug a furrow with her foot-boards and her face. That mud patch was alkali!

My comrade ahead heard the rumpus and came back, and after we got Betsy on her feet and the half-dried mud detached from parts of her, also the handlebars straightened, she was ready again. But she had a new and dreadful appearance. There was not more than a square inch of glass in the lamp and it was knocked awry and jammed and battered shockingly. Texas who was an authority on cyclones said that we had the appearance of having weathered a good one.

At 1 p.m. after sweeping over a long level stretch of almost perfect road, we entered Fairmont. The town was closed tight; the Fourth here was being honoured on the fifth! There was no noisy celebration. Indeed the place had the appearance of Sleepy Hollow quietude on a sunny Sabbath afternoon. I immediately made a raid upon the post office, but like all the places of business it was closed. Rapping on the door and ogling through the front window brought no one to life. A few bystanders told me that the office would not be open till next morning. I enquired where the postmaster lived, and the house was pointed out to me at a little distance, but I was assured grimly that knowing where he lived would avail little.

One spokesman put it flatly that I was a "good one" if I could get my mail today. Up the street I went, here and there enquiring casually on the subject, and one and all they agreed. What, I asked, was the matter with the man that he could not be persuaded? Nothing. He was merely a stickler: when the office was closed it was closed up tight. Nothing short of an earthquake or a presidential message could force those doors.

Some time I had to spend. How much I could not know until I got within the rigid portals of that office. Here was a sniff of adventure: an adventure not of the Road but of the human kind. Riding in the hot sun puts a rough edge on the temper. I would beard this official lion who, though doubtless armed with right on his side, might somehow be overcome. I would see.

But first I had to say farewell to Texas, and here quite by accident I discovered that he was all but on the rocks — temporarily, of course — or in the colloquial, "broke." With "six bits" in his pocket (the Western equivalent of three quarters of a dollar), he was striking for Oklahoma! Worried? Not he! He had friends along the way in Kansas; he would make it all right, he said. And I honestly feel that he accepted the loan that I insisted upon, quite as much to relieve my feelings in the matter, as to serve his own ends. So exit Texas, red whiskers and all, in a barking haze of dust to southward. May we meet again and share a longer trail.

Then I went to beard the lion. An elderly woman showing the wear of the years came to the door and I breathed out my heartburnings. It really was a sad tale: I had come all the way from New York, I said, to get that mail today. So had she and her husband come from New York, she hastened to explain in her first breath, and though I did not care a button where she came from, I knew that I was drowning and clutched hard at the swirling straw. But the good man was now asleep; she dared not waken him.

I understood, but I returned to the attack and presently elicited from her that her life partner, although I doubt the latter half of this relationship, would be in the office about 5 p.m. and *perhaps* he might give me my mail. She could not commit herself. So though inwardly I was in a humour to go in and yank him out of his mid-day snore-fest — I just knew he snored — I said, "Gracious no! Don't waken the dear man if he is asleep!" and assuring her that I would waylay him at the office door, I asked a question or two about her relation to distant Manhattan, offered about ten thousand thanks, quite a few apologies, said all the complimentary things about the trees and shrubbery I could manufacture impromptu, and then made myself scarce.

I was more interested in that little park than in anything else in the town. And what a credit it was, for every stick and sprig of greenery, save the grass, had been planted in the earlier days of the young town. Now there were shade trees and I stretched out limply on the cool sod, for the afternoon was very hot, and filled myself with the feeling of the place. Box elders, ashes, elms and catalpas stood sturdily about me showing the wonderful adaptability of the soil for tree culture. At one entrance stood a bronzed monument on a granite pedestal inscribed "To Our Unknown Dead" and beside it two time-worn maxims, features that gave to the place a distinctive touch, a link to bind the carefree days of the prosperous present to those darker nights of trial in the '60s of the last century.

Because of the park and the treed streets, the town was alive with birds. Indeed I would have thought it improbable that so many of the woods species could have been found in such a prairie oasis, had I not made a survey of the place and met them. During the afternoon I saw or heard the bronzed grackle, flicker, sparrow hawk, robin, mourning dove, cuckoo, thrasher, Baltimore oriole and blue jay, and as I had no field glasses and many of the birds were not now in song, doubtless some other species escaped my observation.

The jays were the surprise of the feathered clans. Two of their nests were in trees over the sidewalk and a citizen of the town informed me with much conviction that these sly, blue rascals of the woods, usually so secretive at nesting-time, here made bold to kill a number of his newly hatched chickens. And every bird of the list had followed the planting of the trees. This thought led me to pondering over the large number of woods birds I had seen or heard about the treed premises on the plains. What countless numbers now had followed the home-steader. Perhaps there was some relation between the oft-told scarcity of birdlife in the eastern states and this new migration of woods birds to the plains.

Nor were these feathered friends the only denizens of the little park. Once as I lay and listened for new voices, a sudden clamour of birds back of me caused me to turn and see a big grey tree squirrel hotly hunted by about a dozen vociferous English sparrows and sev-eral grackles. He climbed a tree for a short distance and then turned as though on second thought, scurried down, skipped to the next tree and raced up airily into the branches quite unheeding the mob at his heels. Grey squirrels are not supposed to rob nests, but these birds evidently did not know it. The sparrows seemed unusually excited and indignant. I noted that my fluff-tailed visitor was very big and fat and compared with his eastern relatives, very much more yellow-brown of coat. His visit recalled the first of his nimble kin that I had met en route, after an adventure with a rattler in the hills of Pennsy.

Then Mr. S. came along and made himself acquainted. Here was a man in his seventies with the hale and hardy appearance of many men in their fifties; was a Grand Army of the Republic veteran — one of the few remaining of the former 80 members of the local GAR association — had been with Sherman on his devastating march to the sea in '64, had come to the prairies of Nebraska among the first when all this plain of present crop acreage and populous towns was nought but a treeless expanse of grass. He had laboured discreetly, accumulated a comfortable fortune and now had retired. But he had worked hard all his life, he said, and now found his new status as gentleman of leisure somewhat uncongenial.

Alas, like many others who, en route through life, have not mixed life's pleasures with its pains, but attempted all the work first and all the play afterward, he was unhappy. Now he could not enjoy himself; he had lost the ability. His play faculty had atrophied with the years. He was in the state of the freed, long-term prisoner who, in spite of his dreams, now found the free world less congenial than his time-worn cell. And from what I gathered of Mr. S. in our short acquaintance, I doubt not that this poor, rich, excellent man did as he intimated he might: go back to toil, put his neck under the yoke, lean on the trace-chains, and some day drop in harness, happy.

We made a rare company, I think. Mr. S. wanted someone to talk to, to unburden himself; I was well satisfied to listen. Like all old men, he lived in the past. To recount early experiences was a thousand times more vital to him than to discuss the Great War. So I had little to do, save use my ears and imagination. There was nothing about me he wished to know, nothing I could tell him, and I hope I may never be found guilty of talking at a man. My entertainment was most excellent. He was a good talker and had lived through stirring times. Days of the level prairie waste "where not a switch could be found for miles," of the early homesteaders and their sod buildings, of the coming of the railroad, the building of mushroom towns. It was all brought to me as vividly as if I had been sitting with a motion picture flashing by before me.

By and by, a newcomer came along, a stiff and pudgy figure with considerable waistline and a face that the Scotch would call "dour." He stopped and asked me if I was from New York and if my name, etc. Yes, there was much mail awaiting me; just come right down with him. And it was only 4 p.m. We went in the back way. That postmaster was the most pleasant man in the town. Whereupon, after I had secured my postal reading matter, with time to think over the situation, and find why I had been given it against the united prognostications of all Front Street, I decided that there are fraternities to be met on the road other than those of a brand of machine. And Frat was coming on the morrow.

▪▪▪▪▪▪ Meter 1618

JULY 6. In the morning I met a saddler of the town who told me hair-lifting tales of the early days and, as a clincher, showed me a furrow through his scalp where a bullet had once come near to finishing him. Life, I fancy, must be dreadfully mundane, flat and stale today to these men after having lived youthful years in the West in earlier times when it was wild and rampantly wicked. All the gun play of the books surely did not originate in the fertile brains of novelists. Although some of these men today delight to recount the early days and perhaps use an impressionistic brush in the colouring, there is a certainty that there are many Westerners, heads of families and respected, who saw and did and endured things that they discuss little today at their fireplaces. For some of the past history of the West is a dark smirch on a fair land.

For the remainder of the morning, I cultivated my GAR friend and then set out to watch the eastern town approach of a dust whirl. At 2 p.m., Frat came along. He was browned to a rich, Navajo hue. He had burned and peeled and burned again. He had three coats of sun-scabs upon his nose and was harbouring something on his upper lip that at first I took to be road dust but later diagnosed differently. In his riding togs, he carried samples of the soil of all the important river valleys between Winnipeg and Nebraska, and his steed also stood badly in need of a grooming. None but the shrewdest could have guessed that he was a schoolteacher.

When I ironically congratulated him on making his seven hundred miles in such record time, he burst out in a long burning tirade against the weather and the roads! He had navigated whole seas of mud! He had had to ship his machine and himself two or three hundred miles in that Red River Valley; he was lucky to be here at all, he said. And then he enquired for the best eating-place in town.

The roads in the afternoon were far from good, but there were fair stretches between the roughly rutted sections, and by camp time we had made thirty miles. But we were not in a good camper's land. A great, black bank of clouds climbed up above the sunset, and thunder rumbled distantly but nearer with every roll. We attempted to make Harvard and had to run for it. I was setting the pace and four or five miles from our port I encountered a stretch of good grade. No stretch of imagination could have called our pace tardy; a few big drops plumping on the road added incentive to flight. In a few minutes as the first big spats fell scatteringly, I swung up over the railroad and looked back. There was no sign of Frat. Go back? But it was raining now and I hurried into a garage.

JULY 7. It rained in the evening and in the night, and during most of it, the roads were as bad again as mud roads well could be. And of all my road days this was the worst, the slowest, dullest, deadest day. To pass the time I tried every expediency I knew, from trying to locate Frat by rural phone to invading the groups at the corners and discussing the war. But it was all impossible. I could not rout even an argument; I would have welcomed a street fight. I may remark, for it is apropos, that the speech of these corner groups savoured I thought quite as much of Heidelberg as of Harvard. At every fresh sally of mine upon the European situation, a discreet and chilly silence seemed to fall upon the tongues of the assembly.

Then I recollected that I had met these disciples of Menno Simons elsewhere, and I confess I have found it hard to love them. Later on, I even drove a bargain with a wheat-grower to go harvesting for him at three dollars a day and board — he had not seen me at meals — but we fell out over the details of the case. He stipulated that he could use me only on the fine days and that I would have to pay for my board on the wet ones, whereas I wanted to work on the rainy days, so we drew off without agreement.

At the end of this weary, lounging, mud-imprisoned day, all I could find to enter in my diary was the following note: "Wind N.W. One shower only in the a.m. Sun came through at 12 p.m. Much advice on roads received. All men are full of it; most of the information conflicts. Frat came in at 3 p.m. with Flying Maria — on a farm truck. He had punctured."

JULY 8. When we set out at 9 a.m. the roads were barely rideable but the soil to westward was growing lighter and running improved. Several times we ran into ruts where the foot-boards turned up and the belly of the machine stuck fast on the combs as the engine raced helplessly. This necessitated our pushing out by hand. But this was pie; the worst lay ahead we felt certain. For a hundred miles we had been hearing stories of the mudhole beyond Minden; its fame had gone clear to Omaha. Direful things awaited any two-wheeler who attempted a passage, we had been assured. There were bridges out, too, we knew. Minden and mudhole had been dinned into our heads so often of late that I felt that for the rest of my life the terms would be synonymous.

And Minden was rapidly approaching. The beautiful little town of Hastings, like most of the others here, was to us merely a filling station for machine or man, and soon we were in the town of the mudhole. Here we found that by making a very long detour we might avoid the worst of the mud, and we were careful to get those directions with exactness.

The longest way around is always the shortest way in such cases and we were delighted. We did avoid that far-famed hole only to run into another one. But again our star was in the ascendency; teams were grading here from both ends of the dump and only a gap of a few feet of impossible riding remained. So wet was the footing here that the three men who levelled the dumpings, and even one or two of the teamsters handling the scrapers, worked bare-footed and with their trousers rolled high above the knees. There was no lack of help when we stormed that bottomless gap; three or four pairs of stout arms made light labour of it.

We thought we had left the mud behind now and said so. Alas! Within a mile or two we came to a grade that was entirely under water! That seventy-foot pool, a foot or more deep, called for some cautious barefooted pioneering. But this road like some dogs and many people had a comparatively mild bite and I managed to ride through it — barefooted however — and then took a snapshot of Frat as he steered Flying Maria to port. In this connection I begged him to take a spill or do something really spectacular and make a real picture, but he said "Not by a townsite!" and came through (barefooted) with all the gingerly circumspection of an old woman negotiating a one-plank foot-bridge.

In the afternoon we started the first jackrabbit. Hurrah! We yelled to make him run and skip; we were in the West now. Both the big, white-tailed prairie hare of the northwest and the black-tailed jackrabbit proper were represented here, and once I noted one of each species on opposite sides of the road at the same moment. They were a welcome addition to our prairie way. When our grandfathers crossed the plains they encountered buffalo, antelope, deer and elk; we at least might have our jackrabbits. Thank heaven he has not yet been exterminated! To see either of these big mule-eared chaps go off sky-hopping airily on his toes, or sit up unconcernedly and scratch his fleas is a touch of the wild that does the heart of the visitor good.

I noted other changes in the life by the trail. Though several of the eastern birds such as the thrasher still were sighted near the tree-clumps and Dick still shrilled at intervals, and doves were routed from the road, there were new friends at hand. The first burrowing owl came to light in the afternoon and we were prepared for a prairie dog and a rattler at once. Several shrikes were noted and the yellowish-coated Arkansas kingbird had almost displaced his equally noisy, grey-coated Brother of the East. Still another bird, and one that bespoke a change of country was the lark bunting. In the afternoon, a male showing his black and white plumage sprang up close by and in the evening we heard one sing. We were truly West now. A rattler was due at any time, and Frat strongly hinted that we really ought to wear six-shooters.

We had eatables in Oxford at about 6 p.m., and then set out to make the next town before lamp-time. Soon we came to a rough, rounding country, a sparsely settled region of poor buildings and far-scattered neighbours. Ahh, the prairie landscape is lovely where it shows the fair face we had seen so long, but when it has a hard and pinched visage as we saw it here, it is pitiable and forsaken. The land had the appearance of newness, yet a settler told me he had been there twenty years. There was much waste land. Jackrabbits and prairie hares, with numerous young in as many different stages of development as the youngsters in a populous French-Canadian village, popped about in the short buffalo grass and waving lupine. Lark buntings became common.

It was a land of the first cutbanks and water-worn ravines. Not a tree or shrub was in sight anywhere, save at the lonely farm-steads. Toward evening, burrowing owls hunted on erratic wing about the grassy knolls, doubtless surprising mice and numerous young ground squirrels out at their last nibblings. A curse had settled upon this country and it was the sterility of drought.

We had reached the dry lands. Soil, deep, rich, alluvial, fine and friable covered the entire face of the earth; had the heavens been kind, these settlers too must have been wealthy. The soil seemed ancient silt so fine that where the recent rains had pounded the roads, little ditches had been cut and the earth lay in the hollows. Here and there, too, whole fields had shed a coating of their top soil, and the brownish mass, sometimes two feet deep, lay in the bottoms of the ravines.

It was a dry country that suddenly had become wet and did not know what to do with it. Such a state is sad. Even now a blue mound that betokened thunder was mounting above the western horizon; another storm was brewing. Ever out of the west came these storms; the thunder-mill of the world seemed to be fleeing before us, hovering twenty miles ahead to westward. Ever westward.

It was here that we ran into the trail of one of the very worst of these Nebraskan storm-giants, a cold trail, for which we were thankful. We had already crossed several strips of woebegone fields, half green, half brown, where the growing grain was smashed and battered into the earth by the spiteful deluge of ice that comes out of these summer clouds. But this path of devastation was so exceptionable that I stopped to read more of the story. Like most hail-tracks, it was narrow. The centre of it had run through a field and along the crest of a knoll, torn through a deserted farm premises and worked off to southward. There was nothing whatever left of the crop save a little brown straw. A dead jackrabbit lay beside the road and though he was too "high" for minute observation, I doubt not that he was the victim of a hailstone.

On its northerly side, the telephone pole was cut and battered jaggedly as though some wanton had attacked it with a long-hafted blacksmith's hammer and beaten it savagely from the top to the ground. Plainly enough, this deluge of ice missiles did not fall vertically or even near it, but was driven slantingly with a terrific force of wind. But it was on the row of small trees that the cruellest work of the skies was seen. These trees were box elder, locust and walnut and appeared to have been set out some fifteen or twenty years. Now they were reduced from healthy green specimens of their kind into broken, cut and ravished skeletons. Even the bark was battered loose; some of them plainly were wounded to the death, although others might possibly survive.

They had the appearance of having passed through a storm of high-power shellfire. Such was one of the vagaries of the sky during this "worst since '98." When Frat came up and looked it over he ventured his humble opinion that our present section of the fair country was not intended for campers-out.

Then Flying Maria suffered a puncture and we lost three-quarters of an hour. According to our meters we had been drawing near a washout where, if we accepted the latest advice, the bridge was gone and the ravine full of washed-in mud. Dusk came on and a night out seemed imminent. I picked a spot on the side of the ravine, and plainly we were between the devil and the deep sea. For if we went to the breezy hilltop inside the pasture fence, we were completely at the mercy of the wind and rain; if we tried to bivouac on the floor of the little ravine we must fight a Russian army of mosquitoes that were already out full of bloody purpose.

I voted the hilltop the lesser evil, but when we went up to investigate we found an army of these musical miscreants so hot after us that it was plain that sleep would be out of the question. From this vantage-point, however, we could see a windmill at half a mile poking over a ridge of fields. It denoted a touch of civilization and we decided at once on a change of tactics. We came down, covered the machines and with our blankets and pillows in a roll, started across the half-dried mire in the ravine bottom in the direction of this chance-offered haven.

We were just in time. Already the west was inky black, and the edge of the rising, leaden-blue wall was quite over our heads. Every few moments thunder rattled and rumbled. When we reached the house, the family was at supper in the lamp-light. I knocked and in response to a rough "Come in!" I stepped inside and explained our plight. In a word I wanted permission to sleep in the barn. There was a dead silence; neither of the two men present did more than exchange glances nor ceased onslaught on the fried potatoes. But I saw in a twinkling that the black-bearded tiller of alluvial at the head of the table was clearing a way for his tongue to tell me that I could not sleep there. So I opened fire first, told him that we were not exactly tramps, that neither of us smoked and could burn nothing about the barn — a tender spot always with farmers — and before he could either hum or haw, I assured him that we would be all right there, thanks, and ran for it.

"Wasn't so mighty sure about it, was he?" said Frat as we headed for the door of the little barn. "But he'll need artillery to get me out of here tonight!" Which expressed the situation quite well.

Then it rained. It poured and drenched the earth while the heavenly batteries hammered away frightfully and huge flashes of lightning chains dashed down the sky. Though no hail fell upon our roof, I could not keep from dwelling mentally upon a certain shrapnel effect I had seen in the evening and connecting it with an impromptu camp under balloon silk on a recent breezy hilltop. By the aid of the flashes that came in through the door, we explored the loft and finding it bare as the old woman's cupboard, we were forced to spread our blankets upon the floor. It was hard, but the passage was draughty and cool and there were no insect pests.

Before we fell asleep we discussed the fun of being gipsies, and we agreed that had we been forced to do these things we would have counted them hardships. But to meet our road adventures as things we were seeking, things of our own choosing — ah, that was a different story. We could lie now and chuckle at the stay-at-homes, also at our host, old Black-whisker and his stalwart son, or it may have been the hired man, who came out with the lantern to tend the horses below us, and who "froze" me bluntly when I put my head to the hatch and told him how kind he was and how comfortable we were.

······ Meter 1756

JULY 9. It rained heavily through the early part of the night, purring gently on the roof long after the electrical fireworks had burned out.

But the prairie never sulks. It may be more fickle than a sweet-sixteen love, but what it does, it does with a will while it is at it. The morning dawned clear and breezy and fresh. At sun-up I gazed out of the open loft door into the stable-yard and finding it swimming, lay down again. A delicious air from the prairie came in through the opening; it was pleasant to lie abed late for a change.

The men came out early and tended the horses and later the rattle of dishes proclaimed breakfast. But we were outcasts in a strange land holding down our appropriated roost by right of conquest. And one of us, badly in need of a shave and a haircombing, was still sleeping on those flinty boards with the calm, snoreless abandon of a babe in its mother's arms. Frat always had an untroubled conscience.

At about 10:30 a.m., the inner pangs that have little relation to conscience sent us packing back to our machines. In our haste to get through the rain, thunder and lightning of this hail-cursed country, we had neglected our larder, and all the grub-panniers could disgorge was a heel of a loaf many days ancient, which Frat thought he recognized as the remains of a loaf he had bought in Fargo, North Dakota. There was also a small tin of sardines and some butter that showed the consistency of some of the lighter lubricants. But it is an old saying that hunger is the best of sauce, and we left not a crumb.

We learned now from a passerby that our only chance of making further western progress, was to go back a mile, turn north and then west and strike for Edison. The sun now beat down ardently with a frying sort of heat; the wind was southwest and more and more resembled the breath from a steamy oven. But it meant that the road would dry out, and about noon we set our wheels turning again, this time eastward. The north and south road was a Tartar; so greasy was it, that in long stretches we were glad to get off the road apology and bump over the hummocky sod.

Here we met our first prairie dog town. Why these pot-bellied little grey plains-dwellers should be called "dogs" and their congregations "towns" I am at a loss to know. Here in the corner of a pasture and around the ruins of a homestead site, many of these far-famed comics sat upon small mounds and called derisively at us. Why did we not stay at home as they did, they seemed to say, and then we would not have to fight the weather.

They had a comical trick of stopping at the mouth of the burrow with head down, back raised a little, and then winking and flickering their laughable little tails. Doubtless there is some citizenry among them, and each individual must conform to certain regulations. But if I could read their code book, I fancy that Rule no. 1 would read something like: "Whenever you sight coyote, hawk, owl, rattler, man with a rifle, or other danger, whistle and run." Some maintain that the prairie dog barks rather than whistles; I confess that to me their vocal gymnastics are little enough of either. But I know what it means.

We had to fight all the way now. But we did it in short snatches, for at our last major consultation over the sardines we had agreed not to attempt any speed records, but rather to take it easy. However there was no easy going. By mid-afternoon we had made a westerly mile and reached a little farmhouse. We were hungry again — we had been nothing else all day — and I went in at once.

There was a mongrel dog in the yard chained to a packing-box kennel, and at sight of a victim he raised a devilish ruction and started to come for me, jerkily — packing box and all. But our disease demanded desperate remedy; I prayed that the chain and staples would hold and I got to the door first. In my blandest, most fascinating manner I told the young mistress of the house that we stood dreadfully in need of filling, and added that we were tremendously willing to pay for it. At which she said that dinner was over some time and that she could not do much for us. This she made plain with difficulty above the ferocious yowling of the cur that now had dragged his house a considerable distance in the direction of my leggings. Could I not buy a loaf of bread? She seemed not too sure of even this concession, but finally I got it.

So we filled our canteens at the windmill pump, while Old Ferocity tore in on a new tack, and then we returned to the road and lined up on a soddy shelf flanking the ditch. The sardines were gone, the butter jar held only a spoonful of lubricant, but there was still salt and pepper in good store. The bread, also the water, I am happy to state were excellent, but truly "man cannot live by bread alone," even with salt and pepper on it. The most pleasant thing I can recall of that meal and the place was that an Arkansas kingbird pair had a nest in the upper frame of the windmill, and I watched the mother marshal her marvellous courage and dart in and settle upon her speckled eggs within a scant foot or two of the noisy whirring planes.

The prairie was wondrously silent in the heat of the day. The southerly breeze, baking hot now at mid-afternoon, and much drier, joggled the trembling heads of the short buffalo grass and moved the stunted lupine, but other than its weary rustling, no sounds were abroad. No vesper sparrows of the greener fields, no meadowlarks seemed here to sing. We welcomed any diversion and when a farmer came along with a wagon, from the west, we took him by storm.

Behind the wagon trotted a running dog, mostly greyhound, fagged and panting and bob-tailed. There are some dogs that can go bob-tailed and appear in the height of fashion, but a greyhound is not one of them. He appears too abbreviated, to have lost a great deal of himself. I have heard it declared emphatically that a rudderless hound could not run well, and my first question, after we had pumped our friend dry on the subject of roads, was about the merits of his dog.

He assured us that his tailless running marvel — did a man ever say anything bad to a stranger about his own dog? — had just caught a white-tailed Jack and was emphatic that these hares were the swifter of the two species. What he would have said had the dog overhauled a black-tailed Jack, I can only surmise. My own observation here led me to feel that the true Jack with the black appendage was a leaner, lanker, sleeker chap than his more northerly ranging brother; but both of them on Nebraska roads as we found them easily would out-run Barking Betsy.

It was fairly dry now, but dreadfully cut and gouged and rutted. We rode the combs till we fell into the ruts and when we got wedged there we heaved out and started again. It was rough while it lasted; the motors roared savagely at such outrageous opposition, and finally we got out and up, although our feet had not often been quiet on the foot-boards. Better running came at once, and in the evening after long detours to escape more mudholes and washouts, we reached Edison. We had made 29 strenuous miles, but again we were somewhat between the millstones. We balanced a night in town against a night on the prairie and decided in favor of the former. Frat said that he had a "hunch" that it would rain in the night and perhaps sprinkle hail like some we recently had noted. And where there is Nebraska hail concerned, I too am a believer in hunches.

▪▪▪▪▪▪ Meter 1785

JULY 10. I was awakened near midnight by a fearsome crash of thunder and a blinding flash, and sprang up to the open window. We were quartered in the southwesterly corner room of the little hotel with windows facing in both directions. The northwestern sky was inky black, and split asunder every few moments by great jagged lightning scimitars that slashed from zenith to the horizon. It had a wicked face, that storm, and I watched it a few minutes. The plain was fairly lighted, for between the greater lightning chains, smaller ones played fitfully. And suddenly as I looked to westward, I saw it coming — the wind. A row of trees thrashed and flailed and then bowed over the fence toward me, and I rushed the windows. It struck the corner of the house fair, so that the building groaned and the windows pounded and rattled. Frat actually wakened a little, that is, he grunted, stirred, raised his head a little at the rumpus, and muttered, "What'd I tell you!" and something else about a tarpaulin and a balloon ascension as he went off again.

But it was all over in a minute or two. Our anchor held staunchly and the gale died as it had come. A few big drops spattered down and that was all; the body of the storm had missed Edison. So I raised the windows again to meet the cooler, fresher air, and while the past parting shots of these plains howitzers were echoing more faintly, I followed Frat off into Dreamless Land.

Early rising had become habit now, and we were ready for the

Road before 6 a.m. It was six miles to Arapahoe; we would breakfast there. We were now in the valley of the Republican River, a welcome land after the enforced sojourn among the arid knolls and cutbanks. The soil was richer — the crop acreage told the story at a glance — woods were at hand here and there and formed continuous greenery along the stream. We were back among the birds, and they seemed thrice welcome.

"Breakfast at Arapahoe!" was our motto. Within a mile we met the path of the night storm; the road became a mess of mud. Only those who have tried such greasy footing on two wheels can quite understand the situation. The wheels would not grip; each wheel insisted on picking its own route. When the hind wheel goes off by itself instead of following in the path of its twin brother, a spill is avoided by only one expedient: shoe leather. The long-legged rider who can best convert himself and steed into a quadruped is the ablest. Strength in the matter counts, for the rider must fight his headstrong machine as well as the mud.

But this mud was both slippery and sticky. It came up in bundles and clogged the hind wheel. There was but one recourse: dig it out and start again. It was slow and wearisome labour. Sometimes we made a hundred yards at an assault, sometimes but fifty feet. Having an intermediate gear at my command, I had much the advantage of Frat. His high gear could not pull him through such a mess; his low gear was too strong and savage. Also, while his legs were as long as Lincoln they were not as long as mine. Two or three times as I rested or waited, digging out state property from that rear wheel, I saw Frat go down; and at such times the smoke that filled the roadway may not all have come from the exhaust pipe. Once I waited and hailed him, and asked him what was trump, and he hoarsely signalled "Arapahoe and breakfast — or I die!"

So I went on, rode everywhere between the fences that a foothold offered itself, fought through a suburban mudhole where the machine grounded in the soft ruts. And in climbing out, I found myself wet to the knees with soupy liquid, and finally did a grape-vine down Main

Street in the direction of an eating-house sign, and then subsided. It was 10 a.m. Frat came in by and by; he was not altogether pleasant to look upon.

To me, the most pleasing feature of this valley, also the little town, was its birdlife. During our fight of the morning while I was taking breath, I gathered some field observations, and now after eating in the town I went expeditioning on foot. The Arkansas kingbird I judged to be the commonest bird, the mourning dove the next; both were numerous. Twice during one intermission I had noted a dove go by over the same course and headed for the same wood, bearing something large and white in her beak, and as doves are not supposed to carry food to their dependents that way I was left mystified. Perhaps the busy little dame was merely house-cleaning. Cuckoos were heard several times and orioles sang clearly from the trees near the road. Upland plover rippled from the air a time or two, and once I saw the author of the unmistakable song on tremulous wing high in the air. The flicker and the Red-head had come back to hearten the way again. But in the greenery of the town I did far better, for shrikes here were squalling noisily and I unearthed a catbird and thrasher pair, some orioles, two blue jays, and best find of all: a mockingbird.

It was our first meeting. He was in full-hearted song, clear-throated and strong. His voice filled the little town and, on hearing him, I was filled with wondering admiration and hurried to find the artist. Up on the top of a red-brick chimney I found him perched, pouring his melodious melody abroad, sowing himself upon the summer winds. Now his throat trembled with the "Drop it! Drop it! Look a-hear!" of the brown thrasher; now it rippled with the ecstatic abandon of the catbird; now it was harsh with blue jay squeal or the cry of a wounded bird; now it was an impromptu but harmonious composition of his own: a sonata to the green plains or a madrigal intended for the ear of a mate hidden away snugly in half-tended shrubbery.

It was charming. Confusion to those men who have decried the ability of American singing birds! What green limit, what "blithe newcomer of the spring" what skylark "blithe spirit" that never was a bird, or what night-singing "light-winged dryad of the trees" could out-sing this good American on the chimney top? Not one of them!

At 2 p.m. we swung off upon our bumpity way again and within a few miles we had left the half-dry mud behind and actually encountered dusty travelling. "Variety, thy name — first last and middle — is Nebraska!" grunted Frat. Here the rains had preceded us by a few days; silt everywhere lay upon the low roads where it anchored after washing from the fields.

Sharp little cuts across the way often had to be crossed and where they were obscured by dusty goggles and grey soil, they used us cruelly. What was more, Frat who in the morning had contracted a falling habit, now by some strange rule of human nerves, insisted on tumbling because the way was dusty. During the time that he set the pace I noted two towering dust-fogs rise suddenly on the road ahead. Each time when the air cleared, I found Frat with an embrace more full of horsepower than gallantry helping Flying Maria to her feet. It was some time during the latter part of this afternoon that I made the entry in the diary: "Frat's nose now a sight!"

Here we had our last view of the Republican. The road climbed out of the valley and turned a brow of the rounding hills, and from our point of vantage we could look down upon the brown, bar-sown river. The near side was under cultivation; the far side evidently was a ranch, probably the remains of a larger one of bygone days, for now plainly enough the dry farmer had tramped heavily upon the heels of the stock man. A herd of fine cattle was bunched in the opening beyond the green cottonwoods that bordered the stream and a dog seemed the sole custodian of these animals, though doubtless a herder was somewhere in the shelter of the trees. It was a new scene even in this changeful land, and now also as I looked about me on the upper or prairie side, I noted the first plants of the arid lands. A cactus or two showed above the short grass and a new vegetable friend, apparently half cactus and half thistle, lifted a large, poppy-like bloom in the breeze. We were at a meeting place.

At 6 p.m. we reached the town of McCook and, after eating, we set out toward Imperial. At evening we were out in the lonely lands again and, working on the assumption there could be little rain or hail or aerial fireworks left in stock in this section of the United States, we decided to chance a night camp. At dusk we came to a green canyon with a little stream in the bottom; the walls were abrupt as the sharp cut zigzagged through the prairie knolls. It offered shelter, and down near the bottom on a soddy spot we prepared for eventualities.

The night was noteworthy not so much for the fact that the thunder rumbled faintly off in the distance and a few drops of rain rapped upon our frail roof, but because the first coyotes sang to us. Their jeering maniacal yelling came out of the night, clear and keen as always and wakened us. A dear old yell that! — a friendship cry, a reminder of other plainsland nights out.

The really true West was articulate at last; we were in it. For of all things, the coyote is typical of that intangible yet assured thing called the West. At any campfire on the east slope of the Rockies from far Slave Lake to the Mexican Gulf he will sing a song or two. An animal that can hold his own against the utmost destructive forces of man — most animals fail even when afforded protection — and can find a mocking song in his heart to sing to awaken his chief foe during slumber hours, is deserving of the honours of war. More or less, I love the rascal that, in spite of the odds, scarcely has been exterminated anywhere, and as long as I am building campfires I hope he will not be.

▪▪▪▪▪▪ Meter 1842

JULY 11. There was a sunrise of marvellous colour-loveliness to greet us at dawn. It was a plainsland day birth where all the sky is in sight and the clouds to east and west and north and south all catch the tints of morning and hold them suspended awhile. And the world of sound was as harmonious as was that of colour. Here we heard the first real singing of the lark buntings. The black and white males were very full of dawn song and the species was abundant. They filled earth and air with a tinkling, rippling, sylph-like chorus that seemed to come from everywhere, yet from no spot in particular. This universal quality is characteristic of other prairie songsters; I have noted it pleasantly in the spring choruses at dawn from the Lapland longspurs.

At Culbertson we found that we had gained another hour on old Sol and had to adjust our watches and lament the loss of an hour's sleep. Our road during the forenoon was up the valley of the White-man's River. We crossed several minor depressions with woods and abundant birdlife, traversed gulches and badlands, but in general, travel had much improved. Yet not tremendously, for we toiled often along poor, rutted roads that in places were very sandy and uncertain. There were some newly graded roads that had never made the ac-quaintance of a steam roller, and some brand new bridges told a story of recent freshets and floods. Also there was still some mud.

Toward noon we reached a river crossing and halted suddenly. The bridge was out: a hundred feet of bridge structure had gone, leaving neither hide nor hair of itself. At each side of the stream the grade merely ended in a twenty-foot drop to the brown eroding torrent which, though now subsided, still hurried fretfully and mined the crumbling banks on its way. On every hand lay the ravages of the flood that some little time previously had torn through this valley. The stream bed was littered with green trees that had been washed out by their roots, and many others on either bank were tottering and leaning to their fate. The green little valley had been ravished.

A crossbar nailed to uprights and standing across the brink of the cut indicated that this thoroughfare was closed, but a detour road that showed travel, turned aside, went through the fence into an alfalfa field, where the biggest stack of fodder I ever beheld topped the rise, and led us to a small temporary wooden bridge across the stream. Upon regaining the roadway we idled for a time in order to take a photo and listen to the birds and to note further the work of the high water. There was a sort of morbid pleasure in the latter.

The little valley was full of birdlife and I saw here both a kingfisher and towhee, neither of which had crossed our path for many days. Quail were calling so plentifully that it almost might have been termed a bobwhite chorus. But equally of note was our interesting discovery, near the grade that led out of the gulley, of flood relics and debris clinging to the trees fully six or seven feet above the ground! At the time they were placed there, the little valley must have been a wide river.

The afternoon brought us through rather a new type of country. It was a land of level distances, of immense fields of scattered, short-stemmed wheat — extensive but not intensive agriculture — of far-removed habitations, of sections upon sections of half-arid, untilled land under neither pasturage nor the plow and given over to the denizens of hot and sun-scorched ground: the grasshopper, the garter and hog-nosed snake, the striped spermophile, the prairie dog, the pocket gopher, the jackrabbit and the burrowing owl.

It was a land bordering on aridity and sterility; the meadowlark recalled the green fields of fertility, but the cactus with its yellow bloom told a different tale and warned us of what we might expect from this plain in a truly dry season. The bloom of the cactus is always a revelation, a strange yet lovely thing to see, and it was so here.

The day was burning hot with a southerly wind. The lark buntings noted here and there on the fences drooped their wings and wore an air of discomfort. But such heat was quite to the taste of certain ground lovers. Four different species of snakes were noted. Two hog-nosed chaps lay on the trail, victims of tires that had preceded us. I have reason for believing that some folks slay this inoffensive puffing "adder" or so-called "viper" or what-not, full of the righteous certainty that the victim is an honest-to-heaven rattler. Common garter snakes were on the trail, and on one occasion a beautiful little green grass snake wriggled into the rut and I was over him before I could avoid it. Also, the rattler was there — so says Frat. Once while he was leading I saw him stop suddenly and run back on the trail a few yards. By the time he had returned and I had arrived, the wily serpent had made his vamoose. But Frat swore to it with a bushel of conviction — had even heard the reptile sing his wicked-sounding tune — that the victim that would-have-been was a huge one.

Toward evening we reached the little handful of buildings

comprising Lamar, and after replenishing necessaries, we went on and made camp at dusk beside a Colorado road. In the diary that I scribbled at in the afterglow while Frat built the smudge fire, I made the odious statement of comparison that this road was the first we had seen during the day. Perhaps I too was a bit rancorous and full of the spirit that had prompted the articulate heart-burning I had heard half an hour earlier as we crossed the state line, when a voice came across the prairie and I think from the rear that said: "We are out of it, thank God! And I hope I may never get into it again!" It sounded like Frat, and though nothing is certain in the matter, I do know that I said "Amen!" to it.

Yet I felt that it was doubtful that we had seen the last of the mud. Much rain had been before us here; the ditches in the hollows were lipping. A flock of teal ducks went by in the dusk and the presence of large numbers of mosquito wretches all pointed to wetness. Also the voices of frogs rang across the plains, and when we turned in behind a good smudge fire, the voices of these long-winded musicians of the pond-holes quickly played us to sleep. But then we required little singing or rocking.

Some time near the middle of the night I wakened. The frogs had not paused for even a breath, and a Carolina rail was now adding his weird night cry to the musical commotion. Far off to northwestward a storm growled and muttered as it worked eastward, into Nebraska, thank heaven! A light breeze sprang from the direction of this newest-born electrical disturbance; it fanned our tarpaulin and winnowed our faces with a heavenly coolness, but we were in Colorado now. And then I wakened at dawn.

▪▪▪▪▪▪ Meter 1937

JULY 12. We had been told a great many times within a week that as soon as we crossed the Colorado line we would find good roads: real hard pike that had been made by the delinquents of the land (strictly overseen, of course). And here we might ride as fast as we could stay on. The latter part of this prediction did not mean much to us. We had been doing just that for some time, had been unable to stick on sometimes at about eight lineal miles per hour. Yet when the last pannier strap had been buckled upon the last item of our gipsy outfit and we were chugging westward over a gravel road, hard and well rounded, we were now more than half inclined to believe that for once — O rare exception! — the truth had been spoken. Hurrah! The speed indicator once more trembled around thirty; the horrid weather and mud in that other state to eastward henceforth were to be but a nightmare horror.

On the road, optimism is born anew at dawn. At sunrise the rosy hue of morning tinges more than the landscape; it is easy then to believe that you can measure off 200 miles for a day's travel — much easier than in mid-afternoon when the furnace winds are blowing. Perhaps the birds are more than a little responsible, and where indeed could one have found the dawn chorus more inspiring? It was not the spasmodic talent of the brown thrasher or catbird of the woodland that had come to us with the light, but a more sylph-like chorus, that tinkling here and there, filled the plains world with faint harmony: that song-service of the day-breaking that is known but to plains folk. It was a symphony of tuneful meadowlarks and tweeting horned larks and rollicking lark buntings, some bursting forth on the wing, others singing from fence post or weed tip. And there were some killdeers crying shrilly and a Bobwhite calling in a pasture, and a bittern and rail adding musical discord from the direction of a rain-filled hollow. It was all good and sweet but now the last of it was drowned by the growling of our impatient motors.

To Holyoke, and breakfast was a spin — until we met the water hole. In a hollow not far from town, the road disappeared under a sheet of rainwater. And did not emerge for seventy or eighty yards. The road was fenced. Plainly it was a case of low gear and a bath. Frat declared that if he must take the plunge he would take it with his clothes off. Why not wade across, leave our clothes, then ride through *à la* Frederick Remington Indians, and dress in dry clothes again?

But the fence posts and the stunted alfalfa did not offer much in the way of a dressing station, and automobiles used this public road. Perhaps that approaching buggy, half a mile ahead, held a female? When we looked hard we were sure it did. Frat hesitated at his own daring. Adam on a motorcycle did seem a bit brusque even for the West; he might scare the horse, he admitted. But it was all much ado about nothing. I compromised, waded through barefoot, found the bottom hard even, with nowhere a foot of water. We had negotiated the pond and were lacing our shoes when our early-rising female friend in the buggy arrived.

This was the land of the half-dry prairies, where the things of the verdant plain warred with the things of the desert, where the dry farmer crossed the path of the stock man and sometimes one side won and sometimes the other. For, where the desert had the upper hand, long stretches of semi-arid waste lay barren: the disputed home of the yellow-blooming cactus, the trembling buffalo grass, the ground squirrels and prairie dogs and a few of the big hawks that hunted them.

Here, too, because the sun beamed down through cloudless azure and the earth was hot, the sun lovers found their haven. Grasshoppers buzzed up in glistening showers, and in the hard, narrow trail that we followed at times during the forenoon were swarms of the females with their ovipositors thrust deep in the soil, and being helpless, they died under our juggernautical tires in the thousands. Snakes were almost very numerous. Now and again we met them in the wheel-track, dead and sun-cured, or sometimes wriggling still after being helplessly broken by the tires of some other traveller. These victims invariably were the smaller snakes; rattlers, the expected guests, spent their time elsewhere.

At other times, the hand of the desert had been thrust back: the dry farmer's broad acreage of wheat — short of stem, but stout of head and bearded — lay green upon the landscape for miles, and in the greener, richer valleys where streams wound their way through muddy banks, and where woods and copses held their own, some of the woods birds of the east gave greeting. We had not yet shaken off red-head; how he had stuck to our trail! We agreed that the world was going thoroughly better with us today. Although we were still on the plainsland, there was variety: that enticing, half-satisfying charm of a never-ending road.

The roads themselves scarcely fulfilled the promise of the morning. But if they were sandy in spots to the verge of despair, we had the consolation at least that they were not muddy, and steadily the procession of the miles slipped by. At noon we emerged through a white, cut-out road breaking upon a wondrous valley and we paused awhile. We had seen nothing like this. Another new world was in view: a world of dryness and heat and distance and loneliness. Below us, cut from the plain, lay a deep crooked valley or canyon, its sides cut and pierced by corrugated promontories sloping down far toward the bottom. No living thing seemed to stir there; it was a valley of silence and colour and rippling heat waves. In the far distance each over-cutting hill was a little bluer than its near neighbour, and tier on tier they melted miles away into the hazy translucence of the horizon and sky.

My recollection of this valley from the plainsland above is pleasanter than of the road down the slope and up again, but soon we were out and reached a thoroughfare that would have done credit to the original builders of highways. In a short time we had swept through the winding hollows, popped over the rounding knolls and reached the fine town of Sterling. Here another fact came home to us. The changes in the road are subtle; we often do not recognize them until the metamorphoses are complete. It was the large number of cattle in the stockyards of this town that brought suddenly to us that the great garden of the central valley of America lay behind us. We were invading the Kingdom of Horn and Hoof; King Wheat held slight sovereignty here.

From Sterling to Fort Morgan was a continuous spin up the valley of the South Platte; the running was so good that we merely slowed at the corners. That we had taken a leaf from the book of the see-it-and-run tourist and ran faster than there was need for in this more comfortable and prosperous land, scarce needs admission. We were merely reacting along the usual lines of human nature; the pendulum was swinging back. We had been fighting so long on retarded spark that to sit up loose and easy and open the throttle a little meant quite a new joy of the road. When at evening the crimson sun set his feet upon the horizon and stood a few minutes to look back over the plains, we were a few miles beyond Orchard, and so we turned in through the wire gate of a fenced pasture to make our camp. It was time. We had made 144 miles since the lark buntings sang to us at dawn. This was more mileage than we had covered for many days.

There is a fascination about sleeping out in the dry country that is scarcely obtained in other places where the camper is in jeopardy of being severely handled at night by the weather. Here the condition of the roads as well as the nature of the sunset declared that we were travelling under an almost rainless sky, but since we had not yet got out of our heads all of the "worst since '98" we spread the tarpaulin and pegged it down as usual. As we moved about at our work there arose from the sparse sod a whispering and rustling of grasshoppers disturbed and routed from their night roosts. We had other and far less expected neighbours, too, for in the dusk a dozen blue herons with slow flop came out from the green timber along the river valley close at hand and trailed off through the darkness toward the north. Full well they knew, even in this land of dusty roads and dry heavens, where lay the good fishing and frogging.

Then we built the smudge fire. It perhaps was more from habit than stress or circumstance, but a camp to be such and more than a lair simply must have a fire of some sort in the dusk, and the few mosquitoes that scented us and came up from the valley gave us the excuse. Perhaps because we felt that it might be the last one needed for a while, we bestowed more tender care on it than usual. At any rate I know we built it well. The experience gathered in more skeeter-cursed states was not wasted. A few twigs and an abundance of dry, sunbaked cow "chips" placed squarely upwind of a squirt of gasoline — there was no romance in this, but it was handy — with the whole smothered under a matting of the acrid artemisia that grew here plentifully, and we had a smudge fire that would smell pleasantly enough and would last well enough to make every long-snouted sucker of blood that should come nosing upwind put his proboscis under his wing and flee.

■■■■■ Meter 2081

JULY 13. Early in the morning we had another sort of visitor. Somewhere just over the border between sleeping and waking I saw an enormous beetle mounting upon the tousled dome of the unconscious Frat. What old Coleoptera could want up there was a mystery; his sole and only aim at the moment seemed to be "Excelsior!" But soon he became entangled, and Frat, coming halfway out of his slumber, reached up sleepily and dislodged him. Five minutes later, Coleoptera returned to the assault and again was shouldering his way through the hairy entanglements that defied him, and I realized the truth.

He was a rove beetle, I think, one of those hard-shelled chaps that finds his life employment in burying dead mice and ground squirrels and such small carrion as lie about on the ground. Without doubt, our black-coated visitor had looked Frat over and decided that he ought to be buried, and now he was merely making a sort of preliminary survey of this, for him, a rather herculean undertaking.

Then Frat, recognizing that he was besieged, stirred, threw off his slumber-chains, reached up and clouted hard. Next he rose on his elbow, surveyed the prostrate Coleop, now on his back and gesticulating wildly with his legs, and then reaching down he picked a heavy shoe and smote his victim with the sole. Thwack! Whereupon there rose from that vile wretch of a beetle a stench to shame the collective plagues of Egypt. The very essence and quintessence of things dead were at his call. Frat, though blessed with but a rudimentary olfactory nerve, declared it positively fierce. Seizing the shoe again, he beat the foe to fragments, ground him into the soil and covered the spot. But it was all useless. Victorious even in defeat and death, the wretch smelled to heaven; so we made a bolt and got out, threw off the tarpaulin and let the dawn zephyrs work their sweetening influence. Henceforth this bivouac was referred to as Stink-beetle Camp.

The footing in the morning was over good gravel roads with some loose material in spots to test the nimbleness of our legs, and presently early in the forenoon we had come upon a new scene that compelled us to pause again. From our stand on the brow of a promontory overlooking the valley of the river, the land lay like a giant relief map below us. The narrow valley was green and fruitful; cottonwoods followed the course of the stream and grass and verdure were there. Speaking, articulate life was there also; for a dozen black and white magpies chattered incessantly — brand new friends these, but to be met again later — and bobwhite, some meadowlarks, some good, old-fashioned blackbirds and a red-headed woodpecker were all pleasingly noisy. A big blue heron flapped slowly over the shrubbery; a hawk circled airily far above.

Beyond this to westward lay another scene: the arid rolling plain, all grey-green in its coat of short tufted artemisia and sage, dotted here and there with cattle, and fading off gradually into the opaque yet intense blue that formed the horizon wall. This was aridity: the beginning of the truly dry lands; the difference between the two scenes was the result of the stream below us. With its banks smothered in miniature forests of tall sweet clover, the stream followed a channel that by dint of much labour had been gouged along the side of the valley. Now it was controlled by human ingenuity and yielded its life-giving waters to the needy soil. How apt the age-old expression "living waters"— the true *aqua vitae* indeed!

We had come to the irrigation lands. Not quite the first of them, it is true, but somehow the meaning of it came home more plainly to us here. Scarcely could it have been better marked, this transition from natural sterility to artificial fertility where, for man to win his bread from the soil, he must throw his genius into the balance. One of the chief differences between savagery and civilization was expressed here at our feet.

Then we saw them — the mountains! The Rockies! Far in the

depths of what had seemed the impenetrable wall of the hazy blue horizon, a chain of white or pinkish masses hung suspended, barely piercing the filmy miles. And coming into eyeshot, the snowcaps and white-crowns of the high-piled giants of the West, the backbone of the continent. It was a sight to stir the imagination, to send up and down the spine those tingling prickles that can be inspired only by the big and deep things: the sublime. We stopped, took off our caps and gazed; the West with its romance and adventure lay ahead of us. We were gazing reverently into a promised land.

All morning we ran with the distant mountaintops upon our right. Perhaps it was their invitation and challenge that opened our throttles. At any rate we paused little by the way, passed through Greely early and at noon swung south toward Denver. Soon we were to sample the going in that fairy land of snowcaps to westward.

▪▪▪▪▪▪ Meter 2182

JULY 15. I have already apologized for my apparent slight of the fair cities on my road and need offer none now for my silence in regard to this lovely western city with its sunsets and scenic glimpses of the mountain lands at its door. Still, as we were being escorted out over the Federal Boulevard by Mr. W. (our good angel in fitting us more completely for the mountains), I felt that our day had been very happily spent. But the Road was calling; those mountains were close at hand. Yet what magnificent deceivers are these white-crowns. They are never just where the visitor thinks them and are always five times as far away as his most pessimistic guess would put them. We had decided to go through or over the northern part of the state. The fact that nearly all the other travellers heading westward on tires went the old route by way of Cheyenne, Wyoming, had decided that. And so now we headed for Golden and Lookout Mountain. Yet though we travelled fast, how those elusive mountain caps seemed to shrink back before us. Shrink, yet at the same time grow in magnificence and tower over the plain.

Just beyond Golden we began to climb stiffly and here we met our first trouble. That winding road carved from the mountainside was too much for plainsland motors. Even at Denver with its 5,000-odd feet of elevation, doubtless their heads had been swimming, but this ascent was too much. Their bark fell to a purr, their strength failed, and they all but died side by side on the slope.

"Lung trouble!" said Frat. "Give 'em more air."

So with a little adjustment of the carburetor we got back the wicked bark that means power, and on and up we went, winding over a perfect road that at times was fenced on the falling-off side with granite pillars and wire cable. Up, up, back and forth, always higher till at last we reached the only spot on that road that was level, the top. Here, leaving the motors, we climbed a few yards to the very tip, then sat down upon a boulder and gazed.

It is well named, Lookout Mountain. The thrill that comes to the plainsman during his first gaze from such a mountain is one that is not given many times in a lifespan. Here indeed was a view! The blue plain rolled away and away till actually it seemed to tip up concavely at the far sky-line, a view quite indescribable. Olympian Zeus never gazed across a fairer, finer scene. No brush could paint its subtleties, no lens copy it: such pictures must be carried away locked in the soul of the beholder.

All forenoon we toiled up the mountain roads, the beckoning snow-peaks ahead, the miles of trail, good or bad in spots, rough or smooth, hard or dusty, falling behind and below. There was variety here, even in the roadbed itself. It was honest mountain scenery now. Clear Creek with snow-water from the peaks, roared below us and broke the stillness at times. The air was redolent of spruce and pine; the shadows were cool. The things that love the shadowy silences were there too. Once as we paused, which we did a great many times, for one cannot commit rank sacrilege and rush the mountains, a towhee called sweetly from the side of the valley where a garrulous magpie was discussing his troubles. And deep below a thrush with a strange new song — most probably an olive-backed — breathed out his peaceful, spiritual song.

Entering the Rockies. (COURTESY: BCA J-01412)

Much of this road was stiff climbing, and late in the afternoon as we toiled up toward Empire, Flying Maria proved too strong for her couplings and Frat had to get out his tools and mend his chain. However, he took it philosophically enough, even challenged me to find a finer spot in which to do a job of tinkering. As I was of little use to him, I went scouting down to the creek to sit on the boulders at its roaring rim to watch a chipmunk, to smell the wild roses and to listen to the restless whisperings of a clump of aspens — good old tree friends these, of many a more northerly trail. When I returned, he was ready. "Be prepared" had been our motto when outfitting; a little of everything necessary to the health of gas motors was to be found in our kits.

Then we climbed again, and in spite of our up-hill road, it was a day of unadulterated delight. We had awakened from our late nightmare; it now seemed a horrid unreality, a land of mud and water and mosquitoes in that hailed-on and sun-scorched plain. In the presence of such cool and lightsome air, such an unfathomable blue sky with its far-scattered white wreaths, such sweet tang of evergreens, that other state to eastward no longer existed.

A new world with a new life was all about us. The pines and aspens and alders were new; the alpine plants on the hillsides were strangers, and I could recognize but few of them. If the pine squirrel appeared quite himself, the chipmunk did not. The tiny golden-crowned kinglets that lisped in the evergreens were the first on this two-thousand-mile trail. The meadowlark that sang a parting song in a mountain pasture near Lookout Mountain appeared out of his element. The magpies that chattered in strange tongues seemed foreigners. It was all new, fresh and pleasing. We were kings of the earth again, joint-heirs with the gipsies to all the joys of the open, never-ending Road.

We had dinner at Idaho Springs, supper at Empire, then loaded some indestructible tinned goods into our panniers in anticipation of an outdoors breakfast, and we set off up the valley again. When the sun was gone from us, the wondrous valley in deep shadow below, and the sentinels still glowing far above, we crossed a rude bridge over a roaring stream, climbed a few feet and dismounted for the night. Several charred remains of former fires told the story of the spot.

Another day of delight was done; the Road was good again. To-night a real campfire was in order; it was a third party in the roadside bivouac. The evening came suddenly cool and the fire's warmth was as welcome as its light and sociable crackle was cheerful. I posted my diary by the light of it; and while thus occupied, steps sounded from the road and we had callers. It took about three seconds to get acquainted. Bill, a native of Ontario, Canada, carried a .30-30 Winchester and had but to open his mouth to make plain that he was not the man his rough exterior betokened. His comrade, Louis, spoke brokenly and claimed as his birthplace Alsace, France, or Alsace, Germany, although he would not have admitted that it was Germany.

So none of us being neutrals, we plunged into the Great War without reserve, and were able to jointly and severally curse the enemy to our heart's content. The Alsatian was stirred passionately, was going back shortly to assail the hated foe. I doubt not that he did so and either won his heart's desire or gave up his life like so many valiant sons of France on the field of honour. What Bill was doing here I could neither guess nor inveigle out of him. When I enquired his game with the rifle, he replied easily — too easily I thought — that there were some cottontails up the trail. When I told him pointedly that I usually went after rabbits with a smaller caliber, he countered suavely with the assurance that he liked to use the same rifle all the time and he did not eat their heads anyway. I fancy the cottontail he liked best was the white flag on the rear end of a retreating mule deer; and I doubt not that a young buck with his horns in the velvet would have suited friend Bill much better than a rabbit — Colorado game laws to the contrary.

▪▪▪▪▪▪ Meter 2252

JULY 16. Mountaineering even with a motor is strenuous play, and while blanket and air-pillow seemed good, somehow we were up with the first dawn light. The morning was chill, the air that came down the valley was cold — the very breath of the white-caps glistening, sun-illumined above us. The first four or five miles were up and down in the rough, dark valley. Then we began to climb again: an ascent compared with which our other climbs had been but play. The summit was not far distant now; every few minutes we stopped to gaze at a new wonder vista.

Somewhere near timber-line or about ten thousand feet elevation, we stopped in a sunny spot for breakfast. A tiny rill of spring water trickled out of the cliff and formed a pool beside the narrow road, and here we made our fire. Above us still towered the unattainable snows; below lay a deep canyon dark with the shadows of evergreens, fairy-like when viewed from above the new tender, green tops and tips. The boisterous little stream growled almost out of earshot in the far bottom. Across from us frowned a barren, volcanic crater-relic of other ages. The trees stood motionless as death itself, no mountain zephyrs fanned even their tips. In the quietness, the lisping of a beautiful little Townsend warbler nearby was very plain, and the sweet voice of our thrush drifted up from shadowy places.

Then the silence was strangely broken. There came a rumble down the road and a shrill unexpected note that echoed far through the valley. The strangers had an old-fashioned, canvas-covered wagon; a man and two wolf-hounds led the way, and two head of cattle were tied behind. The driver, perched high, urged on his steaming horses. But it was the male occupant of the crate on the wagon that drew most attention. He had a good voice and he knew it, did that rooster, and often as he could find breath — which was very often, for the rarified atmosphere troubled his lungs not at all — he let go mightily. A strange awakening to the silences in these solemn places where perhaps cock clarion had never echoed before. Perhaps some princess of the mountain realms had been imprisoned in that old volcanic castle across the valley and was doomed to lie in durance or asleep till a Red Prince of Rhode Island should come and call her to liberty again. If so she was called.

There is little cleaning up after a roadside meal, and when the panniers had been fastened we climbed again. Up, up, up over the interminable slope we chugged and barked, over rough stones, or log bridges above angry, tumultuous streams sandwiched into bits of better road, around sudden uncanny turns, up gruelling drives, now confronted by one snowy monarch across the valley, now by another.

It was all uphill going now, and stiff climbing at that. There were no breathing-places or "Thank you, ma'ams" here. They had told us that the last mile toward the pass was the steepest, and we began to hope that we were getting near the last mile. Presently we made another sharp turn and rushed up a steep climb, skirted a brow over a hundred yards of atrocious road, came out in the open, and mounted a rounding, bare knoll: the Continental Divide, the Summit of the Berthoud Pass.

To have a snowball battle at timberline on July 16th, elevation 11,400 feet; to be photographed and to take photographs of the event and surroundings; to contemplate the trickling water on one side of the slope starting on its mighty journey to the Atlantic, and the water on the other side starting for the Pacific; to pluck marigolds and buttercups blooming in the chilly seepage from the big snowbank that clung to the northerly side of the knoll; to see, and hear, four thousand sheep in one mass of moving grey animation on a new summer range of pale-green pasture far on a neighbouring mountain but little below us; and to fill the eye and mind with beauty and wonderment

Mack Laing at the summit of the Rockies, roof of the continent.
(COURTESY: BCA J-01413)

in contemplation of this roof of the Rockies, surely was to spend an hour well. An hour! I could have camped there a week, sat upon a stone and enjoyed every minute of it. Then we started down the Pacific slope: whole western worlds lay before us.

Nor were all the wonders and beauties left behind with the summit. The long, crooked descent was almost as full of interest, though usually we were too busy with the band-brake to have eyes for much other than the road. For however difficult the ascent, the descent, where eternal vigilance is the price of life and limb, is always even more nerve-trying on rider or driver. At Fraser where we lunched, we found that we had dropped three thousand feet, and a resident here pointed out the spot far above to eastward, where, even above timberline, the railroad crosses the Divide. The great white sentinels of the morning were behind us now. It was a wonder world of big things.

From Fraser we followed an up-and-down-dale road through open or half-wooded ranching country where we made better time and saw proportionately less. But at evening we came to a wonderland again. Leaving Sulphur Springs, we turned abruptly into the hills and at once struck a climb as gruelling as any in the Rockies. Up, up again, turning, twisting, winding along the side of the mountain we toiled. A thousand feet seemed won when we reached a hairpin turn on a shoulder overlooking the valley and the town whence we had come, and we halted again.

Below us to eastward, mysterious in the light of the half-hidden sun, lay a valley more beautiful than dreams. Its charm was in the mystery of subtle colour. From the wonderful sky-tints of sunset to the coolest blue of the valley, the picture was of a fairyland in reality, tangible — ours! We gazed dumbly. When our eyes grew familiar we turned our heads sidewise and received anew the fresh colour thrill. And we gazed until the sun dipped below the horizon and impelled us to turn away.

Soon we reached this new summit and emerged from the woods into the open, and the new sensation here was that of coming out upon the roof of the world again. Distance again seemed to have lost

Mack and Frat shaking hands at the Berthoud Pass after climbing
the Rockies. (COURTESY: BCA J-01409)

its meaning. Hill upon hill — elsewhere they would be deemed
grown-up mountains — timberless, sterile, but clad in the grey-blue
of the sagebrush, rolled away in sharp undulating swells into the sunset. It was beautiful, wonderful, terrible: colossal, blue-grey billows on
a Titanic sea; magnificent, and yet with something lacking. It was the
kind of thing that catches our breath and starts a tear and we know
not why. For there was a lonely, Death-in-life feeling in it: the dead
face of a beautiful, soulless, childless woman.

But oh the variety of the Colorado road! Within three miles we
were literally sliding down again precipitously from this roof and
aiming at the river glinting below. In the dusk the road skirted close
to the rushing stream (the Grand River) and on a green-sodded bank
near the water's edge, we made camp.

There were a few mosquitoes on hand to welcome us as we spread the blankets, but they were half-hearted and did not last long, for the night came down chill and keen with a sharpness that presaged Jack Frost on the rampage. And also we had wood on hand to make body to our smudge fire. We were glad to turn in early. It had been a day good to look back upon.

The one idea, ever-present, overpowering, holding the fort in the focus of our domes of flitting ideas, was that we were in Colorado and had climbed over the Rockies. There was a sense of satisfaction in the thought, and also another of regret. The like, perhaps, could not be on our trail again. But this we knew: the Road was good again. While a spotted sandpiper down the stream peeped in an anxious way that betokened something amiss in the family, and the night hawks grunted as they swung and darted over the valley, we lay and lived it all again till the winking stars came bright.

▪▪▪▪▪▪ Meter 2298

JULY 17. But if the dusk had been chill, the dawn was frigid, for there was a frost rime on the tarpaulin (we had not pegged it out but used it as extra bedding), and the green grass was stiff with white frost. The first ponds we met after breaking camp actually had a coating of thin ice upon them. However, this condition, like all others in this land of the Queen of Contrasts, did not long prevail, and we were soon warm enough. To Kremmling was a scurry through uncountable white-tailed jackrabbits. The rascals seemed to delight in a contest for a few yards with the noisy motors. Then at the wooden bridge beyond the town we halted for a gipsy breakfast.

It was eight o'clock and in that clear air of the higher altitudes the sun already was hot. Here we made the toast to the accompaniment of a quaint hodgepodge of bird voices and songs; in fact it seemed one of those transition spots where almost any bird might find a home. Plainly we had left the mountain realm behind, yet two or three magpies shouted in their mischievous, bickering way across the valley from the dry hills.

But there were others of the lower lands. A flicker shouted with amorous conviction nearby; a kingfisher came clicking over the water to alight on the bridge railing and, at sight of us, to depart as though he had been shot at; a spotted sandpiper was peeping excitedly from the river margin; and a beautiful mountain bluebird spoke up from his perch on the fencewire. How intense! How exquisite the cerulean coat of this Westerner; the sky never was so blue as his back.

But best friend of all, the little song sparrow sang from the willows right at hand. We had missed him for many days in the mountains and beyond, and this little chap did his best to make amends. Though the usual song of "Maids, maids, maids, put on the tea-kettle-ettle-ettle!" was noticeably abbreviated and stopped at the "tea," the effort was welcome indeed. What he lacked in repertoire he made up in enthusiasm. It can be done rarely, for not even the bang of a can of spaghetti, which exploded like a cannon in our fire, could shake him.

The forenoon at least proved fairly consistent. Hour after hour we chugged along on an assortment of roads over the arid, rolling mountains. They were dreamily picturesque in their wondrous, vari-coloured soil and sage-grey and juniper-green trimmings. And they were hot! There were roads of black soil and grey and yellow and red soil and the hundred various tints of each; the canyon walls glowed in warm colours and always there was kaleidoscopic variety. The dusty roads, the sagebrush, the stunted, gnarled junipers of the hillsides and every sign by the way told the tale of aridity. Where in the river valley a settler had braved this lonely land and by means of irrigation coaxed fertility from the soil, his field of greenery shone below us like an emerald in a ruddy setting.

In an open valley our way led by one of these green little sanctuaries and I went in. Plainly it was not a new claim; the buildings, the planted trees told of early effort here. A small tributary of the Grand had been diverted from its former bed and now little rills and trickles in shallow ditches were bringing life to the timothy and alfalfa and garden stuff. Great cottonwoods rustled mockingly to the searching dry airs that came up the hot valley, and in their tops a warbling vireo trilled his summer-singing pipes. His was the last tune I should have guessed to find here. Doubtless the scanty pasturage of the hills was the mainstay of this wilderness home.

A sweet little girl of twelve or thirteen came to the door, persuaded a sour-tempered collie that I was not to be eaten, and gave me road directions. O dwellers in wilderness homes, advance guards, scouts of the settlements, how little are you appreciated by your brothers and sisters of the world's other half who dwell in crowded places!

Some of our going now was over real mountain roads and dangerous. On one occasion we literally hugged the sheer slope, and the narrow cut that served as leeway was the sort to set one thinking, while trying not to. Dizzily below in its bright canyon rolled the turbulent Grand. The descent was abrupt. At such times, an imagination is an awkward and undesirable possession, and I could not prevent my own from wandering as far as the band-brake and coming back to stir up a shiver or two.

Stories of wagons having to be taken apart here by the teamsters in order to effect a passing came to my mind, and what two opposing chauffeurs would do still remains a mystery. Here more even than on the hairpin turns and narrow ledges of the Rockies, the warning words of Mr. W. our Denver friend, came home to us. "Ride the INSIDE track up there!" he had said; and when we objected that it was contrary to the Road law of the land, he said, "I know; but do it!"

And on this flirtation with the hill-tops above the Grand, where there was much rolled-down rubble, any stone of which might have shied a careless front wheel aside and sent us on a far journey, we did as we had been bidden. A trust in Providence is undoubtedly an admirable thing, but under such circumstances, it is also well to look to the band-brake and keep your legs handy.

State Bridge next, said the map, and we had been told in the morning that we would reach it easily before noon. That we did not measure up to what was expected of us worried us little, for most folks seem to regard a motorcyclist in the same class as the aviator and disregard roads entirely. At 1:30 p.m. we were still in search of the town. By and by we skirted the river and pulled into a little compound of log shacks that denoted a ranch. The buildings were over-decorated with blanched elk antlers and some scary chickens ran about. Somebody lived there, and Frat who was leading, dismounted stiffly. A stout lady instantly came to the door. But then of course we knew that there was a woman about; in these out-post places the travellers can sense the difference between bachelor quarters and a woman-blessed abode at a half mile.

"Can you tell us how far it is to State Bridge?"

"Yes, this is State Bridge."

Frat has a robust constitution and a blunt sense of humour. He merely staggered a bit as he turned about and asked me if we would eat. Truly, the traveller must reconstruct his ideas here as to what constitutes a town. Road guides compiled in the West are scarcely dependable; at least they contain a trifle more Western humour than geographical fact. Also the newcomer must reconstruct other notions, for though the "hotel" was a shack with a roof of split poles with earth piled on top, there was a telephone on the wall, and we were served with a satisfying enough meal.

But it was those white horns bleaching outside that stirred me most. What antlered heads had fallen here since Indian days! O to roam these painted hills with pack and rifle in September or October when the elk lords of the wild would be bugling and challenging the echoes in these lonely valleys. There is a large streak of hunter-pioneer blood in me somewhere. At such times and in such scenes as these it gets up and yells.

We started into a brutal, uphill grind at State Bridge and later we met many scarcely less severe. The afternoon brought similar running, save that perhaps the sun burned a little deeper and the roads were dustier and rougher. It was a joggling, nerve-wearing trail that wound and twisted and turned upon itself among those rough, gaudy hills. The only bits of greenery in the valleys were the result of irrigation. Sagebrush stretched in shimmering miles, and the only tree to face the hills was the juniper. How stunted, gnarled, sturdy, full of fight it seemed. With its tattered bark hanging loose on some of the larger trees — they seemed as old as the Beginning — it stood like a dishevelled, defiant thing. Yet the juniper was a lovely thing as well. It was alive. Its dusty green clumps dotted the hills everywhere, and I had but to fancy these same rugged, hard-baked heavings of the earth without the juniper to realize at once its place in the landscape. Volcanic rocks, porous and rough on tires and shoes, lay about on the trail and beside it.

But in this land of changeability no condition long prevails. About five in the afternoon we were in an open, gently rolling valley where woods of aspen with much under-brush and flowers and many woods birds announced that we had reached a rained-on land. Ahh! What a difference. Never before had we realized the meaning of these summer showers of blessing so unappreciated in other lands.

During the afternoon we had turned away from the Grand and run in a northerly direction. Toward evening we came out upon better roads in a half-settled valley and just at sunset reached the town of Yampa. On a sagebrush hill two miles beyond this centre we made camp. Quite in contrast to the preceding night, this one came warm and still. No snowcaps spied upon us from the distance, but close at hand some jagged rock spires, remnants of bygone days of volcanic fire flood's erosion, stood tall in the dusk and took over the sentinel watch of the night. Before slumber-time, we went over to a farmhouse a hundred yards off and at a little stream running through the yard, splashed and rubbed ourselves into respectability and parted company with a wondrous collection of road samples. A lad came down with an extra towel to assist in the near-godly occupation, and then he came back with us to our machines. It was plain that we were rather a new species to him, and on finding us harmless, he must needs look us over more intimately.

▪▪▪▪▪▪ Meter 2376

JULY 18. Four hundred and thirty-nine miles of Colorado's changing wonders, said the road tally, and many more yet to come. We were abroad early. One soon learns the value of the mornings in this land where the sun beams warmly at eight o'clock, hotly at nine and from then is relentless until about five in the afternoon. So just as a duck hawk or a falcon on speeding wing went skimming by over the sagebrush cover, bent on pinning one of the numerous little ground squirrels coming out to greet the sun, and a marsh hawk on the same hungry mission went slowly careening by also, we too set forth to see what the day's hunting would bring.

I think we felt a trifle loth to leave this green valley, for however much the outdoors man may love the remote corners, however much he may sigh for an unfrequented island safe from the maddening crowd, or for a lodge in a wilderness, we are, after all, human at heart and social beings. A fertile valley with some crop acreage, trees and houses, and with a few good old red-winged blackbirds and grackles, bluebirds and swallows for lipping measure, all made an appeal that at one time we would not have admitted. When we had been a day up in the high places where the gods dwell, and another in the splendour of the barbaric hills, a green valley seemed no anti-climax. And then as I have indicated, the heart of the Road lover is as fickle as a sweet-sixteen love.

Roads — the measure of mankind since the world began — how we loved them where they were hard and smooth, and we ran fast, full of the joy of the morning; and how we anathematized them when they were dusty and chucky and full of hidden bumps and bangs and the skidding machines trickily threw us. But there was more good road than bad in this rolling valley, and shortly after 9 a.m. we came into the town of Steamboat Springs.

It was here that we began to encounter rumours of breakers ahead.

"After you reach Craig and get out into the desert, you are going to get it rough!" was the sum total of the consolatory advice we received. But though we had not ridden two thousand miles without learning that a road is never as bad, or as good, as it is said to be by these press agents of traffic conditions, yet there seemed no other verdict in the matter. And so after replenishing the sinews of locomotion and straightening a bent pedal or two, we set out for Craig.

Craig is what in the West they call a jumping-off place. Between this town and Vernal, Utah, lay the so-called desert, a dry land with little settlement. After a session of third-degree methods in the two garages of the place and elsewhere (it is safe enough now in the West to bore a man to death with verbal inquisition if you are sure you will never see him again), we elicited that the roads were trails, that the water holes were few and far between, that we must ride somewhere between seventy-five and one hundred miles before reaching gasoline. And as for sand, that nightmare horror to the man on two wheels, all assured us with a prepare-to-meet-your-god sort of grimness that long before we raised any dust in Vernal we would be one hundred percent efficient in sand-riding. What was more to the point they all agreed that we ought to consult Bill, the stage-driver (auto) who was on that trail almost daily. They said that he knew every foot of it. And he did.

So after this interview and supper, we set off from Craig. One beauty of roughing it through such a dry land is that one need not worry about making such and such a place in time to secure accommodation. It mattered little to us where night fell. One clump of sagebrush makes as bright a fire as the next does; the ground is as soft, or as hard, here as there. And no, we did not expect rattlers to invade our night privacy. For though there are rattlers in Colorado, it would seem that by far the greater number of them are in the pages of fiction and also in the minds of certain tourist visitors hailing from Eastward. Once or twice here and several times elsewhere in the dry states that somehow hold the reputation for wildness and wooliness, we heard the query between various visitors:

"See any rattlers?" and the ingenuous reply: "No, but we heard them often!"

Six miles of good road, Bill had said, and we found it so. Then we turned into a stretch of rounding knolls and tackled the road that to a motorcyclist, of all roads, is perhaps the worst: the sand trail through the sagebrush. He cannot ride the sandy rut, nor ride out of it. The front tire seems full, not of air but of deviltry. With fiendish persistency it tries to climb out of the rut, and in so doing skids drunkenly from side to side. It is impossible to balance. The rider must get down his feet and flail and drag them in a ludicrous gait: a cross between an intoxicated walk and an old woman's hop-step-and-jump. Anything is fair in this fight as long as he keeps his steed on her feet and keeps moving — ahead. A few miles an hour is as much as even a hardened rider cares to make in such going. For sand-riding is a gruelling game. It may develop aches and pains below the belt faster than any other known form of athletics, but at least it is an almost positive cure for dyspepsia and insomnia.

We made five miles of it. During that long hour or more we lived to the full what is popularly known as the strenuous life. Yet there were slight compensations: this adventure of the legs was winning our way into a new phase of this changing land. It was a new mood of My Lady Changeable. In this lonely land (though Frat, whose legs as I have explained, were shorter than mine, declared with conviction that it was "god-forsaken") we had come to the homeland of jackrabbits and sage grouse. As a vanishing wild species, the latter were very welcome.

As it was their nesting season and we saw no young, it was evident that these birds, like some of the other prairie grouse, are given to bachelor clubs and sociability at morning and evening. These congregations that stood at half a stone's throw and ogled and talked foolishly to us (when we were stopped) were not families or flocks so much as fraternities. The jackrabbits, all black-tailed chaps now, scooted here and there everywhere, or sat close at hand as we rested, wagged their attenuated ears and shifted their fleas in brazen unconcern. Once a big badger went humping off through the sage, and a few minutes later, Frat rode into one of the rascals' excavations and in consequence stood on his head in a clump of sagebrush by the trail.

Also we met a team of mules. At sight of us, they stopped short in deep contemplation and studied us hard with eyes and ears. So did the driver. It was evident that our rough and tumble manner of progression was as unfamiliar to him as to his long-eared friends. I was wondering hotly whether or not he was going to have the grace to give me even my slender half of the trail, when — Presto! I had it all. The outfit went from the way as though blown out and headed for the mountains. The frightful expletives and exhortations hailing from the driver were of little avail. The very best he could do was swerve his sky-hopping conveyance a little, and according to the law of parabolic curves, doubtless he came back to the trail within a mile or two.

In the dusk we came to the place of a lonely homesteader, one of that intrepid sort who seem to have faith enough in Providence to defy the weatherman and try to grow wheat in impossible places. At his warm invitation we spread our blankets upon a matting of rye hay near the little frame stable. He was glad to see strangers, and as he unburdened his heart, I wondered more and more at the strangeness of some men.

It was the loneliest claim I think that I ever beheld. Yet he and his wife had been here three years, had grown nothing to speak of, but were full of hope for the future. Had the sage grouse and jackrabbits and perhaps other game been denied him, existence must have been difficult. Yet hope was there. Hope, an inexplicable thing! What surprised me most was that for years this same pioneer of lonesome land had been a railroad man. Which only goes to show that we all hitch our wagons to the unattainable and sigh for things that cannot be. A little field of cleared sagebrush land where every green blade was a bait for a hungry rabbit. A little rye hay, short and stunted, this and hope — alas! But we were weary to exhaustion. On our couch of rye hay, a luxury to us now, not even the coyotes that came close and insisted on serenading us intermittently through the night could spoil such slumber.

▪▪▪▪▪▪ Meter 2466

JULY 19. The sunrise brought a sky of colour glory, of tender, warm tints and hazy cloud-wreaths all steeped in rosy glow. We oiled our dusty steeds and mounted, a bit stiffly, it must be admitted, for that trail already was beginning to tell on us. The morning road brought a repetition of sand fighting, and after a time we reached Lay Ranch and breakfast.

In this connection I wish to state, for the benefit of mankind, my conviction that any man wanting an unfailing cure for sluggish liver or rebellious digestive apparatus ought to rise early and ride to his morning meal over seven miles of Colorado sand trail on a Barking Betsy. He will be cured. That is, if he survives. If this treatment will not affect the wonders of the advertisements, then surely he is doomed. So take or leave this bit of medical advice; there is no charge for it. And as for us, never while smothering the yell in a clamouring stomach did hot cakes taste better.

While thus pleasantly engaged I was much taken with the excellence of some photographic enlargements of Colorado big game that decked the rough log walls. Upon making enquiry, I was delighted to learn that I had stumbled into the stamping ground of Mr. M., perhaps the pioneer of big game photographers in America. In a little cabin close at hand I found him: an old, grey-bearded, pleasant gentleman with a touch of John Muir or John Burroughs or Henry Thoreau about him, a veritable Bank of England of golden experiences with the big game that twenty-five years ago inhabited this region. Alas, such experiences never can be duplicated.

In the short three-quarters of an hour that I had to spare, he showed me a museum: antelope, mule-deer, elk, cougars, bobcats and bear. What weary waiting at the water holes he had known, what disappointments with his old-fashioned machinery, and yet what successes. He took me to the log stable to see the nestful of phoebes, and though the brood had just vacated the cradle on the beam, we found them on the wire fence outside. He had killed a rattler that morning and was about to go and hunt another that had been seen by one of the ranch hands. He was a surveyor, or had been, but plainly his real work had scant relation to lineal measure. His heart was in the Highlands, or more exactly about the water holes in the valleys.

Yet there was a ring of sadness that touched me. His only published work on his beloved hobby had told the truth too well to be a financial success, and he had not tried again. But I doubt not that when this good old man has been gathered home to heaven — and I hope that chimerical institution has a department somewhere off in a quiet place where such spirits may continue their harmless hunting of black-tails and bobcats — I doubt not that his books will sell to the nth edition and someone will be able to see Europe after the war on the proceeds.

Then we buckled on our armour again. Indeed it was a fight all the time now. There was sand and sand and more of it. We were wearing out. And it is a fact that as vitality runs low, appreciation of the aesthetic vanishes: another case of the wolf coming in at the door and the dove going out through the broken pane. By and by we came to the Bear River, crossed and held a war council. Our engines running on low gear had eaten fuel at an alarming rate; plainly our tanks could not carry us through. Either we must turn aside from our trail and go to Maybell and get gasoline (the map said that there was a town or supply station there), or later sit by the road and await the coming of our stage driver. He in fact had warned us against taking the Maybell route, declared it impassible for two wheels. And so now we compromised and decided to go into this source of supply and then return to our present trail again.

This we attempted to do, but the trick was to find the cut-off road. By and by we noted a small frame shanty back a little distance from our trail, and leaving Frat I cut through the hummocky sagebrush. I was forced to walk the last hundred yards, and a rather rough-appearing individual came out a few yards, stood and waited for me. He gave me directions and without a word to spare, but why he should have come out to meet me puzzled me a little till when I reached the road Frat said: "Hey! Did you see what that fellow put in his pocket as he came out of the shack? Well, I did. It was a gun. I suspect we had better paint these army britches blue while we are in this country!"

So we turned aside as directed but soon the trail degenerated, if that were possible, into a sandy mess, and we found even low gear so cruel to our machines and ourselves that we abandoned them and walked. It was now about three miles to our destination. Already we could see a cluster of buildings shimmering dizzily through the heat waves, and anyway walking was easier than fighting.

Though we did not find the "town" of Maybell, we were very well satisfied with the store and storekeeper. For not only did he sell us supplies, but as we were leaving he invited us to ride back with him. He was going out that way he said. It was not till after he had delivered us bag and baggage at our machines and turned about and wished us good luck did we realize that he was doing it gratis and out of the largeness of his heart. Truly it takes the really hard places in the world to reveal the man in a man. One does not get below the skin so readily on Fifth Avenue.

So we returned to our original trail again and renewed hostilities with the sandy way. It was not a pleasant way. The day near noon now was hot, calm, silent and the superlative of each. When we choked our overheated motors and halted for breath and to ease our aching nethers, the heat rose from the earth like the radiation from a box-stove. Behind us in a yellow train of golden fog, the dust hung suspended. On this account we had to ride widely separated, and the silence lay so dead that it was oppressive. Our ear-drums tingled to the tune of ethereal bells. Every heartbeat in our veins seemed vocal.

Yet even in this lonely land we found living things to hearten us. Magpies, ravens, a dove or two at intervals and some sage thrashers and sparrows were noted, and the raptorial chaps were out in force. Several little red sparrow hawks were routed from perches on the junipers by the trail; a vulture now and again came and made aerial observations upon us from on high; and on one occasion we watched a large hawk with much bluff and to-do chasing a golden eagle.

The only variety furnished by our road after we had eaten a mid-day lunch below the tarpaulin, was that we met rougher country and hills that were tartars. On account of the sand and stones in the deep-cut, winter-washed trail, the uphill drives at times were almost impossible. In addition, we were nearing the dregs of our endurance.

Unlike the giant Antaeus, we were flickering out on account of too incessant contact with Mother Earth. That is, our legs were, and to ride here with feet on foot-boards was a trick beyond human skill.

Also, the canteens were empty. The demand on them had been constant, for there is something in the mental and physical make-up of a man that makes him doubly thirsty when he knows that liquid refreshment is scarce or not to be had. "You'll never miss the water till the well runs dry" in the words of the ancient song, is telling but half the truth, for you will never want to drink so deeply as when the last dribble is in the well. I cannot imagine that Tantalus in Hades really suffered as he is supposed to have when he stood in drinkable liquid to his middle. Had he rather stood in a spoonful, then for a surety he would have been in Hell.

Cedar Spring was somewhere in our way, but three or four times the trail had forked and now we were not even certain that we were steering for our port. There is, I think, no more mean, unwholesome feeling can creep into a man than the half-certainty of being lost. It is primitive, an heirloom of the Grey Dawn days. But because there seemed nothing else to do we kept going. For, as Frat said, it was as easy, and more manly, to die on the trail looking for a spring than to give up and wait for one to come. All the other Colorado heroes that we could recall in the books, who had been forced — by their authors — to wrestle with grim and thirsty death in the dry lands, had always fought very hard. So we emulated the heroic example and, between rests, tore away. Now that I have a somewhat different perspective, I feel that there was no alternative. A clump of sagebrush or a stunted juniper, even at its best, is a poor stopping-place when the mercury is way over one hundred degrees.

At last! In a hollow below us at the rounded end of a shallow canyon, a dozen white-faced cattle were standing in a patch of grass — green grass. Water glistened, the hillside was dotted with dark junipers, and we knew that we were right. Cedar Spring was before us. In very short order we took possession, then at the canyon-head found the source of the water where a deep hole lay dark and cold. Ahh! If

Mack Laing drinking from his canteen: Colorado proved to
be a thirsty land. (COURTESY: BCA J 01411)

any man wishes to know the true value of a spring and a real appreciation of spring water let him turn not to the much-sung rill of wood
or mountain with all its poetry and age-old romance, but rather to a
deep fountain in the desert lands — even Cedar Spring.

Two killdeers, some doves, a bluebird and a cock sage grouse were
routed from the place, and it was easy to imagine the innumerable
wild things that before the coming of white-faced cattle had used
these sweet waters. What proud antlered heads of mule-deer and
great wapiti had lowered here; what antelope bands with their white

rear-patches shining in the sun had skipped down these slopes; what coyotes, bears and big mountain cats had lapped to their satisfaction. As we washed a dusty salt rime from our skin and sipped again and again, I built up in my mind the pictures of the past as they may have been when only game trails headed down the hillsides toward this source of living water.

Of all the qualifying adjectives, not even barring expletives and anathemas, that have been applied to these dry, hot lands, there is one that to the outsider who invades here can never grow trite: it is a "thirsty" land. Fierce and unconquerable was the passion for liquids we possessed. I profess that ordinarily I am not like old Rip Van Winkle: "naturally a thirsty body," but my throat and whole being held burning desires to be measured only in calories and horsepower. I could never see the excuse for a drinking saloon in a city, but I believe that now the sight of one of those abominable signs with its hideous artistry — mug, bubbles and all — would have been hailed with intense delight. We had verily robbed the white-faced cattle at the spring, yet within a mile or two we were again gulping copiously from the canteens.

Sundown found us with drought-like throats and with canteens empty again, fighting down a wide, hazy valley, when three homestead shacks in the distance loomed over the sagebrush and gave our flagging limbs a little fresh vim. But though we tried each in turn all these premises were deserted. The first had a concrete well but the dribble of water was fragrant with decomposing mice; the second well had dead mice but no water and the third place had no well.

So we went on again and just at dusky dark we came to a spot on a knoll where a large space, much tramped with stock and showing the remains of fires, marked a camping-ground, and we stopped. In a sharp cut below, a patch of skylight was reflected: Twelve-mile Spring. Yet when we went down the much-worn cattle trail, we found the walls of the cut and the soil even at the water's edge glistening with an incrustation that said in large letters: Alkali. Beware. But I was thirsty. I sampled it gingerly and to my surprise found no salty or bitter taste.

Frat too tried it, said he could find little wrong with it and confirmed my sense, or lack of it.

And so we drank, for it at least was wet. Whether or not our taste buds had closed up for the night or gone on a holiday, or simply withered, or our judgement was so sun- and thirst-warped that we could not recognize truth, I am unable to state, but certain it is we paid a large and disproportionate price for our tipple. For that varied assortment of minerals, in spite of its seeming innocence, had in it more sly malignancy, more anti-slumber potency, more belly-aches and other curious things than any brew that ever was concocted in a witch's charmed cauldron.

▪▪▪▪▪▪ Meter 2514

JULY 20. Another dawn song of the coyotes, another wondrous sunrise and whispering of desert voices from the ground, another sagebrush fire and short-course breakfast, and then we took to the sand trail again. The first few miles were a repetition, though we soon passed a ranch fence on the other side of which were a number of range horses, then Colorado showed that she had lost little of her variability. The trail now led into a valley that was different. The roads were of clay, the hills were the same: yellow, faded soil much marked and cut and scarred by water. Though the road was hard, it was cut at intervals by cruel chuck-holes, and the hillsides, too, though hard baked, were much crumbled and weathered by rains and snows that evidently came with another season. Also the sagebrush gave way to little clumps of the short, leprous-looking, salty shad-scale.

Ravens croaked hoarsely and wheeled here and there around a hilltop, and in one spot a flock of them apparently were quarrelling with two vultures. Once too in this vale of dreariness, a great vulture, with plainly marked whitish under-coverts on his wings, flapped up from a knoll and swung almost overhead. Rightly or wrongly, I saluted the great American condor or California vulture. Truly a noteworthy chap this, one of America's vanishing unfortunates. These birds added a touch of gruesomeness to the desolation, and although the road was so good in stretches that we were able to run with a little speed, I think we were glad when we got out of the place.

Early in the forenoon we came to Box Elder Ranch. The difference between Box Elder and the rest of that barren land was that a small stream running out of the hills had been ditched down and made to do service in irrigating a small farm. In addition to box elders, there grew Lombardy poplars — wherever in the West there is an irrigation ditch these tall trees raise their spindle forms — and there were flourishing willows and even wild roses, also garden vegetables and grain to show what the thirsty land could do when given the aid that Providence denied. Here we had another and real breakfast, then took up the trail again. The end now was nearly in sight.

The most noteworthy thing in the next stretch of running was that our passing was a procession through a series of noisy prairie dog towns. There were whole cities. Their yelping filled the air continually, and they sat up close at hand, patted their fat bellies, although heaven only knows what they had in them, flicked their stub-tails and ogled saucily at their strange visitors. Also I recall that at a little shack here by the way we met a little board sign with a scribbled: "Gas for Sale". Demure and modest enough was that advertisement, but when we went in and filled our tanks, it was to the top-notch, upset tune of "four bits" (fifty cents) a gallon. Tinned gasoline, no less, transported here by our friend Bill, of the Craig-Vernal stage.

About noon we stopped at another shack by the trail. But this one was different. From the distance of a mile, its string of white washing shouted "woman and home" to the hill-tops. And it was a home, and though the man of the house was absent, I'll wager that he was proud of it. His wife, a young woman of two or three and twenty, pretty and homey, met us frankly at the door and, without any hesitation, took our canteens and filled them from the supply of cool water within. The small stream of spring water ditched down from the hills explained their attempt at settlement here.

How were they getting on? "Why, very well," she replied, glancing around at the little garden that somehow seemed to be making a heroic fight of it, and we tried to be encouraging. They had second water rights, she said.

Any neighbours? "Yes, there is a man who has a claim up at the foot of the hills; he is three miles away. The next neighbour is across the valley about six miles."

Ever get lonesome? "Not now; I used to at first — a little. My husband is away a good deal."

The inside of that pole-and-mud little house was as clean, the tablecloth as immaculate, as any in the land. It is wonderful and noble and touching this optimism of the West. These are the intrepid ones who are bringing the emerald patches into the sterile valleys — at long intervals, no doubt, but growing larger and closer and greener with the years. They are pushing back and loosening the dead, sun-withered hand of the desert. There will be no slackening, nor retreating, of these bearers of green things, for theirs is the faith in the future that endures.

How cheerily they accept their lot; how full of optimism is their talk. Optimism, the booster spirit, just plain bluff, call it what you will, it is as strong in the dry lands as in the richest valley beyond the Sierras. Settlers seem to imbibe it from the air or from the water. We met a chap at a ramshackle premises who had thousands of sheep in the making back in the hills, another who reckoned his cherry crop in tons. What he did with the proceeds was not very evident. Another who told us without the twitch of an eyelash that his business was "locatin' gold-mines." Alfalfa yielded, goodness knows how many tons to the acre, mines were pointed to proudly as the richest in the state or the world, etc. etc. But I think the climax of this sort of thing came to us at our meeting with the sweet little woman in the mud-and-pole home by the trickling stream of spring water.

Onward we followed the valley again in the same forsaken, sunny land of shimmering colour vistas, till early in the afternoon, towering over the horizon far ahead, there burst out a glistening, snowy mountain peak: a crown of the Uintas far off in Utah. Through that still air — there was not a cloud, no sound but tingling silence — we seemed to see off into blue infinity, and distance to have become mere empty space. Then below it against the many-coloured hills flanking the valley we saw a spot of greenery: the K Ranch.

Here we stayed long enough under the big poplars to have a chat with the stage-driver (he had passed us on the road the previous day while we were at Maybell), then we sped off over what I judged to be the dustiest roads in the state, bound for Jensen and Vernal, Utah. The roads were more travelled now, graduated from the two-rut sand trail into the dust and chuck-hole class worn fairly equally from side to side, and we at least had room to flail around. But we were through the Colorado Desert. "Onward" was the word. We came down through strange, bare hills of wondrous-coloured clay along the Green River, passed through the little town of Jensen. And then Colorado, my Lady Changeable with all her moods and strange ways, fell behind into the blue, mystery haze that ever enshrouds her.

Almost with the crossing of the new state line we had entered a new kingdom. It was a wide valley that, as we approached Vernal, became a checkerboard of green farms trimmed by tall trees and all circumscribed in the distance by strangely unreal, gaudy, age-worn hills that seemed as lonely and forlorn as the ridges of an abandoned world. Which in truth they were, for here life was in the valleys, while death and ancientness was apparent in the hills. It was life won by dint of hard labour. Water here was the price of life. Green farm-crops met our eyes again; a miracle seemed to be performing by the dusty roadside.

It was the kingdom of the trickling ditch and the tall Lombardy poplars: Utah. Miles away in the distance we could trace the boundaries of farms and the course of the ditches by these tall, green sentries, which stood as regularly and as straight as a company of regulars under the eye of their captain. We had reached the land of the Mormons, the people who, for all their curious beliefs, have made the sterile desert lands blossom like the spring. Civilization, even if somewhat quaint and strange to us, was a joy after the lonely lands of the last few days. A load of alfalfa was now a fine sight after our late vistas of sage-grey plains and shimmering, over-painted hills. That white peak in the distance was far enough away through the translucent blue to be enjoyable. We had flirted with white peaks already; this, the kingdom of the green ditches, was a new love. All which perhaps goes to show that twenty-five hundred miles can do little toward stabilizing the affections of a road-rover.

At 5 p.m. after a few miles running over the dustiest footing that could be imagined (this road powder, fine as flour and several inches deep curled out from our tires like smoke and spattered against our leggings with the feeling of water), we entered Vernal, and since Flying Maria, after the fearful usage in the rough country, had a worn clutch that required attention, we immediately repaired to a garage, then to a hotel and a bathtub. Already we had noted a new atmosphere about the town. It was Western but seemed to lie under a spell of easy contentment, a Sleepy Hollow quietude that somehow pronounced this centre in the desert an ancient place. And how well too it was named. Vernalis: spring. Would that every town and village had as fitting a distinguishing mark. So many of them, alas, are named after some old man So-and-So, who in his time between lying in a cradle and under a tombstone, did nothing more egregious than to keep clear of jail, and perhaps quite by accident to raise pioneer crops upon the townsite.

▪▪▪▪▪▪ Meter 2598

JULY 21. We spent the day in town. Frat found Flying Maria lamer than he had supposed and was busy. So was I, but in the way of trying with the aid of the doctor to eliminate from my system certain salts and sodas of Twelve-mile Spring, and I must here digress a little on the devilish intention of these mineral waters. Brother of the Road, never, never, on any account whatsoever allow yourself to be alkalied! Leave such springs to the birds of the air and beasts of the field and white-faced cattle, all of which have special linings. Rather than drink, die of thirst by the trail like a hero and let the turkey vultures give you a Persian burial. For then you die but once and honourably. If you imbibe you may die otherwise and often. I did. And I say "devilish intention" advisedly, for such infernal mineral compounds pick and choose their victims.

Here were the two of us, Frat and I. We had tippled equally, and today he was complaining of an abnormal appetite, while I lay in the shade of a tree toward the west end of Front Street and hoped that Frat or the repair man would so jimmy Maria's internals that he would have to wire Milwaukee for repairs and wait a week. I was *hors de combat*, done, all gone. I had expurgated all but my ghost.

About mid-afternoon, I made the acquaintance of the Commercial Bureau. A Commercial Bureau or Club in these Western towns and cities is usually a society that has for its aim the spreading of knowledge about its particular neighbourhood. Usually it disseminates wind. It is calculated to extol the possibilities of the place for settlement and to induce the stranger to become enamoured of the place, to separate himself from his coin of the realm or to come with his wife and children to live there. Usually it has the colonizing knack, and also it is a repository of fact more or less well established. Here usually you may get for the asking a road map of the state and enlightenment on any subject of local nature from the length of last year's potato-vines to the number of pairs of boy twins in the county's current crop.

The Vernal Bureau was no exception. Mr. H. came along and made himself acquainted. Whether or not he was a diplomat, I can only guess, but for a certainty he recognized the wisdom of the old Latin maxim about the relation between sound mind and sound body. For instead of extolling irrigation lands, sheep ranches or gold mines, he looked me over and then marched me straight away to the office of the good doctor.

After I had been given a soothing opiate potion calculated to drug my indignant internal fixtures into forgetting that they had been outraged, Mr. H. took me down to his house. He seated me below the shady fruit trees, went into the house and returned with a quart bottle of ice-cold Jersey milk. I was consumed with a burning thirst desire — had been so for days — and that bottle, I will take my oath to it, had four inches of cream toward the top! O Brother of the Road, could mere lacteal fluid but taste like that always, then I too would be an idolater and worship Isis! And Mr. H. did this all with a quiet assurance that made me forget that I had wanted to die, and that convinces me now that he had met other travellers who had become too intimately acquainted with Twelve-mile Spring. In fact I felt much better at once.

Alkali ailment, like sea sickness or a half-fledged love affair, has the happy advantage of being checked sometimes or even cured outright in a twinkling. I felt able to ride now, and at about six in the evening, Frat having finished repairs, we cranked our machines, turned our backs upon the green little town and took up the trail again out into the badlands. In half an hour we were again in the drear, forsaken hills of red and yellow clay. In colour it was a vast, begobbed painter's palette lying ridgy under the blue sky. How lonely, how lovely, how kindly and pleasing to the eye, how cruel and soulless in heart was this new desert world.

Once having outdistanced Frat, who had halted to correct some adjustment or other, I stopped awhile to look and listen. A death's silence hung overhead, a little desert sparrow chippered nearby and some ravens croaked dismally in the distance. And between sounds the silence hung so dead, so ringing in the ears, that it hurt.

Nineteen miles from town we came to a small irrigation ditch in a wide valley, and a bare patch of earth marked with campfire remains told us to halt. The night was so warm and dry that we needed but a single blanket. The tarp was now useless. We slept here upon a comfortable bed, for though thistles are popularly supposed to be bad medicine as bedding material, we found them not so here. Russian thistles grew in green mats along the ditch-run and beside the trampled ground. They had followed the wheels of traffic in wetter seasons, and a matting of these springy, spiny weeds placed under the rubber poncho made a bed to fulfill most of the eulogistic statements about certain mattresses found in the back pages of the current magazines.

■■■■■■ Meter 2617

JULY 22. There was a rumble of wagons in the night and when the coyotes wakened me at 4 a.m. there were two desert schooners close at hand. The horses were tethered and the owners asleep. Three ravens came hurrooing from the hills to drink at the ditch. A dozen little grey-coated horned larks came tweeting into the cleared ground to alight and pick about tamely within a few feet of us, and the desert was breathing again. It was morning, and leaving our neighbours still wrapped in their blankets and tucked away in the upper decks below the rounding roofs, we took to our dust-trail.

That the roads were fairly abominable for two-wheeled travel, I will state once and finally. They were not sandy, but rather dusty and chucky. The hard soil was ground into powder, and in consequence the road was rutted, filled with loose dust many inches deep. Here and there, a concealed stone or bit of adamantine soil that had defied the grinding of wheels gave us a bump or knock that banged us out of the saddle. All in all, the travelling was easier than it had been on the sandy sagebrush trails in north-central Colorado, but the difference was not tremendous. In the diary at night, I said: "All day in dusty, skiddy, stony roads; going painful" — and first impressions are said to sink deep and oftentimes to record the truth.

We were in the desert again. At Vernal where they routed us very carefully, they advised us humanely that probably it was worse than we had come through in Colorado, but it was not now consistently desert. Early in the morning, we came to a small attempt at irrigated settlement where several claims were in the making. I felt that the birds were the truest indication of its success, and also an indication of the change in the status of the wild things that is wrought by the coming of man. The burrowing owls were more numerous than else-where, the green crop lands had enticed the desert mice and perhaps the prairie dogs to come here: the owls had followed their prey. The swallows came because the buildings afforded nesting-sites, because the ditches provided mud and the stock decoyed insect provender. The killdeer came solely for the reason that they found drinking water. But the family of meadowlarks seemed rather out of its element. A snowy mountain peak fifty miles across a barren desert did not seem the right setting for these tuneful sprites of the green plains.

After almost two hours of early running, we came to a little stream and halted for breakfast. This creek — we did not learn its name — was a natural watercourse. It was quite muddy, was bordered by green thickets of cottonwoods and willows and rimmed by stretches of round cobbles. Upon a dry bar near the water's edge, we stood our machines, kindled our fire and lay down to get acquainted with this new phase of Utahan desert life.

There was a magpie convention in session here this morning. What its object could be remained mysterious, though I think the birds were mostly concerned with the liquor question. They must have come for miles, for their clatter and laughter filled the air and the wood seemed full of them. I have a suspicion, too, that as we were on an oft-used campground, they regarded the morning the most propitious time to call. And among such gossipers news flashes across the desert in a twinkling. A hundred yards downstream, there stood a big dry cottonwood, and ere long its branches were clustered with these long-tailed, long-tongued conventionists. Fully fifty or sixty, I judged, were in this tree alone. Nor were these black and white scalawags our only bird neighbours. We had found an oasis as full of feathered life as some havens we had met east of the Rockies. Song sparrows sang from the willows. And if there is a patch of willows and some water anywhere in America without these beloved chaps, I have yet to find it.

Doves cooed unseen, warblers lisped and sang, and other bird voices came to ear that I could not identify. I was a stranger and far from home. A noteworthy chap took position in a clump of thick shrubbery near the bridge from which he scolded harshly like a cat-bird for several minutes, and when I went to rout him I found an excited towhee. But he was no friend of mine — some unknown, hoarse-throated Western species instead. There were still others and I am not sure whether it was the chickadee or the singing thrush that capped the climax. We heard both. The thrush sang a solemn strain much like that of the ethereal veery of the East and probably he was a willow thrush or western veery. As a representative of green woods and damp, ferny glens, he seemed more astray here than the meadow-larks had earlier.

By the time we had eaten, I had taken a sort of superficial sound census of the valley, and now I set out to ingratiate myself into the treetop gabble-meeting. This was folly. At my first move in that di-rection, the company exploded, and with derisive yells and chuckles scattered to the four winds. They "smelled powder" on the instant.

Then we started up again. Our progress — somewhat painful — through Roosevelt, Myton and Duchesne brought little variety. I re-call though that at the first mentioned metropolis we lost our golden opportunity to harvest a bunch (or is it "band" or "flock") of cowboys over a road wager. They had come into town for some gala occasion, and as the two-wheelers were less common on that trail than cow ponies, we were surrounded in a moment. The species of cowboy seen in the movies is not much in evidence in the West today, and this was the nearest approach to the films we yet had seen.

There was much good-natured chaffing and many offers to swap steeds, but when we mentioned roads, they said with one voice in chorus, that to get over the first mile beyond town, we would have to push. Yes, push. It was a new grade, dry as dust, autos got stuck, and it could not be done on "them things." Any money? Yes, they would back their convictions, every one of them. They had seen the road and we had not, and so with our bluff called — I believe this is the correct Western way of it — we had to content ourselves by telling them to watch our dust. And I hope they did, for though that mile was per-haps as ugly a mess of dry dust all plowed into ridges and honoured by the name of road, as could be found between coasts, I flailed through it without mishap. And after the dust-fog had drifted away, Frat followed.

Shortly after we left this town, a fine show of a thunderstorm mounted above the hills to westward and boomed ominously. There was something unbelievable about it. Every sign on the landscape gave the lie to summer showers, the roads fairly shouted it. Yet we had to believe, and on coming to some poplars beside a hurrying stream in a little ditch, we turned in and waited. Waited and yet improved the hour. Cleanliness is supposed to be as near godliness on the trail as elsewhere, and so we got out our kits. If you are careful not to locate too close to an anthill, the shady side of a poplar is a charming tonsorial shop, for if it was so airy and dry that the lather withered upon our faces altogether prematurely. It was a small matter.

We found that the desert sun and breeze had been working a toughening and tanning process on our faces, and now we could have whittled off our beards with a fair jack-knife and never shed a tear. Also we parted with much road material. For though perhaps trail-dust, if viewed with the eye of the Scotch house-wife, might be classified as "clean dirt," nevertheless it was good to be rid of it. By the time we were dressed again, the last thunder rumble had died in the hills, and the threatening blue-black sky had faded. The sun had not ceased his shining.

It turned cooler immediately, and it was apparent that rain had fallen somewhere ahead, but not till mid-afternoon did we cross the storm-path. In a shallow, winding depression, that in time of rainfall was a watercourse, we came suddenly upon a hurrying muddy little torrent. The first of the turbid flood had arrived, and even as we watched it, it grew deeper, so we hastily rode through. A deluge had fallen at some spot in the distant hills and for hours had been rushing down the valley.

We had been advised strongly in Vernal to follow the route that led up the Strawberry and thence down the Spanish Fork, and so toward evening we were working up the rough trail that followed the former stream. We had our evening meal at a Y in the creek where a green valley of greasewood lay about us, and the cliff swallows wheeled overhead at their hunting to fill the youngsters reposing in the nests fastened high above us on the striated walls of the abrupt cliffs.

Then we tackled the Heber Road. Compared with this thoroughfare, the rocky road to Dublin was a boulevard in the residential section. In spots it was but a respectable pack-horse trail. It was crooked; it picked its way over rocks and through stunted timber and was innocent of scraper or grader. We bumped over the rocks that we could not dodge, pounded up and down steep places, plunged through a narrow, but deep and very wet ford, crossed two bridges built of corduroy (rough, unhewn logs) that shook us till every vertebra rattled, and at length climbed up a hill road and halted for the night in a grove of pinion pines.

We knew our campground as soon as we set our eyes upon it. Man like every other animal is a creature of certain traits and habits. Others had camped here before us. Wild animals are full of the same thing and make their paths in certain spots rather than elsewhere. It may be that we all follow the line of least resistance or it may be something else. Now in looking backward I recalled that many times we had turned into an inviting spot and found that numerous other bivouacers had preceded us. History has been written in charcoal since time was young. There was no water here, which meant that there was none anywhere near, for man camps at the drinking places in this land as surely as the game trails of deer and wapiti lead to them. We thus had to depend on our canteens.

And just in the dusk there was a rumble in the stillness and soon we had company. The men, father and grown son, were bringing a load of lumber down the Strawberry, and they too had arrived to camp at this spot. Upon their load was roped a cask of water — much appreciated refreshment for the steaming horses as well as for the drivers. I went over at once and tried to make friends and learn their story, but they were either shy or taciturn and nipped my advances with such a chilling frost that I soon withdrew.

Our camp was above them and as I lay in my blanket I watched their preparations for supper. While the son tended the horses, the father built a fire and then hoisted an iron pot of water over it, and then they took from the wagon a freshly shot jackrabbit, stripped and dismembered it, and put it in the pot. To me, looking down as I was into the glare of the fire — for it was dark now — it was veritable Cannibal Island cookery. I know that I could have made a much better culinary job of it in a frying pan. A hard-times meal! Pioneering in stern reality. Yet looking into the future, I can picture this young chap as a grandfather with a town in the irrigation lands named after him, and see him with his children's children on his knee telling the story of the hard days when he teamed lumber over the Heber Road and lived on hope of the future, desert air and boiled rabbit.

▪▪▪▪▪▪ Meter 2680

JULY 23. We started early. The land we were about to traverse was called a desert and we anticipated a hard day of travel. Yet the landscape here was delightful and full of lovely features that hitherto we had not seen in the dry lands. Our road ran through the scattering pinion pines and junipers, and every moment we were allowed glimpses out over broken lands, soft and subdued in tender colour, tempered by the morning sun and dotted and clumped with the dark tufts of evergreens. Soon we toiled up a deep-washed trail in a broken valley that had all the appearance of having been mapped off into sheep pastures and little parks and gardens. But it was the grey of shadscale and sagebrush and the green of greasewood, and the dead colour of burned rocks rather than flowers.

Although it was beautiful and lovely, yet it was desolate. No living things stirred. I looked in vain for a deer on the hillsides or even a slinking coyote. But the valley lay there as dead as though created so in the beginning and was determined to remain so till the end of time. Every juniper, every sagebrush clump seemed as ancient as eternity.

In one spot, a rainstorm a day previously had crossed our path, but fortunately it landed upon a sandy section where the soil was not greasy, and it even improved our travelling. Most of the trail was very deep-rutted, sandy, full of evil-purposed stones and chuck-holes, but the country was pleasant to the eye, full of the charm of lovely colour. All forenoon we chugged up a green valley of greasewood with blue hills at hand and in the distance — blue, blue as clear colour squeezed from the tubes of the painters of the universe. Yet though they were intense, they were softened and subdued by distance, but the eye grew familiar, and to see the true colour values we had to turn our heads sidewise or look upside down. To get the most out of such landscapes, one ought to be an acrobat, ready at a moment's notice to stand on his head. Each time the ends reversed he would be greeted by a new colour dream, a fairyland as inspiring as a brilliant sunset.

After a drive up a fiercely stony road we reached Rock Hill Ranch. Here we had dinner, and also happily we were able to fill our gasoline tanks. This was one of those outpost places for which the West is notable; crude necessities shorn of trimmings were to be had here. The few buildings were shacks of rough logs, and there were not many of them, for this was a sheep ranch — there were thousands of them off in the hills, the owner said — and these animals required no shelter. In a corner of the building where we ate, was a little "store." This consisted of a few rows of tinned goods: the sort of stay-with-you indigestibles required by men in rough places to keep the partnership between their bodies and souls intact and firm. Rough and ready, crude but complete.

Here too I met a touch of that Western something that I have indicated previously, the thing that in moments of extreme benignity I call enthusiasm and optimism and at others I call by an uglier name. Our host was a native of the state, big and disproportionately fat. A fat man is out of line in a desert; we look there for lean and swart men. He was as rough-hewn as his environs, glad to meet outsiders and to sit down while we ate and to tell us what he knew without asking any bothersome questions. When we enquired about the roads ahead, he waxed eloquent. Roads? We were over the worst of it — pretty good, weren't they? And we now had clear sailing right to Salt

Lake City. "Those things" (that is, our machines) "ought to take you through awhooping in a few hours," he said. "Simply a boulevard, boys! Simply a boulevard! That's what it is. It's the new government road, level as this floor!"

At this remarkable news I turned to Frat. He glanced down at the floor then looked our host over with an attention somewhat keener than usual, and when next he caught my eye, he winked his shooting optic exactly one hundredth of an inch, and though it was coffee time, he picked up the salt-shaker and placed it right by my plate.

Boulevard? Rot! Within a mile of that centre of mutton culture, we toiled again in beastly roads. Frat went down and plowed about in the storm centre of a golden dust whirl. Whereupon when he got upon his feet and heaved Flying Maria into the same state of road preparedness, and had coughed and spit quantities of yellow road material out of his inner compartments, he said unseemly but fitting things about the proprietor of Rock Hill Ranch. One had to have a sacrificial victim in such cases, and that fat grower of tough mutton had to go to the stake. The truth was not in them. These wind-jamming Westerners were too imaginative for him. By Golly, they believed their own lies! And he ended with a vile attempt at a pun: boulevard — the fat lobster must have meant a "bull-yard."

But both road and the nature of the country improved somewhat. After a twirl over an open, swelling stretch of treeless, prairie-like miles we came to the lake reservoir, and turning, skirted it to the government dam. How blue and fresh this liquid appeared after the desert; what golden possibilities for the future lay stored in it, what Western dreams to come true. We were on the government road now, and though it did not fit into our apperceptions of things pertaining to boulevards, it at least had been graded. But it was narrow, and dry soil graded does not make a road until it has been rained on and packed. And though I was already possessed of this bit of knowledge, I had to learn it again.

In turning a curve on a knoll too rapidly, Betsy's front tire lost its hold and after we had stopped doing a base slide exercise, I picked myself and Betsy out of a golden dust comet that was a veritable Halley's affair. At least so said Frat, and he came up fast and ate my dust that he might tell me so. He had never raised any storm like that he averred; he had seen it at over a mile and thought it must be a sand blizzard coming.

Then we struck off again toward the distant hills: the watershed. And here we met him. He rode a roan pony and sat in the careless, easy, glued-on way that is not seen much out of the cattle country. Behind him trotted a grey pony with a small pack outfit, and, yes, he was clad in real honest to heaven cowboy togs — almost all we had seen at the movies. He might have been Bill Hart himself; from his hat-band to the heels of his riding shoes he was right. He was a real cowboy! So we fell upon him. We knew the trail well enough — there was only one — but we stopped to enquire.

Twenty-three or twenty-four he appeared, soft-spoken, good-natured, almost suave, and dismounting at once, he answered all our round of rapid-fire questions with a smile. Yes, he had been riding since he was six years of age, had wrangled wild horses in Utah, ridden in the round-ups clear to Winnipeg, etc., and now he was travelling light and camping where he pleased. Lucky chap! The romance had come back to the trail again, and in about three minutes I was willing to trade a gascart for a certain grey cayuse nibbling about in the sage in quest of a mouthful of eatables. But he forestalled me.

"John, come here," he called finally to the grey pony, and John, wise-appearing and considerably beyond his coltish days, lifted his head and came to his owner at once.

"John, tell these gentlemen how old you are," and the equine chap thus addressed, after a preliminary shift or two on his front feet, pawed away with his right foot to the number of seven or eight.

"Shake hands," and he lifted his front foot high and extended it.

"Show them how you scare the Indians." He drew back his ears and showed a mouthful of yellow teeth.

"Show them how you like the ladies." He edged nearer and nuzzled his master's cheek.

"Very good. Now show them how we dig a well in the desert."

John hesitated a moment at this, and a far-away weary look came into his eyes, but a little slap jogged his memory wondrously. He put his left fore-foot behind his right fore-foot, then began to pivot about on his front members.

"Go to it now!" And John bored away with vim and really made quite an auger-hole in the dry soil.

When we had exchanged pleasantries about the merits of our differing steeds and prepared to go on our ways, he handed us his card. It read:

Professor B. — Professional horse-trainer.

And it might be hoped that every "Prof" has his business as completely at his fingers' ends.

Toward evening, we reached the beckoning hills. Like many other things viewed from afar, hills are deceivers: their blueness, their mystery and appeal are apt to vanish on too close acquaintance. Soon we were toiling up among them over a dusty road and shut in by mere ordinary timber. A rainstorm descended upon us — warm raindrops scatteringly thrown with half-hearted intention — but though we halted and got out our tarp in anticipation of a downpour, it was needless preparation. Scarcely enough rain fell to dampen the road.

But it was an excellent stop, for we had reached strange and new pasturage to rummage in. Woods and life of this sort had not been on our path before. The native poplars that stood tall and straight were a change from the gnarled junipers of the desert and also a reminder of northerly woods. Flowers were on every hand: blooms of white and pink and purple smiled from among the trees. There were white masses of yarrow and wild parsnips and also pink geraniums and a dozen other half-familiar, half-strange faces that I could not call by name. Birds too were all about us. How good and gladsome was a robin song again. Fully a dozen hummingbird sprites buzzed and chippered and darted about with a sizzling sound as they sought out the flowers of the hillside.

We might fittingly have named the place Hummingbird Ravine. A white-crowned sparrow sang sweetly again and again, and even came out on the bare road to pick about and show himself within a few feet. Soon, voices and songs came to my ear inviting me to ramble a little. We had halted near a culvert where a small stream of merry water raced down the ravine. It was born at a spring bubbling from the hillside above us, and this little ripple of pure, life-giving water — trite, but I like the term — was the real source of all this birdlife and song and plant loveliness.

Presently Frat led off again up the hill and soon a tremendous dust-cloud ahead and a disgraceful amount of klaxon and muffler rumble announced excitement. When I hurried up into seeing range, for the air was thick, I found him hard on the heels of a flock of sheep. My education in the matter of sheep had been neglected, and I do not know what a thousand fleeces look like, but it seemed to me that Frat had fully that many stampeding up the road ahead of him. They would not quit the path. When he tried to edge through, they invariably crowded in front of him; they simply bobbed along at a ten-mile gait, raised the dust and the devil and held tight to the road. Now he added his voice to the din, but it had no more effect than the klaxon and cut-out.

All that was necessary to clear the way was one leading sheep with sense enough to get off the road, but the leaders somehow lacked inspiration. Flying Maria was fairly on their tails, and every moment one or two at the sides fell back winded, but still there were enough left easily to reach Salt Lake City. It was a clear case of the survival of the fittest, and gasoline power seemed bound to win. After a time one leading sheep jumped from the trail, and every sheep followed. Frat's comment (a little later; I could only guess what he was saying in the wake of the sheep) was: "Well, I have read of sheep in Africa that store up fat in their tails; in Utah I reckon they store it in their heads! What next'll be on this boulevard?"

Soon we reached the divide and looked afar over the blue hills and valleys. Oh the beauty of it again! Not since we had paused at evening to scan the fair face of Colorado in the western foothills of the great Rockies had we met so fair a scene: so vast, so majestic in its high-piled undulations, so blue. It was a swelling, diversified series of ranges, each painted evenly in its own separate tone of purple and indigo.

The sun was hidden. The dark valley lay intense in colour full of awful gloom and mystery. They were too blue, too veiled, too mystic to be real, and I almost feared to start off down that yellow trail into such a valley of shadow. Far away, like the first star twinkling from the evening heavens, gleamed one lingering snow-speck: a beacon-light of hope above this gloom world of indigo. It is well for us that such scenes come only now and again. They come seldom enough to lift the soul suddenly out of the level of its ordinary dull abode. Such scenes constitute the high points, the climaxes of the long trail.

With wondrous suddenness, this mountain range brought us into new realms. We were among the tall evergreen trees again; their dark foliage had been accountable for the somberness of the hillsides. The scent of their pungent resin was abroad in the air. We followed a stream strangely turbid and brown. A sawmill stood near the road to remind us instantly of a certain load of lumber we had seen toiling down the Strawberry. Real woods greenery, maples, alders and cottonwoods and fragrant-breathing shrubbery hovered about the stream and stood grey and dust-coated by the trail-side. Down, down we chugged, ever valleyward. We met a cattle outfit, passed a group of three or four cowboys camped and cooking supper in an open spot by the stream, and so set to find a site for ourselves.

Just about this time I noted a strange, unnatural blueness and greenness to the near side of the stream, and as I crossed a little rushing tributary that ran below a culvert, I got it in the nose and chest. It smelled to heaven, did that liquid. To the eye it was liquid crystal of angel purity; to the nose it might have been the drainage from a cesspool in Hades. Sulphur dioxide and hydrogen sulphide and other sulphurous atmospheric mixtures that are supposed to belong to Nick's dark abode were breaking loose from that deceitful water. Betsy breathed a whiff or two of it and then rushed at a reckless pace down the dusty road and presently came to a stand at a sweeter, more tempting spot by the stream-side.

As a campsite, I admit that this one was somewhat a failure. After the cool of the evening had settled, the breeze turned and blew down the canyon. On its rustling wings, that night zephyr carried each moment a new supply of sulphur compounds that, to speak lightly of them, were highly objectionable in slumber air. Frat with his blunted olfactory organ had the best of me and told me to "Go to sleep and forget it!" Oftentimes I have longed for a nose with the keenness of a fox's that I might read correctly the scent story of the woods as Reynard does, but here I realized that sometimes such a nose would be a vile possession. My own now was far too good. Not until my outraged nerve became surfeited, tired and full, did I fall asleep. To sleep, and dream dreams tainted with the rosy optimism that might be expected to follow a surfeit of carbon bisulphide.

▪▪▪▪▪▪ Meter 2737

JULY 24. The weatherman tried to send a shower of rain in the dawning of the day, but plainly it was a forlorn effort and we rose early from our fragrant roost and continued down the dusty canyon. We still rode in a strange land. More sulphurous tributaries fumigated us as we sped by innumerable little cataracts of blue and green crystal liquid that sparkled as though diamonds were flowing there, and by and by a sordid brown torrent engulfed our brilliant and odoriferous little friend and we saw it no more. Then we encountered the red sandstone battlements.

High above us, cut and carved and gouged by giant forces of other years, these great ruddy walls lifted their bare brows in the sunlight. There were caves and crannies up there that suggested Arabian Nights Tales, abodes of wild men and robbers and wild animals and eagles' eyries. Once as I paused to scan these new features, I heard far aloft the harsh scream of what I judged to be a red-tailed hawk.

Doubtless a family of young were safe in some nook in the inaccessible face of the cliff. Then as we came to habitations of man in the way of little ranches, the road became smoother, and between high green hills rimming the valley we came down to the railroad. For some time it had been a stranger to us.

At a little spring by the roadside we stopped to make breakfast. How mighty the virtue in a little spring in a thirsty land. Close at hand was green shrubbery, and a family of young warblers were twittering, while goldfinches sang their summery songs from the wires that followed the railroad. Chipmunks and grey ground squirrels frisked about a stone pile a few yards distant, impatient, I fancy, to get the crumbs of our rough and ready meal. For many, many others had camped there before us. This seemed a touch of life as we had known it in other lands, but when we raised our eyes to the colour-steeped hillsides, it was to be reminded that we were in the dry country still.

Indeed we were approaching the very heart of it — the human heart, if I might call it so. Salt Lake City, the metropolis of the desert lay close ahead. And to every thinking soul this city of the desert is a mystic thing. If he anticipates a visit, the miracle is ahead of him; if he has seen it, the wonder only grows. We were anticipating that a good road lay before us. After some of the trails we had fought recently, this new means of locomotion was trebly sweet, and we sped off to the town of Springville in its green valley among the poplar battalions of the ditches. We were again in the land of the streetcar!

In this little city we got more than usual for our money, for we had run right into an imposing celebration. The city was holding Pioneer Day festivities. Somehow I think that this parade that we stopped to ogle moved us more than such a thing commonly does. Since leaving Denver we had been roughing it. We had cast away many of the niceties of so-called civilization; we had slept on rocks, gone unwashed sometimes to bed, spent days uncombed and unshaven. We had toiled and fought with the trails, sweated in the heat, been thirsty and assimilated alkali. We had lived without frills.

I repeat that as we watched this creditable pageant that depicted the things of the pioneer past: milestones of progress in this fierce land, we were stirred deeply. In fact I know it, for when the Queen of the Festival came by in her chariot surrounded by her covey of lovely maidens, Frat declared that he thought he had had enough road rambling, had pioneered the dry lands to his heart's content and wondered if any homesteads were available close to the city limits. I too had looked for prickly things rather than such lovely blossoms in the desert. But the pageant passed. I reminded Frat for the fourth time that a good road lay ahead of us, got him started ahead at last, and soon we ran through the populous city of Provo and on to the shining star of the desert, Salt Lake City.

We came in over a wide yellow road of gravel that carried us through a weird land. A broad, bright shimmering valley lay before us, full of radiant colour and all atremble with the heat waves from the burning desert sun that shot its fire down through a transparent sky. Not a cloud lay anywhere to be seen above the far, dim horizon. The land near and far, but especially the far hills gave the impression of having been baked into gaudily coloured tiling and bright mosaic. Which truly it was, for when we paused, the heat rose in our faces in a burning draught — burning, yet not so unpleasant as the thermometer indicated. For man is the most adaptable animal in the world, and now we too were acclimatized, sunbaked and hardened and glazed to a turn.

It was a great, bright, cruel, yet lovely desert, for here came the overwhelming sense of the miracle of it. This expanse as far as the eye could ramble out across the quivering plain, even to the feet of the red and yellow hills beyond, was cut and plotted with threads of greenery that in the foreground resolved into ranks of the tall poplars, the fittest emblems of the reclaimed lands. Green plots and patches between, buildings hidden in the greenery of orchards, and grazing animals all added their silent voices to the story. The desert truly was blooming. It was a parallel to the prickly, stunted, ill-shaped cactus of the arid and waste places that in spring breaks out in blossoming loveliness. It impressed me as being something too strange for our mundane trail, something that did not belong to North America. I was gazing across a far Sahara into some Biskra oasis of the East.

▪▪▪▪▪ Meter 2818

JULY 25. Today was noteworthy for the reason that we first met Tan. While we were occupying a goodly section of the outdoors roost provided by the House of H. for dust-begrimed itinerants of the road like ourselves, during which time the internal organs of Flying Maria were in the process of rehabilitation, a certain blond young gentleman from Pittsburgh came in. Rather I should say that a patch of sunburn and a smile came in, and Tan was behind it. He also rode a two-wheeler, had come from Denver but taken the more usual, northerly route through Cheyenne, Wyoming, and thus finding better travelling had made faster time over this section than we had. He expressed a wish to accompany us to Frisco, and as no such request could be denied to such a smiling fellow, we agreed at once. But we slept out, we explained. Well, he had never tried it, and the ground to him had the comfortable appearance of the cobbles on Penn Avenue back home, but he would try it. He had a good constitution; he would buy a thick blanket.

Also he gave the further reason that we were soon about to tackle the Great American Desert where the rattlers, coyotes and jackrabbits were particularly large and ferocious, and we would find strength in numbers. He asked us about our guns and flicked out a little .25 automatic Colts. When we told him we travelled light, his face for a half instant almost lost its smile. He came near being serious. It was plain that his task, which he had invited, of protecting the lives of three men in the desert with one little gun and two boxes of ammunition was the first great real responsibility of his young life.

JULY 26. We had decided to follow the northerly route of the two between our present city and Reno, Nevada, and in the evening we set out on the road toward Ogden. We were bound thus to traverse a course around the northerly side of Great Salt Lake, and we hoped to see a little of the Great Desert. We still followed the valley and we spun off over a perfect road of concrete with a brilliant sunset on our left hand and resplendent hills of a hundred colour tints on our right. It seemed a fair promise to us in this new adventure to come in the lands of Out and Beyond.

The real desert lay ahead but as yet we ran through the green miracle lands of grain and corn and clover, of fruit trees and poplars. At dusk we picked a roost in a pasture plot on a sloping hillside, just within the roadside fence. There was a trickle of water from a pipe above us on the knoll. An orchard with promise of much fruit rustled close beside us, and a row of poplars was at hand to whisper. Friend Tan looked over my choice (as the senior member of the trio, the honour of choice had been given me) and declared that though the ground was not as soft as the bed that his mother used to make, he would be a camper-out if it killed him.

Most of my recollection of this bivouac under the desert sky centres on Tan. He had to face the momentous question of making his first bed on terra firma, on ground baked hard as brick, and with one blanket. He made the most of the situation. And no sooner were we well begun than certain eastern friends called upon us. It seemed almost beyond belief that we could be attacked by mosquitoes here, but facts are stubborn, and we had the truth brought forcibly and pointedly to us on the sharp beaks of these devilish adversaries.

They had been bred in the irrigation ditches and had lost little in the new environment. Tan said that they were "rotten." Though it was scarcely the word for it, "rotten" covered the general situation fairly well. We had no smudge fire material, and sleep for a time was rather difficult. Long before any one of us had won it, Tan had observed that he had found bones in himself that he had never suspected before, and muscles that had not been discovered when he studied superficial anatomy in the Art Institute in Pittsburgh. The last thing I recall hearing was a half-asleep, half-despairing:

"Hey, fellows! What do you do when your points of contact get fearsome sore?"

And Frat said: "Put on fresh ones."

■■■■■ Meter 2833

JULY 27. The land of the trickling ditches is full of contrasts and anomalies. The desert night air did not come chill as I had anticipated, and at dawn I was wakened to the tune of woods birds. When we give credit and praise to the spirit that has carried man into pioneer lands such as these, let us not forget the birds that have come with him to share his fate. At the farmhouse a little distance up the road, a wren was singing his chattering, explosive songs with unusual abandon; a robin song full of the cheer that is beloved from coast to coast drifted about and enlivened the morning; from the poplars came the ripple of a vireo; a mourning dove in the orchard cooed away with an ardour that suggested a second wooing and a second, belated family; a warbler of some species strange to me sang unmistakably from the fruit trees; and a Western chat talked in strange tongues. This latter chap, true to the laws of his skulking tribe, hung about the shrubbery in the orchard, never showing himself, and only his medley of honks and chatters and whistles told his identity.

All this I listened to in the pleasant dawn, and then turned to the pleasant task of persuading Tan and Frat to come back to the plane of realities. I am sure we must all own to a tingle of wicked pleasure at the task of dragging a fellow being out of his beauty slumber. Frat was as usual, but Tan was very far down. On the third summons he "groaned and stirred" like Coleridge's dead men. Then after a trial or two he got to a sitting posture, heaved and stretched, then drove a mask of awful agony from his walnut visage, replaced it by a golden smile and said:

"Well, boys, I'm going to live through it anyway! But I know I'll never be the same!"

We breakfasted in the city of Ogden. In our early running, we traversed some of the finest and most fruitful irrigation lands we had yet seen here: the sturdiest poplars, the tallest, rankest corn and fodder, the most heavily laden fruit trees. Some of the fruit already blushed red with a message to us as we sped by. But later in the forenoon beyond the city of Ogden we ran out into the newer lands where the methods of the dry farmer were utilized more extensively — over larger acreage and with less return. Here were the outpost farms: the hands of husbandry reaching out, clutching, transforming, thrusting back the arid desert. Broad wheat acres were here, the crop already garnered. It was scant of stubble but big of head and kernel, and on the road in fat sacks high piled on lumbering wagons drawn by four-horse teams we met the threshed product.

Corrine was our last town of note. Then our road became a branching trail and we went out into the desert. The country we traversed was flat, but at noon beyond Blue Creek we ambled up a long, winding trail to a higher elevation. Travel was easy enough. The footing was hard-baked and only the yellow dust was unpleasant. But in mid-afternoon we found to our chagrin that we had lost our course; our trail faded in the sagebrush: a double auto track that eventually looped on itself where the preceding traveller had made a right about-face.

It was indeed a strange place in which we had landed. We were upon the ancient Shore of Great Salt Lake: a bluff of rock and gravel sparsely covered with sagebrush that dropped abruptly to the ancient-washed plain below. Once the lake had lapped at the feet of this promontory, but it had backed away till now it merely gleamed faintly afar in the distance, and the deserted bed remained. This was flat as a floor, green and grey and yellow in spots and dull sickly white in large areas that even at a mile or two suggested salt-fields. The blue and purple distant hills were intense in their colouring. It was a scene fascinating and yet cruel: charming in the brightness and loveliness of its colouring, but cold and forbidding in its barren saline bitterness.

We held a council of war on the brow of the bluff. It was evident that we were upon an old trail that years previously had gone down the slope here, but subsequent rains of winter had cut the slope away

Mack Laing gazing into the distance across Great Salt Lake, Utah.
(COURTESY: RICHARD MACKIE)

and left an impossible descent. Frat and Tan were for trying to get their machines down, two men to a machine, but the senior member, more full of the discretion of years, deemed it a good place for the exercise of the veto. About the time we had decided that a return was inevitable, we noted a team and light vehicle approaching on the far flat below, and so we waited. They crossed the white flat and at a little distance scaled our bluff at a half accessible spot we had not noticed, and then swung across toward our trail.

From the occupants of the light wagon, we learned that if we followed their track we would pick up the main trail about five miles distant on the farther side of the flat. So because it is always more pleasing to the heart of the adventurous to go ahead over no trail than backward over the best, "Forward!" was the word. In a moment, Tan's sheaf of dusty thatch was bobbing above the sage with the eager celerity of a shot-at coyote, and we followed as best we could. Tan had ridden from Pittsburgh without a cap and the desert could not make him change his ways.

We had an interesting time getting down to this flat front yard of the Great Lake, and our interest flagged little while we were upon it. Almost every sort of road surface was represented here, even when we were not riding upon the old abandoned railroad track and heaving our steeds over near-impossible crossings. Then we came out upon the salt floor. An incrustation of granulated salt, some inch or two in thickness covered the earth; it was smooth yet spongy and the machines called for more fuel than while running on hard surface. Frat and Tan threw up their hands, then put them in their pockets or sat arms folded and leaning back steered their snorting steeds from the saddle and described hippodrome gyrations here and there across the white plain in a way that quite suggested familiarity with the Greatest Show on Earth.

This airy gyration came to a sudden ending, however. Frat rode ahead and so ended first. A small rill across his path had but recently

Frat and Flying Maria discovered that there was mud
underneath the salt flats. (COURTESY: BCA J-01414)

dried. The surface was as innocently spotless as the rest of the field, but the under-filling was mere mud. Flying Maria went bang into the little bed and then stopped short. Frat did not. In fact Maria stopped so much shorter than Frat did that she did not even fall over; instead she stood upon her feet sunk to the engine and in a mechanical sort of way seemed to be saying "What next!" It took more than one heave of two of us to get her upon solid footing again.

Late in the afternoon we ran in a greasewood desert. It was beautiful after a fashion, this pale green clumpy vegetation above its sun-baked yellow earth, with the intense hills always looking on from the mellowed distance, but it was the beauty of death, lacking something vital, a trifle uncanny. One must get used to the desert. We had passed through Promontory at noon — one of the towns that they said was robbed of its railroad — though we saw no town. Elsewhere throughout the region there were signs of habitation at rare intervals, but at 5 p.m. we came to something new. Here were some fresh-water springs with well-filled craters, and an enterprising settler had conceived a reclamation project. The bang and clatter of a gas engine filled the air. It was drawing up the precious liquid and dispersing it to the surface of a new farm in a way that seemed to prophesy success and profit for the owner. As yet, however, there were no evidences of the productiveness that later were to follow. The project was new, and when we tasted the clear water we found it slightly saline.

The country during the afternoon was not entirely devoid of life. We saw two ravens, several black-tailed jackrabbits, some sage thrashers and desert sparrows. Every living thing in such a land is an event. Where there is water there is wild life, and we had passed several springs. We dusted into Kelton just in time to secure a meal before dark, and now because on two or three occasions during the late afternoon a slight mizzle of rain had fallen, the storekeeper kindly ordered us to sleep in an unused shed nearby. To which we of course readily assented.

"Say," said Tan as we were making night preparations, "this country on a road map doesn't look quite the same as on the ground, does it?

If I just had to live in this focus of two or three cow-trails that these humorous Westerners call a town, I'd be the storekeeper; he is pretty much the whole corporation. Fancy being a town all by yourself! Shall we take in the movies this evening or hit the blankets?"

After deciding that we did not just feel like movies, we chose the blanket course. All I remember of the hours that followed between dark and day-dawn was that I wakened six or seven times and each time the coyotes were holding choir practice nearby in the moonlight. It was Handel's *Messiah*, I thought, or other equally practice-worthy compositions, but they made altogether too much of it and toward dawn it cloyed. Tan, who had heard nothing like it in Pittsburgh, wakened at the first trill of the sopranos, fumbled around for his little gun and enquired hoarsely if we thought the brutes were coming after us, and if they would come into the shed. At which Frat snorted unfeelingly and turned over on his other ear. Frat had the best of us. He turned his good ear down, his deaf organ to the coyotes, and so slumbered like a babe is supposed to. As for Tan I doubt not that he shivered himself unconscious by and by.

▪▪▪▪▪▪ Meter 2970

JULY 28. The last coyote was singing a belated solo to the sunrise when we turned out. While I was watching some cliff swallows darting around the wooden buildings and wondering why they should choose to leave their ancient cliff battlements to colonize the eaves of such mean habitations, Frat commanded me to examine my hind tire. It was flat. So it was nearly half past nine when we took the trail again.

For three hours we toiled without incident along this dusty, double wheel-rut through the greasewood and sage. The hills apparently always were near but we rode in the level flat and never had to climb. Jackrabbits were our only companions till we reached Rose-bud Ranch. It was now noon and we halted to eat. What a veritable rose-bud in the dew was this green spot in a thirsty land! Here was the inevitable spring; its little rill had been dammed into an artificial pond. Real, yet scarce-to-be-believed bulrushes stood in the shallows and waved in the hot desert wind; shade trees grew upon the pond side of the rounding bank. The clatter of birds was in the air. Here under the pleasant shade of a fine willow, while a pair of Arkansas kingbirds and a pair of their eastern brothers quarreled noisily over who really owned the place, we ate our rough meal.

The history of a country is written along its rivers and springs. Here was the spring that guided the foot of man in the region. The ranch was founded on it. The dusty autos carrying dusty tourists that at intervals followed the disreputable trail hither, headed for it from afar. It was a Mecca to everything that lived in the land. The buildings were crude and uncouth, the typical rough and ready makeshifts of the raw land. The remains of a stone grist mill stood at hand to bring us a little of the romance of earlier and more primitive days. But ranches in this country are not what they seem. We were told that six thousand sheep as well as a number of cattle were back in the hills on the higher ranges.

Herds and flocks in plenty. Instead of the rusty horseshoe nailed over the stable-door, they might better have depicted the cornucopia in the shape of an ox horn. Yet what anomalies do we not meet in the waste places. South of us within easy eyeshot across the few intervening miles of shimmering, heat-crazed shad-scale and greasewood lay a limb of the Great Salt Desert. We could look out through a gap that was framed in red and purple hills, into the heart of it — as bitter a heart as could be found in any earthly landscape. White and wan, glimmering, rippling through burning heat-waves, it lay ghastly and dead, a Death's Valley deserted by man and God. The sight faded out in the dancing heat-ripples, sky and horizon and salt-plain mingling in a weird devil's dance in the far distance. Here and there across the more immediate plain, sharp, vertical funnels of dust rose in tall whirling columns, mighty pillars of gold holding the earth and heavens asunder. It was not a scene to hold one very long in contemplation. I was glad that our afternoon's trail lay in the other direction.

We were advised now that very bad roads lay ahead. One adviser

Frat fighting through a dry irrigation ditch in Nevada, while Tan
cheers him on. (COURTESY: BCA J-01405)

Tan negotiating another bad place in Nevada. (COURTESY: RICHARD MACKIE)

whom we deemed well-posted on the highways here, doubted our ability to get through on two wheels. He advised us very strongly to take a round-about route, which he described, and when we reached the railroad, to take to the ties. It was twenty miles to the railroad. So after meeting some other parties that had just come in, we set out again, and riding far apart to escape each other's burning dust fog we came to grips with the new trail. It was the worst road we had seen for some time. The soil was hard as brick yet cut into dust and ruts and chuck-holes that banged us about unmercifully.

It was a case where the best rider and the best mount, the nimblest, strongest legs and the stoutest arms won out most handily. More than one of us was thrown. It was also a fearful test of the temper; and to the eternal credit of our new friend Tan, I want to record that Tan arrived at the end of that twenty miles smiling. He had not seen the like, he admitted, since he had ridden some of the back streets of Pittsburgh. But then Tan will see something funny enough to smile over at his own funeral.

We held a long council at the railroad crossing. Our really bad road was scheduled to begin now. Indecision held the court for a time. Those Southern Pacific ties seemed made for almost anything else than motor-biking. To ride was one matter; to get caught by a loco-motive was another. Absurd as it may seem, it really is a difficult matter to remove a four-hundred-pound motorcycle from between the steel of a railroad track. We knew this too well. We put our machines between the rails and tried to get them off again single-handed over the rail on short notice. We practised until we found a method whereby it could be done with a fair amount of speed. And yet we hesitated. It was an auto approaching on the trail ahead that decided us. As we watched it bumping and staggering, Frat declared that it made him seasick in contemplation. He said: "Hit the ties! Lead on Macduff!" So I cranked and led off over the bumpity ties. Frat was to follow, Tan to take the rear.

At 3:30 p.m. I jolted into Lucin, but there was no sign of my comrades. In coming in I had turned a right angle where the railroads intersected; so I left my machine in the "town" and cut across country on foot. It was good to get stretched out on shoe-leather once more, and anyway I had a nature puzzle to solve. Since leaving Salt Lake City, several times I had seen tiny darting figures by the trailside. I hoped now to find one, and sure enough, before long there was a rustle among the dry shad-scale clumps and a long-tailed darting little creature scurried hippity-ippity for cover. I cultivated him gingerly at first; and then I tried rushing him. But both methods were about equally futile. He would have none of me. That he was a slender long-tailed lizard I was assured, that he was bottled-up lightning and possessed of the impossible knack of being in two places at once I was also assured, but there my biological research ended. I called him a swift and let him go at that.

Two miles down the track I found Frat mending a puncture. But it was more: he had picked up a large-sized nail that had pierced the outer casing and both sides of the inner tube and torn it as well. Generally crucified it, he said. Frat was not now in balmy mood. Mending a chewed-up tire in the Utah sun is not the mere matter that it is in the directions on the cement tin. He had gone past the sun-warmed and mellowed stage and turned ascetic. He made sharp remarks more or less original about the fool who put nails on the track, about the fool who suggested riding the track, and against the fool president of the fool road for keeping such a fool track.

Tan meanwhile was wandering around nearby with his gun, hot on the trail of a rattler. He simply had to get a rattler. This we were to learn was his one dominant passion. Since leaving Pittsburgh he had been on the quest, and now he was well nigh in despair and desperate. So far he had seen a lot of good places for them to be, and heard numerous things that buzzed, but flint-hearted Fate was against him.

When we reached Lucin we found other touring visitors of the Road in town. Two Jewish families of the well-to-do order from Brooklyn, New York, had driven across the continent so far, and now having weakened, were loading their large and powerful autos upon flat-cars and they had taken to the Pullman, bound for Reno, Nevada.

Pater explained to us the hundreds of dollars this portage was about to cost him, but declared that he had had enough of the desert. He had no desire to be a hero, he said. In the last twenty miles he had been forced to use the shovel about seventy-seven times when his big car dragged her underparts and the drive-wheels spun helplessly.

That indignity had been the last straw. The blowsy over-flowing matrons and two or three grown-up daughters sat in the half-hearted shade, fanned themselves, perspiring copiously and asked us if we didn't hate such a horrible country. To which being somewhat possessed of an evil spirit at the time, I could only reply that I liked the country exceedingly. The roads were a bit rough in some odd spots, I admitted. One had to be a good driver in order to get through easily, but even at that I would rather ride ten miles here than one mile in East Side Harlem — recalling at the moment the time when Betsy and I had turned turtle and spilled on the cobbles near the curbstone in the stinking Bowery.

The station agent at Lucin was most kind, and gave us train schedules and advice and soon we took to the ties again. At nine miles I stopped and waited, for it was not possible to ride here and look back, and after a little time Frat came along at a thirty-mile humpity-bumpty clip. But there was no sign of Tan, so after waiting awhile, fearing an accident, I turned about and rode back. Six miles down the track I came to him. He had his machine off the ties, and he was whistling softly: "You wore a tulip, a big yellow tulip" as he diligently mended a puncture. He too had picked up a big nail and it also had played havoc. By the time the tube was patched, darkness was drawing in, and the two of us had to make camp.

As I lay in the darkness and watched Tan's evident delight over his big blazing campfire of greasewood, I was filled with strange ideas: how deep-rooted is a man's love of fire, even when he has no use for it. Perhaps Tan thought that he had a use for it, for the coyotes already were singing shrilly to the growing moonlight, but I think rather he gloried in it because it was fire. A primitive passion gratified. But then we are all a motley composite of primitive passions glossed with a coating of inhibitive restraint, a coating all too thin and transparent at times.

It was, therefore, a great day for hairy man back there in the dawn vistas of time when first he learned to make a fire. We love it yet just for the same reason that children do: because in our short lives we must go over the same ground, more or less abbreviated, of course, that our pithecanthropus relatives did. And they loved it because it meant life and survival. Tan's fire represented one basic difference between man and brute: without it we would have gone to bed like the grey wolves.

▪▪▪▪▪▪ Meter 3042

JULY 29. When we reached Frat in the morning after dodging a freight train, and enquired for his health and happiness, he said he had had a fine night of it, so we headed west again. Soon we reached Tecoma, the next centre of desert civilization, but there seemed no one much alive so we tried to beat a freight into Montello. I was leading, and as the track really was not badly ballasted, I held the speedometer at thirty-five miles, sat tight and trusted in Providence. But Providence sometimes is a bad banker.

Suddenly I spied another freight approaching, but it was on the other or left-hand track (the road was double-tracked here) so I heaved in a big breath and kept travelling. Crash! The engine came on and by, almost staggering me in the whirl of air, and the next instant I was paralleling the pounding boxcars that were passing at a speed that seemed fearful.

The wind was south, or directly across our course: it picked up the smoke and dust and whirled it into my face; bits of gravel came like birdshot. That was the longest train I ever saw! I was praying for that belated caboose when, to my horror, twenty feet ahead of me I saw a cattle guard! I shut off, crowded the brake and locked my hind wheel, but with Betsy popping like a crazy machine gun, we skidded for the guard. The outraged hind tire shrieked in agony as it sledded over the ties and gravel, and it crept from side to side.

We do not live many such moments in a lifetime. To be face to face with violent destruction is not pleasant. I had a horrible presentiment that when I encountered the guard I would flail about and then mix up with those thundering wheels. In such short space I did not then see that this cow-trap was one of those Western contraptions, bottomless and with a roof of well-spaced 4-by-4s lying edge up and parallel. In fact, I did a little exact observation.

There are those who have maintained in print that in drastic moments they have reviewed all their own personal criminal history and seen all their evil deeds rise up in array before them. As for myself, I do not believe it possible. In the present case I had time to get little more than started on the formidable list. Just when I was speculating on the sort of messy corpse I would be for Frat and Tan to gather up, I shot into the guard and with Betsy halfway down and stuck fast, I found myself clinging desperately to prevent a skin-the-cat over the handlebars.

Then the caboose hammered by. How I got Betsy out of her predicament I do not know but I was not gentle about it. Necessity is said to know no law and that freight train behind me was coming fast. By and by after it had passed, Frat came along, but there was no sign of Tan. He, as we found later, was back along the track mending another puncture. So we rode into Montello, found some breakfast and waited.

We were in Nevada now. The main road through the place was a mess of white powder, but we were told by those who should have known better that good travelling lay ahead. We had dodged the worst of it by taking to the ties, they said, and though neither Frat nor Tan felt that he had dodged much of anything, and I was not so sure of it myself, we decided to keep to the road henceforth. It at least was clear of three-inch nails and cattle guards.

The country was still barren and rolling with the watchful hills looking on from the distance. There was a striking similarity to north-central Colorado. There were sagebrush slopes again and green junipers dotting the hills, with the usual jackrabbits to bounce off by the trails. But whereas our footing in Colorado had been sand, here it was hard soil which, though it was cut cruelly into holes at times, in the large made better wheeling.

Before reaching Cobre we encountered a short section of road so wonderful in its ferocity that I stopped after getting part way through and used the Kodak on the others as they waded and fought forward. For they waded. No rider could face that jumble of white dust-furrows with his feet on the foot-boards. The dust rippled and rolled and splashed, curling out like white steam from a locomotive funnel on a winter's day. Only the upper half of the rider was dimly visible above the whirl of powdered road. Each chap's face was worthwhile too. On such occasions Frat looked bold and matter of fact as though eating up such a road-mess was a mere trifle for him; Tan spread wide his million-dollar smile as though he liked it. Just beyond this tangle, we overtook one auto slowly towing a second, while some of the occupants, including a pretty young woman in khaki, walked.

When we reached the town — the reader must always be very mindful of what constitutes a town in this country — Tan discovered another puncture, and so we were able to get acquainted with our fellow travellers. They were a party from Kansas City, Missouri, travelling in two autos, but now they were broken down and stalled and had to wire for repairs. It was rather a professional party.

There were four doctors, as well as the strikingly pretty nurse, and when I look back now with cold, clear judgement on the facts in the case, I refuse to believe that Tan's latest puncture was a bona fide hole in the inner casing of his tire at all.

In fact, at one time I thought that we would have to break up our road trio and leave him there, or else camp in Cobre too. But we were two to one, and we finally got him out of town and safely on the Road again. Now, however, we put him ahead. At which he tore off madly in a dust-comet, and we saw him no more till we reached Wells.

Two miles beyond this real little town we made camp by some junipers. Outwardly, Tan was all right again; but after the sagebrush fire had died and we were stretched in our dusty blankets, and a little burrowing owl was lifting up his voice, I heard someone in our camp

Frat and Tan enjoy a sagebrush fire near Wells, Nevada.
(COURTESY: BCA J-01407)

groan, "Boys, Oh Boys! What a pair of eyes!" And I know it was not Frat because he never gets worked up so over a woman.

Alas, how human hearts meet and are sundered by rough circumstance! Here was our fellow traveller from Pittsburgh, though half asleep, slowly reconciling himself to the probability of remaining celibate through life, his only ray of consolation a certain Kansas City address in his left shirt-pocket, all because we would not allow him to remain in Cobre to discuss gossamer nothings with a dusty young woman in khaki. As I saw her, she was noteworthy in but two directions. She was pretty, which with the sex is common enough, for all our mothers were pretty when young, and I recall also that she declared that she took a bath every day even if it was only in a teacup. Which really *was* noteworthy. We made no such pretenses. Truly it is hard to be a naturalist with human beings around; the latter have more strange and interesting ways than birds and batrachians. Pope was right: "The proper study of mankind is man." Also woman.

▪▪▪▪▪▪ Meter 3111

JULY 30. It was chilly in the early dawn when we rolled out of our blankets. While I was busy trying to get a picture souvenir of our camp under the junipers, Tan built a fire and warmed himself in body and spirit. Tan had a weakness for fires. Then when the sun was gleaming on a snow-spotted peak far to the southwest (probably an upper point in the Ruby Mountains) we took to the road. And it was a good road. It led us through a land, the like of which we had not recently seen: an irrigated valley with dark soil that brought forth crops of green fodder and alfalfa and yellow wheat and with horses and cattle in good measure.

These are the necessary concomitant of man and good, black land. Necessary, for how inseparably has the destiny of man been welded with his domestic animals. As humans, perhaps we are in the habit of overestimating our own side of the relationship. I fancy that if one of the inhabitants of Mars swooped down over such a fine valley on his first terrestrial visit, he probably would mistake the relationship, judge the Holsteins and Percherons the owners of the estate, and diagnose the land-owner in his modest domicile in the corner of the farm as some sort of queer little biped stock housed in a decorative beaver lodge.

This morning Tan gave the first act of his Wild West performance. There were more jackrabbits here than we had seen for some time. A jack can scent an alfalfa field at wondrous distance, so the ranchers said; they had come here for a purpose. So had Tan. If he could not shoot a rattler's head off *à la* the movies, he would work vengeance on a jack. So we heard the snapping of his little pistol as he rode ahead, and in spite of the dust we crowded him close to see the show.

Tan was proficient enough on the draw, but the little white rabbits in the shooting gallery back in Allegheny, though small, had behaved differently to these big, sky-hopping jacks and he simply could not discover the combination to land them. Jack would bounce out easily into the road, his black tail flipping loosely as he cantered on his toes in a manner that seemed to say that he had to take a morning constitutional anyway, and might as well run before this fool, popping thing as any other. Bang! And somewhere close to him a puff of dust exploded. Down went his tail, back came his mule ears and he shot out of his dusty tracks. Bang! And he flew, then took a tremendous side leap and whizzed off for cover.

The jack had survived the onslaught of the Colts. At each stop Tan took to load the little gun, we congratulated him on his shooting. He was somewhat nonplussed over the amount of gunning it took to kill one rabbit, but he said he would be doggoned if they were all going to get away. He had a lot of ammunition left yet.

After running nineteen miles through this cultivated land, we breakfasted in Deeth, then set out for Elko. After leaving the settlement behind, we traversed a rolling land of sage and juniper. There was little sign of habitation, that is, of the human kind. But Tan, who still led our trio, halted about 9 a.m., and when we came up he was laughing and he said, "Hey! What does a coyote look like?"

We did the very worst we could impromptu for *canis latrans*, and I think perhaps Frat added a few touches that would not tally exactly with the American Natural History but Tan cried "That's him!" and told his story. One of these grey haunters of the sage had ambled across the path and then slipped in behind a brush-clump and stopped to watch the procession go by. But our leader stopped at once, drew his Colts and sent a stream of .25s in the precise direction of that sage-clump. At which the grey rascal got out of there with speed and dexterity. He travelled in several directions at once, Tan declared, and at each shot that coyote tied a knot in himself. All of which was doubtless true, as there is nothing on earth a coyote hates quite so much as being shot at.

Elko proved a real town with 4,000 inhabitants — or so they said. We arrived at ten in the forenoon but had to halt for repairs. The rough going had torn and disrupted our panniers and so we at once sought out the saddler. When, after having eaten, and we were ready again, Frat discovered a flat tire, so it was not till 2 p.m. that we got under way. Which seemed a long, impatient wait, for there is something in this sort of life that breeds impatience of delay. We longed to be up and going always. We were seeing things extensively rather than in detail; our harvest was one of general effects.

We had an enjoyable afternoon. The weather was cooler than usual, the road was good, and the scenery was delightful. In a general way, we were now following the course of the Humboldt River. Ten miles from town we entered the hills and followed the windings of the stream. Life was full of pleasure, and in mid-afternoon by way of celebration, we left our machines, cut through a pasture where crickets, no less, were singing, and came to the river. Here we stripped and revived in full measure the pleasures of the old swimmin' hole. Nowhere does water feel so grateful to the skin as in the dry and dusty lands.

Nor did we realize what strange creatures we had become until we stripped. In contrast to our mahogany hands and arms, faces and necks, the skin upon our bodies gleamed papery white. We were a new piebald race. We spent half an hour here to the best of purpose. Quite aside from the morality and sanctity of ablution, it is good to feel and act like a youngster once in awhile. We even had a rough and tumble before we got away, in which Frat, half-dressed, ended on his back on the bottom of the stream, clothes and all.

While Frat was drying some of his renovated apparel — the bath was good for all of him except his traveller's cheques — Tan stalked off through the sage with his pistol in hand, and presently behind a screen of shrubbery we heard a steady, measured string of shots that suggested target practice. But when we reached our steeds again our comrade stood up proudly and displayed his game: a half-grown jackrabbit. We had to admit now that he could shoot; he had nailed the creature squarely in the eye. It had been asleep in the cover where there had been no disturbing dust-puffs to terrify, and so it had waited till at the fifteenth shot Tan had got the proper elevation and windage. He had redeemed himself; he whittled off a foot to carry in his pocket and the black tail for a souvenir of the Wooly West, and we went on our way, everyone happy. At the next town however, our comrade of the gladsome smiles mailed a fat and spongy letter; it was addressed to a young lady back in the East and though I can swear to nothing, I was convinced at the time that I could have guessed what was in that envelope.

It was eating time when we reached Carlin, and after a meal and another short delay while Tan rode back four miles to find his tire pump, we slipped away into the grey lands again and made camp in the sagebrush. When we were tucked away, Tan, on his broad back and looking up into the twinkling stars that were blossoming out in their blue meadow, exclaimed: "Well, boys, I never thought it could be like this!" And he spoke from sheer happiness of soul.

There were no fetters, no burdens upon this somewhat intangible part of Tan's composition. He was always happy; his face said so. He smiled because, like the great reformer, before God he could do no other. The inward illumination beamed through seventeen coats of sunburn and much dust. He did not try to be happy or long to be happy; he *was* happy. When we spilled and went down in the dust-smother like Bois-Guilbert before the lance of the terrible Desdichada, he laughed; when he himself went down he laughed. The sun was a joke because it burned blisters on his nose. Life was all a joke — comic opera or perhaps burlesque. He saw only the high spots in life and they were all humorous. He never swore; he had no need to. "Dog-gone it!" was the very worst profanity he was ever heard to utter, and he reserved this for crucial and supreme occasions. This evening when we were near slumber land, he suddenly burst out in a chuckling rumble, and when Frat said sleepily:

"What the devil are you boiling over about now?" the reply was: "You, saying 'Glug-glug-gurgle' from the bottom of the Humboldt River — pants and all!"

Shall any one of us ever forget these desert nights out under the stars? Not likely. For the desert, hateful as it seems at times, somehow takes one to its heart in a strange way. Its nights are best of all. Many a time I felt genuine sorrow that the demands of my physical being dragged me off to slumber so early. I was usually the last to cross the border, but we were playing a rough, hard game and slept like marmots in the winter. Rather I would have lain longer conscious to listen to Shelley's "solemn midnight's tingling silences" or Milton's fairy bells tolling the "music of the spheres." The nights here always tingled; the silence was good for a man. "There is something better than music in the wide, unusual silence," says Stevenson, "and it disposes him to amiable thoughts, like the sound of a little river or the warmth of sunlight." Poor creature he, half man and half angel, with the soul of a giant and genius fettered to the pitiable physique of a weakling youth, he knew the potency of nights out under the heavens, knew the beauty of the desert silences, but O the pity of it, he knew them alas too late!

▪▪▪▪▪▪ Meter 3191

JULY 31. A flat tire in the morning held us until 8 o'clock. While we waited on the slope we noted that we had several visitors. A number of jacks popped up their heads and waggled their long ears in different parts of the grey slope — plainly a challenge to Tan, and he brought out his artillery. With the air of a man possessed of a reputation, he raised the little weapon, screwed up his face and let go. Nothing much happened. He fired again a few times with the same result; the jacks went on with their feeding. Then one chap came hopping aimlessly as though in a brown study, straight down the hill. He ambled around us and came to a full stop on the other side of the trail. Tan was frantically loading a new clip. Frat said, "Aw, give the poor cuss a chance!" and reminded the would-be assassin that the victim's eye was now a fitting mark.

Bang! The little pill kicked up a trifle of dust a few inches ahead of Jack's nose and he took one hop and a half forward and quizzically sniffed at the spot, and wiggled his nose. Bang! The pill landed a foot ahead and he repeated his smell quest, very much mystified and in earnest. Bang! The bullet rattled beyond him and he popped up on his hind legs to see what on earth was over there. He examined the spot, stopped, looked and listened, flicked one long ear and then dropped down on fours again just as another missile went about where his ears would have been had he continued upright. This bullet struck a stone beyond him and whined, and Jack, convinced that the place on that side was possessed, ran across to *our* side of the road.

Here recollecting suddenly that one of his fleas had been too long in one spot about the back of his neck, he proceeded to make the parasite change his quarters and accordingly set to scratching the spot vigorously with his left hind foot. He was too busy thus to notice Tan's next leaden message. But at the moment when he was going to change and try it with his right, another bullet knocked a spoonful of gravel flying, some of which struck him, and he darted off very plainly scared, mystified and disgusted generally with the place. The show was over. Tan said, "Doggone-it!" and put away his gun.

The country we traversed today was far from a desert. It was a land of flat valleys of fertile soil, mostly barren on account of dryness, but supporting rank, heavy sagebrush. The saying in this country is that where this shrub will grow, there wheat will grow; it was plain that if Providence had sent a little more moisture in summer, crops in plenty would have been assured. Some of the valleys grew natural grass and we passed ranchers busy haying. Little meandering creek-beds traversed the flats — dry now, but evidently full enough in springtime with water from the melting snows on the bare, barren hills — and willows grew in thicket fringes along their courses. Birds were at hand again. We saw mourning doves and heard their cooing, also shrikes, kingbirds, nighthawks and magpies.

It was good to meet the magpies again. They are typical birds of these out-of-the-way corners. Cunning and sly like nearly all the members of their tribe, such as crows and jays, they are always ready to watch you and perchance revile you harshly from a safe distance, while waiting to visit your campsite after you leave. Like the rascally crow, they have sagacity written all over them. How beautiful their coats and graceful their forms! The dash of white in their dress takes away the morose, piratical appearance of the crow or raven. Their beautiful slender tails give them a jauntiness possessed by none of the jays. But here perhaps appearances are deceiving. At any rate the wisdom of the ages seems stored naturally below their black crowns. In the desolate and forgotten corners where they see a human face but once or twice a year, they seem just as wise in his ways as they are where they see him every day.

At 11 a.m. while traversing a greasewood flat, I had my first bad puncture. The air left my hind tire with a prolonged whish and I bumped upon the rim in a twinkling. A sharp stone had cut a triangular hole through the casing and pierced the inner tube. By the time this was mended and the emergency shoe bound in place, we were ready for dinner and reached it just in time at the big, white ranchhouse beside the trail. Here we found a Chinese cook and a ranch foreman with a Belfast brogue. The latter in spite of his rough exterior was interesting enough. I had a longing to tarry here awhile among the cow punchers and investigate some of their moonshine, but time was a consideration. At 2 p.m. we passed through the town of Battle Mountain and toward evening made camp twenty miles to westward.

▪▪▪▪▪▪ Meter 3270

AUGUST 1. We awoke to another wondrous sunrise and found ourselves in a wide, flat, half-green valley with clumps of thorny shrubbery scattered close at hand. Bird voices spoke up, and in that vast country of stillness seemed quite to fill the air. A shrike or two were rasping from a distant thicket, and some warblers lisped and whispered to remind us that we had not met one of their relatives since leaving the environs of Salt Lake City. A crow family not far away were noisy as they always are in the morning, and it was pleasant to hear the rascals again. But when some meadowlarks piped up with overflowing hearts it was like shaking hands with an old friend.

Those clear flutings seemed to drift out and fill the wide valley. Nor was this all. While I was busy once again with my wretched tire, Frat called out in an uncertain, mystified way and said, "Boys, have I been drinking?" And on looking up I found his vision riveted on the sky; and here coming along out of the east, very low, with huge wings beating easily, was a big, white pelican! A pelican in the air at a few yards is an enormous-appearing bird, awkward and ungainly of shape, but magically easy in motion. The big creature paid little heed to us, but before it had quite come overhead, Tan exclaimed "Great Gosh! What is it?" and cut loose rapidly with his Colts. At which the big bird swerved a trifle and went on his way.

Another flock of a dozen came along shortly and it seemed probable that we were near a rookery. I asked Tan to put up his gun. Although these were the very last birds I should have guessed to see here, it was quite evident that such chaps knew their business. Somewhere among these endless, barren hills lay a lonely lake with probably an island for nesting site and fish for the catching. The birds we encountered doubtless were returning from a night's fishing elsewhere and carrying full pouches to the nestlings.

At about 8 o'clock we struck off at a good pace down the flat valley. The road was good and bad in spots until our path led us along an old abandoned railway from which ties and steel had been removed, and here it was all bad. There is nothing in the diary of this forenoon's adventures except the curt remark that "I went over the dump." But it is written firmly enough in memory. For I skidded in the rut, went over the side and Betsy plowed down in the gravel on her side and face. This of course had to happen at a fill where the grade was highest — some fifteen feet — and we came to a state of equilibrium (badly adjusted) about halfway down the slope. Betsy had lost her eye, and the whole lamp was knocked gee-haw. What was much to the point, too, was that we could not get back up again, and I was alone, the last of the three.

So we went on down. Gravity, the band-brake and a pair of legs attended to that, and then we took to the ditch. Two hundred yards ahead at the lowest point of the grade I then tramped a goat-path up the slope at an easy angle. And then, though I had my doubts about it, I put my steed to the test. Where sheer power was called for she had seldom failed me. Nor did she now. In low gear with throttle wide open we came roaring up on the top of the dump.

I recall this day with some chagrin and bitterness of spirit. It was the uncalled for spilling on the railway dump that began it. I found that I had lost my ability to ride. I would not admit it at first, but the facts were against me. I tagged along behind, and my comrades had to wait. They asked what was the matter, and I had no answer. I could not understand it. I had a three-speed machine; they had but two. On other occasions I had rather prided myself on the ease with which Betsy took me through the bad places. I held advantage over them, yet today I rode like a beginner or like a drunken man.

I seemed possessed by a demon of helpless ill luck. When I tried to miss a rut I went into it; when I tried to ride in the centre of the road, I invariably ended in the ruts. My legs saved a hundred spills, but I was fast wearing out trying to make the pace of my companions. On the last ten miles of the way into Winnemucca where we arrived at 1:30 p.m., I was thrown three times. Being thrown in the dust is not conducive to self-satisfaction. I decided that the problem was psychological; I had lost faith and consequently ability, so I let it go at that and fought away bitterly.

After dinner we set sail for Lovelock. We were advised strongly to take the new road. Whether this was a judicious move or not I cannot say; but we took it. In my notebook later, I said that the first ten miles of this trail agreed in every detail with Sherman's definition of war. What was worse, I could not yet ride; I was growing no better — fast. At first, Frat and Tan chuckled over it and made unkind remarks about Betsy's battered face, but now they offered consolation or said little, which hurt much worse. We were back in the desert again, the same ancient valley of salty shad-scale and sparse greasewood, the same ever-present hills of wondrous hue looking on from afar. It was all lovely as ever to the eye, what I saw of it, and at sundown, utterly worn out, I followed my comrades into a new scene.

It was one of the strangest places we had met on our long trail. We had entered a wide valley from the side and came out upon a bare plain so level that it appeared to be the surface of a lake. The valley turned gently toward the southwest and this level floor followed as far as we could see. The soil was bare and whitish in colour and glistened in the slanting rays of the sun, and as if to increase the similarity to water, small green islands of greasewood at intervals dotted the level surface. Save for the purple hills it might have been a good old Manitoba marsh in mid-winter.

The soil under our tires was hard and smooth as a billiard table. Pavement never was like it, and I opened my throttle, wider, wider than it had ever been opened before, and spun into the sunset. Faster! Faster! The change was heavenly. I was flying now; my tires seemed not to touch the earth. In a few moments I shot by Frat, then overtook Tan and stopped him. Such a scene was too good and rare to miss in the darkness. I wanted to camp and see this ancient lake bed in the sunrise. Also I wanted a rest.

We drew in beside one of the little greasewood islands, and while I stretched out my aching limbs and tried to admire the afterglow in the sky, Frat tinkered with Maria's troubles and Tan built his fire. It was only now that the stories of the rabid coyotes had any real meaning for us. For we had heard of them at Winnemucca and again at Pronto in the afternoon. At the latter place (it was merely a station), several men had gathered for the usual Sunday afternoon conference and they warned us jointly and severally on the perils of sleeping out. Coyotes were mad, afflicted with rabies, were biting stock, dogs and even ranchers and herders, they said.

When they learned the extent of our armament, they suggested with Western candour and frankness that we were fools. Frat reminded them that Providence watched over intoxicated men and imbeciles, and that we probably were safe, but they were in earnest. I too had scoffed then at such danger; but now when Frat and Tan brought the machines into a three-sided cordon with the fire on the open side, I felt that the move was a good one.

As Frat was hauling at the front of Betsy he suddenly exclaimed: "Hoho! No wonder you can't ride! No wonder!" Then he laughed. "If you would gee-up that front wheel you perhaps could!"

Frat's sarcasm was almost cruel, but perhaps it was in order. For when we examined that detestable wheel it displayed the alignment common to wheelbarrows. During the day it had been rolling along with the lateral leeway of an intoxicated sailor.

▪▪▪▪▪▪ Meter 3343

AUG. 2. I awoke before sunrise and sat up to see this new land of surprises, desolation and wonders. I felt elated in spirit. I could ride now, and I had not been eaten up by a coyote. They had sung in the night just as usual and quite as atrociously, as though they were not mad. Yet the first object my eye landed upon as I sat up, was a coyote. The rascal was sitting complacently on his trousers at about a hundred yards, looking us over, wondering what queer thing had come into the desert. How I itched for my rifle! When I reached over quietly and shook Tan he merely groaned and stirred a little, but at the word "coyote" I touched a concealed spring and he came up with a jerk, gun in hand like some brown-faced wild-eyed Jack-in-the-box. He had fired two or three shots before he was awake.

Br'er Coyote had not a vestige of cover; he merely shifted ground. And as an English drill sergeant would say: "He made it snappy!" He made himself as scarce as he could in the shortest possible time, and at each shot he did a little better. The bullets whizzed and whined along the smooth plain. Tan was not sparing on the ammunition. I got behind him and shouted encouragement. At about the third shot, Frat wakened wide and clapped his hands and banged on the klaxon. If the animal had been hanging around in the night to see what we were by daylight, he found out. Whether he was a mad coyote or not, I am unable to say, but I think probably he was. He at least had plenty of provocation.

We had an outdoors breakfast and before leaving I examined some of the little green islands close at hand. I found some holes of small rodents and the excavation of a badger but no other sign of life. Our coyote and a stray jack or two in the distance constituted our neighbours. Not a bird note fell on the ear; the valley held the silence of the plains of the North in winter.

The sunset of the previous evening had been magnificent, the whole sky turned to coloured glory; the morning view across the white expanse was scarcely less enchanting. We were a little loth to quit the place, and now decided that it would be a capital performance to ride off up the valley to Jungo. Gas and oil could be obtained there at a store, we had been told. As a matter of fact, Jungo's one building had been hovering in our eyes since daybreak. A mirage lay upon the valley: things were not what or where they seemed; Jungo was aloft, suspended between earth and heaven in a way that would have been a bit unreal had we not been used to the exaggerations of Western landscapes.

So we turned up the white way and headed for the store about five miles distant. What a racecourse! We simply had to fly here. Lying low on the tank to cut the wind, although it was dead calm, we opened the throttles till they would open no more and flew. There is a fascination and exhilaration about spinning through space at seventy miles an hour. We are all speed fiends at heart. In five seconds now I was paid for my tribulations and lost cuticle of yesterday. Tan raced till he saw that it was going to end too soon, and anyway the air pressure dragged at the roots of his hair. Then he folded his arms and gyrated about here and there like a skater. With one voice we voted it glorious, the more welcome that it came unexpectedly, for who would look for such a racecourse in the desert?

At the store we replenished oil and gasoline, and Tan annexed a set of rattles. At last he was possessed of the coveted souvenir. Of course in so far as he had not collected the rattler himself — shot off its villainous head in the approved style — the trophy was rather an anticlimax. But, well, Pittsburgh was a long way back. He might find a rattler himself yet. Tan was almost as much an optimist as he appeared to be, a rare quality in a man. But there was one thing I was assured of: he would not find the time *today* to hunt diamondbacks while I trailed behind and fell in the dust.

It seemed hard luck when we had to part from our lake bed and pick our way on the trail again, but by and by we reached the river and found a fair road. After a time I overtook my two comrades who were stopped together. They had a new desert trophy. Frat had a fine sample of a Nevada badger which he declared he had just shot with Tan's gun. In proof of which he showed both the gun and the badger, while Tan smiled approval and gave a fairly accurate moving picture imitation of envy. The creature was still limp and freshly killed and Frat may have had a fairly good circumstantial case all right, but when I wanted to hold a post-mortem examination he said to hurry up and take his picture so that he could prove it to his friends. Which I did, but I have a well-founded belief that this grave-digger of the desert came to his end, not by a Colts bullet, but by being run over by the last automobile that passed on the road.

About noon as we neared Lovelock, Frat came down on his rim and we halted for repairs. It was no pleasant place for vulcanizing inners, for the day was bright and fearfully hot, and a clump of waist-high greasewood at mid-day offers but a doubtful shelter. While Frat worked at his tire, Tan lay down in the sun and went to sleep. Had I myself attempted such a feat, I know that my outraged body would have yielded up its perspiring ghost, and I should have ended my terrestrial journey in the cemetery at Lovelock. Not so Tan. His ghost was more firmly anchored, and he loved the sun like a crocodile. For after I had grown tired watching the buzzards — a brand new one came along every so many minutes, circled, looked us over and departed — I called to him to help me catch a lizard that I noted scurrying nearby. At the second summons he got up, twisted the sleep agony from his countenance, drew his pistol and was ready for anything.

I was determined to capture this specimen at any cost. It was my long-tailed friend again and nothing slower than electricity was any

Frat with a Nevada badger he claimed to have shot. (COURTESY: BCA J-01402)

match for him. Back and forth from clump to clump we chased him, and at every opportunity Tan let go with his gun. He never was mean with his ammunition. Frat gave up his cementing and joined in on the double, possibly because it was safer to be on the heels of the hunt than to be anywhere else in the neighbourhood. Finally we got the creature cornered in a clump where he waited, pending our next move. I begged Tan to put up his weapon. He could not hit such a target in a million years, I said. But he, as I have said, had the vision of the optimist.

He fired again as I was speaking. And shade of Robin Hood and his Merry Men and of William Tell and Leather-stocking and the rest of the crack shots! — he notched the animal fairly through the forward part of the tail. The hunt was over. Strange as it may sound, the victim was almost helpless when shot thus, and we quickly gathered him to his fathers. After all this, he was only a beautiful little spotted lizard chap with a tremendously long and delicately pointed tail. The length and character of this member suggested that perhaps he used it kangaroo fashion as an aid in jumping.

We reached Lovelock early in the afternoon, but we all had work for the vulcanizer and did not get out of town till evening. This town, like numerous other mining centres, was respectable enough if one kept to the front street. Some of our observations would not look well in type. It seemed to be what is often referred to as a "wide open" town. It was wide enough to have driven Hannibal's oxen with their flaming head-gear through almost anywhere without singeing even the leaves of the scanty shade trees.

In the evening less than a mile from town I had a forceful reminder of the old story about the horse that lost a nail from its shoe. For several days I had been riding with a bolt missing, one of the two that held my handlebars firmly in place. Now as I rode in the dusk I encountered deep sand-ruts, was thrown and snapped the remaining bolt. Betsy now was *hors de combat*. What was to be done? Camp here, I said, beside the road. There was a soddy strip here between the worn trail and the railroad fence and I signified my intention of sleeping right on the spot. But the other two overruled me. Better push up to the gate, they said, and camp inside the fence. It was only about one hundred yards, and so I pushed.

When we had night preparations complete we returned to the Road and were debating over whether to return to town on foot, when down the road in the darkness we heard a sudden commotion.

Horses were running and a light vehicle was clattering. We could hear the blowing of the animals as they galloped; the thud of their hoofs indicated top speed. In a moment they burst upon us and we scattered like rabbits. It was a runaway team and light wagon with no one in it, and they followed the fence so closely as they pounded by that Frat went over the top as Tan rolled under it.

▪▪▪▪▪▪ Meter 3422

AUG. 3. There was a pair of kingbirds chattering belligerently in the morning when I wakened, and later as we were packing up camp, an oriole whistled several times from across the railroad where a string of well-grown poplars followed the irrigation ditch. This bird was another surprise. No denizen of the desert he, but like the others of the plains mentioned previously, he had followed man into the dry lands. In the springtime the patches of green from these tall trees had caught his fancy during migration and he had tarried to live and conquer a new world. I judged this bird to be the western Bullock oriole. His whistle did not sound quite familiar; we had left our old Baltimore friend behind long since.

I was scarcely surprised now to meet nighthawks and some small flocks of blackbirds: Brewers and yellow-heads. In these small flocks I realized several things. There were tule swamps somewhere in the neighbourhood or the yellow-heads would not have been on hand. In their dilapidated coats, I recognized that nesting was over, old and young off together, and summer already on the wane. It had been welcome to the Jersey hills when I had spun off on my long trail. How short is a season!

By very careful handling, I found I could ride Betsy back to town and so we returned. It was 2 p.m. when we got clear of the place. During our vile durance there was but one note of real consequence. About noon a fine flock of white pelicans swung up from southward. They were fairly high but their great size seemed to bring them close.

There were nearly two hundred of them, and for some time they floated about, circled, sailed and hovered in the blue sky over town and gave one of the most pleasing exhibitions of magic flight that one could see among North American birds. Their white coats glistened like snow in the sunlight; their immense, black-tipped wings scarcely seemed to flap at all as they passed among each other in a pretty aerial quadrille. It was a fascinating sight though I observed that not many of the inhabitants of the town took note of it.

During the afternoon we had good enough running. For miles we followed the valley of a dry lake bed again, but though the trail was fair it was not the racecourse we had enjoyed before. Once off on our left we caught sight of the blue glimmer of water, but though we paralleled it for a time we presently lost the sight, came out of the valley and entered a new domain.

It was the desert again but unlike it in the past. It was a black and forbidding land, volcanic, recently baked, with the rolling slopes of ashes and burned rocks scarcely hidden at all by the stunted shad-scale clumps. It had the appearance of coming fresh from a volcanic oven, which doubtless it had, and had not yet acquired the yellow colours of the older desert. And drifting across those brown slopes came the hottest wind we had encountered. It was the breath from a furnace. To ride against it was to get it with forced draught, with blow-pipe intensity.

About 4 p.m. we came to a tiny rill of blue-green water cutting our trail and we knew we had reached Sulphur Spring. The rill was so hot that we could barely endure it on the skin. Forty yards up from the crossing was the spring source. It was a pit some twelve or fifteen feet across, quite deep, and it was boiling — not merely in the bubbling sense of the term, but red-hot: 212 degrees Fahrenheit. It steamed even in an atmosphere that was far beyond one hundred degrees. The boiling pit was of little use to us but the rill was luxury. Soap dishes and razors and pocket mirrors came out of neglected kits and for a time we enjoyed ourselves. It was the first opportunity we had had for some time, Frat said, to find out just where the desert left off and the sunburn really began.

Sulphur Spring, Nevada. A shave, shampoo and general overhauling were in order for Tan and Mack. (COURTESY: RICHARD MACKIE)

At evening we passed the deserted and dilapidated buildings of former salt works, and at dusk, finding no suitable campsite were obliged to drop down on a slope on the barren waste. A strong cool breeze was now blowing, and we were glad to camp low in the shelter of a hummock. For whatever may be the desert day, hot and trying to body and soul, the evening always settles in like a benediction, cool and delightful. Tan of course made a fire, although he had to work hard, and as we lay in our blankets we had a new feeling. We were nearing the end of our trail. Until today no one had felt it; now we lay and discussed it. We had been ready to get out into the desert, into the Big Silent Places. We were ready enough now to leave it. California lay close ahead. California! What an abundance of things were called up in the magic word. On! On! to California.

▪▪▪▪▪▪ Meter 3477

AUG. 4. We left our desert bed early. There had been little incentive to tarry, for though the soil had been loose there were angular stones in it. Even Frat, who always slept a mile or more under the surface, declared that he had wakened twice in the night from a horrible dream in which someone was kicking him in the short ribs — with trench boots. Tan said that he felt almost half as bad as he did on the morning after his first night out in Utah. But soon we turned our backs upon the flaming magnificence of the morning sky. The sunset the previous evening, across the valley had been one of the most splendid too, and strangely most gorgeous in the eastern heavens. And with a fair trail before us we headed for the land of the sunset.

By and by we came to a Y in the road. One sign said Reno, the other Hazen, and we took the former. We had been told so often lately that when we reached Reno all our road troubles would undoubtedly be over that now it had become a matter of faith, a tenet of our religion, and we longed for Reno. We knew that at Fernley we would connect again with the Lincoln Highway, so when the road again branched, we chose the Fernley way. And for eight long, wide and solid miles we rode a deep, soft sand trail where not for fifty yards could we give our feet a rest. It was the old, gruelling, fighting game that Frat and I had played ad nauseum in central Colorado. But it came to an end sooner now.

We were reaching civilization again. Toward Reno, after passing through Wadsworth, we encountered a green, irrigated land much like the Salt Lake region. At 10:30 a.m. we passed into the far-known city of Reno and I repaired immediately to the motorcycle agency. The chuck-holes, arroyos, ties, cow-guards and whatnot had done their work. When we removed the remains of the coiled springs from the front forks, there were eleven pieces in one and fourteen in the other. Which was no reflection at all on the springs.

Before leaving in the afternoon after my repairs, Tan came into the agency and exclaimed: "Say, do you know that it is 104° in the shade right at this minute! What in fortune was it yesterday at Sulphur Spring?" We could not answer, but today was comparatively cool. Only the extreme dryness of the region renders such extreme heat bearable. Tan's figures were correct; he had consulted the thermometer of the weather-bureau.

We made ten spinning miles over good roads out through a new sort of country, then Tan contracted a puncture. Stopping now went much against the grain, for we were entering strange and interesting paths. The great deserts lay behind; the land of the Sierras already was reaching out a welcoming hand — as it does to all strangers. We could see it in the landscape and feel it in the air. On to the Golden Land of the Sunset! was the slogan in our hearts and on our tongues, and yet here we had to sit beside the road, inward impatience smouldering almost into flame.

To help matters, Frat also thought it a good time to tinker. Flying Maria had not been hitting in manner orthodox. It was the timer, he said. He knew it was. Of course probably the breather-spring in her carburetor needed a turn or the gasoline shut off a notch, but when Frat diagnosed the ailment as timing gears, why timing gears it was and the timing remedy had to follow. Out came the tools, out came fifteen screws and off came the cover of the gear case. He loosened the magneto cog, and the next moment found three cogs lying in the sand at his knees.

To put them back — ah, that was the rub. He recollected now that he knew as much of timing gears as he did of calculus or of the fourth dimension. Tan was equally wise on the subject, and I admitted my ignorance. Tan laughed; Frat did not. I could not, for I wanted to see California before the World's Fair in Frisco ended. Put them back! But all the permutations and combinations of cogs were dead set against him.

It is always easy to give general advice under such circumstances. The easiest and handiest words in the English language are "I told you so!" My advice to him was to borrow Tan's Colts, get in the road and stop the first auto with a man in it who showed any suspicions of

The Nevada desert was a poor place for Frat to tinker.
(COURTESY: BCA J-01403)

a knowledge of timing gears. After which I went up the hill to see what I might rout from the shrubbery.

But Frat started to examine the cogs critically, clean them, whistling a low tune the while. Whistling in the dark is a common human trait. By and by, Tan joined him and they both whistled. When I returned they were excitedly discussing timing and telling one another all about the subject. The number of times they had put in those three gears and taken them out again is beyond me to state. Between times Frat pedalled himself into a fever trying to make Maria bark, but she would not even growl. They talked an excited jargon of "One cog ahead," "one cog back," "breaker-points," "piston-head up," "piston-head down."

An automobile went by and the driver called out "Want any help?" but Frat shouted back blandly, "Oh no!" So went the late afternoon. And about sundown as Frat was weakly pedalling, we were all startled by an explosion within the interior of Maria and off she went. She stuttered terribly and coughed and spit fire, but the thing was done. Tan gave a yell and danced a war-dance on one foot. With a little more adjustment now, Frat rode up the trail and back and then declared Maria sound, better than she ever had been. The moral of this story is that bluff sometimes wins.

But it was too late now to travel, and so we made camp. It was while we were stalled here that a honeymoon couple with their dog-cart came by. Their method was somewhat unique. Mr. and Mrs. B. were on a walking tour; they had set out from Reno and intended to walk to southern California. They had loaded approximately one hundred and fifty pounds of personal effects into a big, square box, mounted it on bicycle wheels and attached shafts and handles — a combination of a baby carriage, dogcart and the doubtful vehicle-species of a Bowery huckster.

Nero, the big St. Bernard, pulled in the shafts; Mr. B. pushed on the handles. Of course, Mr. B. did not say that he was on his honeymoon, but crime will out. A newly married man usually is so guilty-appearing that there is no mistaking him. From his age, I judged him to be forty, and considering the locality, it might have been his second or even third adventure, but even so he could not hide it.

They were enjoying the trip immensely, they said, but Nero did not say that *he* was. I was sorry for the dog. He was young and scarcely grown. Already he was footsore from his load. He was not a Nero but a Martyr. 150 lbs.! Mr. B. said. When, oh when, will folks learn to go outdoors with just enough, learn to simplify life instead of complicate it, and leave the indoors behind where it belongs? I was on the point of asking him why he had not brought the piano and the chickens, but I noted that the little woman was concerned about the dog and so spared her.

I have no doubt that they had a gramophone in the box, or perhaps the pet canary or the parrot, or even the wedding presents. I felt my ire growing hot at the outrage, and this was not all because Mrs. B. was so young and pretty. I would have put Mr. B. himself in the shafts, Mrs. B. at the handles, and given the footsore dog a ride. I felt that with one-third of 150 lbs., I could have honeymooned from Reno to Timbuktu and back and had a good time all the way — that is, providing I could find one of the sex as pretty and wholesome as Mrs. B.

Their main idea was correct: it was the rock of ways and means that plainly was going to upset the boat. There is real romance I suspect in such a honeymoon well-managed. To go off in the sunshine, two together, like the doves in the springtime, and bill and coo on country lanes where there are no Pullman neighbours to ogle and eavesdrop, no smirking hotel ninnies to whisper wisely, "Newlyweds!" Ahh, if ever I have a honeymoon it shall be such a one.

▪▪▪▪▪▪ Meter 3533

AUG 5. We were gone as soon as Tan could fill his tire. The desert sunrise lay off to eastward but we had turned our backs upon it; a new land was calling us from the West. As we popped off down the yellow road, I noted tall pines standing on the hill opposite. They were all lit up with the gold of morning. These were new trees to us, strangers. Nothing like them had stood sentinel anywhere on our transcontinental trail. We had the feeling of entering a new world.

A turn or two and a beautiful trout stream of purest crystal and we came to Verdi. Then after breakfast we went on again up-grade; we were climbing the foothills of the Sierras. The Sierras! There was magic in the word for us Easterners. It made a pleasant stir in the imagination, felt good on the tongue. It conjured almost as much for us as the word "California!" There was so much that was new here that now when Frat stopped to put that magneto cog one notch some other way, I was glad of it. Those long-leafed yellow pines with the red trunks and tremendous green cones, large almost as my fist, standing scattered on the hillside above the clumpy sage, and also some new shrubbery, were calling for investigation. Two or three thrashers sat upon the tops of the smaller pines, and with voices that were harsh and strange, they shouted disapproval. Their coats were not of eastern cut or colour, and they, too, were new to us.

When we reached the first divide we had to pause again, for Tan's latest patch had worked loose, and while he was at it, Frat had to play with those cogs. But if I was not glad, I felt something selfishly akin to it. It was the most pleasant place to tinker or to write a diary that we had found in about thirty-five hundred miles. So I sat on the red needle-carpet below a big yellow pine and scribbled and listened to my new bird friends. How welcoming strange it seemed to come to these things so soon.

Far over our heads towered these tall-straight pines, the most beautiful in America. Their ruddy yellow bark seamed in decorative alligator-leather patterns glowed warmly in the sun and shone from afar. Their long needles whispered softly, and filling the air, made the forest sweetly articulate. A cedar or two in strange dress were in sight, and underneath grew mountain laurel and a species of Amelanchier, both also in unfamiliar garb. My bird friends spoke through the wood at intervals but they were like old friends in new clothes. On the way up we had met a kingfisher — good old faithful, he! — and a flicker. But the flicker was a red-shafted or Western species. And here in the pines on the hillcrest, juncos and chickadees and nuthatches called out, but they also spoke in new tongues.

Suddenly Tan produced what was left of a road map, scanned it eagerly, and shouted: "Boys, we're in California!" We were, so we stood up, solemnly took off our dusty caps and looked away to westward down the mountain woods-road across the valley to where an indigo hill shut off the view. Mecca lay ahead. Being bare-headed as always, Tan could not uncover, but he gravely saluted. Then he said:

"When I told them back home that I was going to ride to California without a hat, they said I couldn't. Guess I fooled them."

"Up in Winnipeg," said Frat, "they recommended a brain specialist for me. Of course a man never knows when he is crazy. I'm here anyway, crazy or not."

It was at a filling station in some little town here east of the Sierras that the garage man tried to scare us. It is the way of a garage man. After taking your money, he tries to "throw a scare into you" by discoursing on the fiery dragons ahead: road dragons of the type of sand, chuck-holes, straight-up-and-down climbs, hairpin turns so sharp you are in danger of riding over yourself, and so forth. When this gentleman of the Road — they have changed their highway manners little in the West since the days of Jesse James — drew on us with: "You'll soon *need* some gas! Wait till you get near the summit, some honest-to-god pimples there. You may have to push! You're not to Frisco yet," we naturally let him ramble along. We were almost used to it now. We had been shot at with ammunition of that calibre ever so often since we had left Denver.

"Well," said Frat wearily as he screwed on the gas cap, "I figure you can't scare me much. I came through Iowa when there were two feet of mud on the level and the ravines were plumb full. Nebraska was worse. Lots of times I had to swim this boat there. I climbed over the snowbanks in the Berthoud Pass, Colorado, with air so light that the motor was giddy and so d— cold that the gas froze. And I had to build a fire every mile to thaw her out. I bored through those sand trails in north-central Colorado, lost her two or three times in that sandbed at Maybell and had to dig her out. I got rained on in alkali country in Utah and had to put skates on her, and just back there in some of the chuck-holes and arroyos of your boulevards I have been looping the loop till my head aches. You can't scare me much now. Bring along your Sierras."

We slipped up and down dale in sunshine and shadow sharply contrasted, until when we were two miles from Truckee, Betsy went lame. By a strenuous use of the pump I managed to make town and then occupied myself mending a puncture. Frat invaded Maria's gearcase again. She was in mighty form now, we judged, as every time he passed his magic hand over those cogs, she came through the operation — rather I should say "ceremony" now, for it had come to that — better than ever. Tan went off and interviewed some young ladies. Oh how clean and sweet and adorable they looked in their white tennis suits. Half a dozen of them! Frat and I could only look on enviously and wonder how such a dusty, unwashed, untonsured, sun-baked, scabby nosed fellow could do it. But Tan knew how: he held the centre of the stage like a seven-times-wounded veteran of the Great War.

At about 3 p.m. we moved on again. Lake Donner lying blue among the pines was very lovely yet not quite what I had anticipated. Perhaps it was the sunken timber that marred it for me. Sunken trees and stumps near shore always give an impression of newness and rawness. But from above as we looked back from near the summit, the effect was very fine, and we stopped awhile on a rocky ledge just to see and admire. The climb itself, compared to some parts of our trail, was a mere joke. Our steeds ate it with avidity and we were up and over in short order.

We made camp early. At a magnificent trout stream of considerable size — one of the innumerable tributaries of the mighty Sacramento — we passed several fishing parties and tourists enjoying themselves, and there were so many campsites to tempt us that we had to tarry. It would have been bad taste, worse manners and sacrilege as well to have hurried through such a country. We noted that several camps were permanent. Californians, we were to learn, take to the hills in summer. At a little store half a mile up a side road we secured supplies, and a short distance back from the growling of the stream, yet near enough to hear its rumble, we made our night roost.

▪▪▪▪▪▪ Meter 3583

AUG. 6. The morning was chill and crystal clear. We were cold in our blankets and colder when we got up, glad to don our heavy sweaters. Several Californian Waltons were on the move even before us, and one of these visited us for a few minutes and went away puzzled and a bit disgusted when he learned that we did not carry rods. How could we fish without rods? How could we travel without fishing? To him we were poor samples of humanity. The kingfisher that rattled away noisily downstream said so too.

Our course led almost continuously down grade, though shortly after breaking camp we met one of two short, sharp climbs. We had crossed the last divide and were dropping down quickly to the plain of the Sacramento. We were in the Coast country, sunset land, the land of the Pacific. How bright the sunlight, how high and far away the intense sky. How deep and cool the shadows; how still and cheerfully solemn the piney woods.

How strange also were our new wildwood friends. A flycatcher with a voice like that of a wood pewee but harsh and unmusical, called from the timber. Once as I paused on a ridge to await my comrades, a dainty little quail mother with a dark coat and jaunty top-knot tripped out into the sunlight with a dozen or more younglings about her skirts, all to dart away and become invisible on the approach of the first noisy motor. Big grey ground squirrel chaps, strangely marked with white patches about the neck, ran across our yellow dust-trail, and small striped ground squirrels scampered over the rocks. One peculiar species of chipmunk with a white rump like an antelope presented an unusual sight for a 'munk as he skipped over the stones. Plainly we were far from home.

All the way down to Alta the road was dusty and rather rough. The much-vaunted highways of the state lay still somewhere ahead. Several inches of dust powder lay in the road before our tires and rose after us in a yellow fog that hung provokingly long in the still, sunlit air. Plainly we were in a country that, as far as summer rains were concerned, was entirely unsophisticated.

Soon we were down upon the plain, the rolling farm and fruit lands of the Sacramento valley. Real roads lay before us. Desert trails were forgotten and we rode at a shocking rate as did everyone else we saw. But there are no halfway measures in this state; here is the home of the superlative. Frat was setting the pace, but about noon, having seen nothing of Tan lately, I stopped at a fruit farm.

Endless acres of peach orchards lay about the rolling countryside and the fruit harvesting was in full swing. In a building where they were packing the fruit, I was invited to help myself. If you, reader, wish really to know the taste of fruit, spend some time in preparation. Go into the desert and sojourn awhile, get baked and frizzled up, acquire a thirst that is never stilled, absorb a little alkali, grow a full-fledged appetite, and then inveigle yourself into a Californian peach farm and persuade the owner to ask you to help yourself, not to the boxes of fruit, but to the overripe fruit that they set aside, too juicy and soft for packing.

Then I was escorted through the orchard by a ten-year-old lad. It was all very commonplace to him — he had to hoe there sometimes, I suspect — but it was not so to me. No one, I think, ever forgets his first meeting with oranges on the tree or figs turning to sugar in the sun. This, however, was not a citrus valley; the orange groves we knew lay far to southward.

But Tan did not come and so I went back to hunt him. Every mile back now I reckoned as three, and I travelled a long way before I saw his Navajo smile by the roadside. He was a bit crestfallen, it is true. He had just mended his twenty-seventh puncture, or it may have been the seventy-seventh. I had lost all count. I was in a fine humour over it. My sarcasm was large and of good flavour. It behooved him to give those tires to the junkman. I did not purpose to spend the remainder of my summer sitting by the roadside waiting on him while he ran an outdoors vulcanizery. He was penny wise and pound foolish.

At first he took it with some concern and assured me that if I must rub it in, I need not be so rough about it, and that though appearances were to the contrary, he really did not like mending punctures in the sun. Then while I stormed, he began to smile and at length to laugh and when I had shot my philippic, climax, benediction and all, the laughing wretch said:

"Very well, now how about your own?"

When I looked down at my hind tire, the sides were spreading out flatly. The unspeakable thing was punctured!

Late in the afternoon we reached Sacramento, and found Frat waiting for us at the motorcycle agency. Before we were ready to proceed, evening had drawn in, so we prepared for an early start for Frisco and spread our blankets in the yard almost underneath an orange tree. Which was rather lucky and providential, for it would not do to camp out in California and not sleep at least once below the tree of the golden apples.

▪▪▪▪▪▪ Meter 3676

AUG 7. We were off with the first day-peep. The Lincoln Highway lay before our tires, a pavement clear to Frisco. It seemed too good to be true when they told us this: less than 150 miles of asphalt-gliding where all we would have to do would be to hang on and sing. We would be in the big city by noon, they said. Frat led off at a lunch-at-the-Fair clip that was calculated to fulfill predictions, and we did our best to keep in sight of him. We had dreamed of roads like these at nights in the desert when our bones ached. Tan came alongside. We could ride tête-à-tête now. There was no dust and we left the noise behind. "Real climax!" he shouted. "That Illinois flat isn't just what I dreamed of California, but this road doesn't remind me anything at all of Nevada!"

As for the "Illinois flat," he spoke truly enough. The land lay stretched out for miles level as a table. But there were subtle yet pronounced differences. We were in a vast acreage of wheat-lands, yet the long stubble with only the heads removed in harvesting was not true of "back East." For harvesting was now over. Here a great herd of grey sheep were gleaning in the grey sun-bleached stubble, and everywhere dotting the fields were cattle and horses getting a fat living in the same manner. It was a prosperous, wealthy country, with much acreage evidently in the hands of the few. "Land poor" farmers they call themselves in the West. Fruit here was not much in evidence.

These landed barons knew how to make an easier living. Only about the buildings were graperies and fruit trees to be seen at all. Here and there across the plain rose the forms of solitary oaks. They were shapely and picturesque yet added a sense of isolation and loneliness to the flatness of the landscape. Standing commonly by the roadside were tall rows of eucalyptus trees. Their tattered bark and strange tropical foliage gave them an appearance that did not quite fit into the scene. They appeared strangers, far from home — as in truth they were.

We breakfasted in a little village at 8:45 a.m. It really was hard to stop even to attend to such a necessary and pleasant function. Yet we stopped longer then we intended. When I went to mount I found that my hind tire had lost its filling. But by and by, we got spinning again, until Betsy again bumped on the rim and another mending job was in order. This was exasperating. It was awful! And when we had started travelling again for a few miles, the wretched thing let go once more. Individually and collectively, we anathematized that sorry bit of rubber.

There are times when I have wished an inanimate thing alive that I might get what is called personal satisfaction. This was one of the times. But you simply cannot get personal satisfaction out of a rubber inner tube any more than you can out of the moon or the Almighty. We heaped it with malediction and cement. But Tan did not. He said he'd be doggoned and helped me mend it. And I just knew that the wretch was enjoying the situation.

We made the beautiful little city of Stockton at noon. But just as we had entered the outskirts of the place, Frat motioned me forward, and when I reached his side he called out in an agony of spirit from a soul bored to the point of nauseation that *his* tire was going flat. So we pulled in at the curb in the shade of some fine trees — the city was beautifully provided in this respect — and set to work again. We had become the joke of the road now. We were playing in a run of hard luck as the card-players say. Tan, who was more orthodox and did not believe much in luck, said that he believed we were riding so doggoned fast that the road burned off the patches. To which Frat snapped out that when he got another blankety-blank patch in place, he would ride twice as fast and keep them cool.

I had time now to observe the beauty of the place about me, the strangeness of the growing things. A species of ornamental palm that waved its feathery arms from several gardens added a little of the tropics that scarcely was expected here. Only my old elm tree friend seemed familiar, so I held up a passerby who appeared botanically bent, and persuaded him to interpret my surroundings. I got as far as the orange tree, the fig tree, the pepper tree, the locust tree, the umbrella tree, the walnut tree and then I gave it up. My head could not hold the names of the lovely flowering shrubs that even this late in the summer adorned these beautiful Western homes. But one cannot digest a whole botanic garden in half an hour anyhow. California! I understood a little of it now.

At 2 p.m. as we were nearing a little town, Tracy, I think. Betsy limped again and in a moment went down on the rim. There are times when feeling so far transcends mere words that the latter are utterly impotent and worthless. This was such a time. There is no English equivalent for what I felt; no publisher could print what I said. I saw Tan and Frat turn into town, and in a few minutes reappear on the highway again and spin off to westward.

I knew of course that they figured I was now ahead and were setting out to catch me. So I fell to work again: to remove the hind wheel with its appurtenances and take out the inner tubing and put it all back, alone. With only the doubtful assistance of a telephone pole, it was work. It was five o'clock when I came from the vulcanizers in town. However, the afternoon had not been entirely lost, for the watermelons and cantaloupes were ripe and plentiful enough in this land of sunshine and hot, asphalt roads.

With Frat and Tan somewhere ahead of me, I set off after eating my fill of the fruits. Throughout the afternoon, a strong southwest wind had been blowing in my face. Toward evening it increased to such a gale that in order for me to ride with any degree of comfort it was necessary to lie almost upon the handlebars in "scorching" attitude. The bright sunshine was gone now and the air was cool. A new feeling pervaded the air; it was the breath of the mighty Pacific. And now to add to this day of road sorrows, Barking Betsy lost her speed and stamina. She barked with a hollow sound as though she did not quite mean it. Her lungs were bad. She called for too much throttle and ran hot. Then it came to me. This air off the ocean was cool and full of moisture. For weeks Betsy had been breathing the hot, dry, light atmosphere of the desert and at high elevation. This ocean breeze was too much for her. So I gave a turn or two on the gasoline and she snorted and pricked up her ears on the instant.

In the evening I ran through a short stretch of half-settled, hilly country not like anything seen before on this long trail. They were not rocky hills, but they were dead and dry in appearance, and in places their crowns had been sheared of a hay-crop. With an occasional fringe of shrubbery at the sides they appeared to lie upon the landscape like huge priest-pates shaven and shorn in manner orthodox. And who but a Californian would make hay on a hill top? At 6.30 p.m. I turned into Pleasantville for supplies, and then after a short run into the sunset with hills away ahead beckoning on the horizon, I pulled up at the roadside and made camp.

I was alone, with Frat and Tan still up ahead, but now I was half glad of it. I had begun my long trail alone; I would end it so. All about me lay the open fields — the most dry and desolate fields, I thought, that I had ever seen at this time of the year. But they had been green and luxuriant enough in the early springtime, for though the soil now was baked as hard as it had been in the desert, there was a luxuriant crop of sun-bleached grass by the roadside. I pulled it in big handfuls and placed it below the groundsheet, and so lay down upon a bed fit for a king, or a steel trust president or any of the other chaps who are popularly supposed to sleep easy, but do not.

The wind died with the sun. It was dead calm now, and a hush as of the desert had fallen upon the plain. A meadowlark sang a go-to-bed ditty in the dusk, and a shrike at some cover not far distant replied harshly. Their voices sounded out of proportion in the silence. Sounds from the farm buildings echoed far, and all about me from the warm earth rose the "Creekle-creekle-creek!" of the field crickets. This added the necessary autumnal note to the grey fields. Down to westward where lay the big city, some clouds hung upon the blue hills, and as the sun vanished it shot its rosy and pink and salmon tints out to right and left and above and painted another of these Western dream sunsets that for some time had been a part of our daily fare. But this sky-painting was brief. It hung there for a few moments above the deep-hued hills, then vanished leaving a world of grey, and so I lay down with my thoughts.

Alone but neither glad nor sorry. For he must be an uninteresting person indeed who cannot chat with himself now and again, and enjoy it. The evening was good, and tomorrow I would drift down to the Golden Gate, look upon the face of the Pacific and finish my journey. And now looking backward in mind's eye along the trail from the grey asphalt near my bed to a ferry-boat upon the far Hudson, it did seem a long way, yet so short, so disproportionately short, to be the girth of such a mighty continent. It had been long looking westward, but now when viewed backward toward the rising of the sun, quite the reverse. Our lives are such: to look ahead from our wondering teens to the far days of grey beards seems like the vista of the very race to which we belong. To look back, alas, it seems but a breath or two, a tear and sigh with a laugh between.

The man who knows not the roads of a country knows not that country. I had sat upon my growling steed and seen a vast and noble continent spin by. It had not always spun, it is true. In fact there were times when it bumped and jolted, but it got by somehow and now I could see it all. It had been a mighty film, a four-thousand-mile reel of wonderland, the like of which may never be seen within four walls.

I could mentally view it all: the black and white cattle in the green pastures of New Jersey; the rolling blue hill country of lovely Pennsylvania; Ohio with its locust-lined roads that seemed made for lovers; undulating Indiana with its pastoral views circumscribed at a mile;

Illinois with its rich, green prairie spread out like the sea; Iowa's green billows of fertility rolling endlessly; the water-washed alluvial of Nebraska — although I confess it, my picture was mostly mud — Colorado's mountain gods with snowy crowns overlooking the sand and sagebrush; Utah with her magic green spots defying the painted desert; Nevada's lonely yet lovely desolation burning in colour splendour at the rising and setting of the sun; and here about me the golden state that seemed more wonderful than any of the others. Lying in the darkness with my eyes shut I could see this picture-procession of the long trail written upon my eyelids.

▪▪▪▪▪▪ Meter 3786

AUG. 8. It was chilly at dawn and I did not rise till after sun-up. There was no need to. It was only fifty miles to Oakland and a pavement lay before me all the way. There was a light mist abroad, and the cattle loomed big at their pasturing. My meadowlark sang again to the rising sun as though the dampness and coolness revived in his heart the desires and fires of the springtime. The low hills were swathed in carded grey mist banks whose sinuous trains came down at intervals and dragged across a little valley. The grey haystacks perched high, broke through their shrouds now and again, and stood bold like little castles along the Rhine. But by and by, the sun broke through with its warm beams, and so I mounted and rode down to the Big City by the Golden Gate and to the sea.

▪▪▪▪▪▪ Meter 3842

THE END

AFTERWORD

by Trevor Marc Hughes

A MOTORCYCLE-NATURALIST was how Hamilton Mack Laing described himself before departing from St. James Place in Brooklyn, New York, and would continue to do so for years after completing his 1915 motorcycle journey across the United States of America. He had first discovered the motorcycle, a newfangled bit of technology in 1914, when he purchased his first bike, a new Harley-Davidson 10-F, and then the following year, a Harley-Davidson 11-F, which he would use to fulfill his dream to ride across the continent.

As a naturalist, Laing had already made a name for himself writing for various publications, describing his adventures in the natural world, many on foot, where he would observe and photograph bird-life. At the time, the motorcycle was an innovative form of transport that would, he believed, give him a new perspective. His cross-conti-nent adventure on the motorbike from east to west across North America would strengthen his resolve to be a writer and naturalist, further his beliefs in simplicity and convince him that the new technology of the motorcycle could connect him with the natural world as never before.

When Laing began his work as a naturalist from a motorcycle, he was among the first to seriously engage with motorcycles. In the United States, 1901 would see the actual beginnings of the creation of motorcycle companies when Indian started production. Across the Atlantic, motorcycle company Triumph had begun producing motorcycles a few years earlier. In 1903, Bill Harley, Arthur Davidson and Walter Davidson created a single cylinder two-wheeled machine in Milwaukee. Coincidentally, 1903 was also the year of the first motorcycle crossing of the continental United States. It was made by George A. Wyman on what was actually a motor bicycle built by the California Motorcycle Company. It took Wyman a little over seven weeks to travel from San Francisco to New York City. When he pulled into New York on July 6, he was the first person to cross the continent using a motorized vehicle of any kind.

Wyman's trip was widely publicized, and people everywhere began to realize that a corner had been turned and that the world was moving into the era of the motorized vehicle. Laing saw that there would be great leaps forward with this new form of technology, and soon after purchased his first motorbike from the recently created company of Harley-Davidson. He would eventually declare: "The man who knows not the roads of a country knows not that country." Laing saw that the motorcycle would offer a distinctive means to gather up the material he needed for his writing. He also realized the motorcycle would set himself apart while he was establishing his career as a writer and naturalist.

―⁓⁓―

I first came to learn about Laing's motorcycle journey when his biographer, British Columbia historian Richard Mackie, informed me of Laing's unpublished account of his riding a motorcycle across the continental United States on a bike he had named "Barking Betsy." I was interested right away. As a motorcycle travel writer, I am always drawn in by accounts of two-wheeled adventure. I am also a staunch defender of motorcycle travel, believing it allows travellers to gain a unique connection with the places through which they travel. The Laing manuscript, Mackie informed me, was written over the winter of 1915–16, soon after he completed the trip. The typed manuscript was tucked away among the many file folders containing the Laing Papers, which Mackie had catalogued and sent to British Columbia Archives in the early 1980s while penning Laing's biography. Not long after learning about the unpublished manuscript, I departed for the archives in Victoria.

Over the next few months I would read Laing's rich tale, devouring the descriptions of life on the road, from his extraordinary ability to identify birds from their songs to his notes on travel etiquette, tips passed along to future riders, laments over deplorable road conditions, celebrations over being able to open up the throttle on stretches of asphalt, and observations of a country before it would enter the First World War. It put a smile on my face.

Partly my intense interest in the manuscript was because I began reading it during a particularly dark and snowy winter, at least by Vancouver standards, and was living vicariously through Mack Laing as he struggled to ride, lift, push and pull Barking Betsy to the Golden Gate. The Kawasaki KLR650 dual sport motorcycle I had ridden all over British Columbia was in winter storage in Burnaby. I was dreaming of sunny skies, warmer temperatures and an open road.

Laing dedicated his tale "To every lover of the Winding Road." He saw the "Winding Road" as a metaphor for life itself. Just before his departure from St. James Place, Brooklyn, when he was looking ahead to a "six-weeks' perambulation on two wheels," he noted philosophically: "How similar to a road is our entire spin through life. We may see the path clearly enough to the turn, but beyond it, the future must reveal." The Road, as he often called it, would become an important part of his motorcycle adventure.

I would do more than read Laing's account. I decided to transcribe it and prepare it for publication. For several months I pored over the manuscript, getting to know Laing's writing style, his observations of birdlife encountered, his references to the land, to the people and places of a century ago, and make note of them in my binder, one I named "The Transcontinentalist" after the title given his file at the British Columbia Archives. I would make several more visits to the archives, eventually finding the photographs Laing had intended to go with the book, and which are included with this volume.

During these visits to Victoria, I also found other articles he wrote during his motorcycle-naturalist period, articles that shed light on how he devoted himself to planning his trips and packing the minimum necessary in his panniers. Throughout my reading, I found myself fascinated by his method of travel: there would be no helmet to wear, no protective gear donned as we know it today and a simple collection of items in his panniers that would sustain him during his six weeks of travel on Barking Betsy.

Eventually I would track down, with the help of BC Archives staff, Laing's original nature diaries. One of these, dated 1914/1915, would, in precise cursive writing, provide details of his motorcycle journey. Here he listed the names of some of the individuals encountered on the trip, individuals whom he referred to in the manuscript only by an initial. I treasured holding Laing's diary of his trip, a small ochre-coloured notebook, packed to the edges with ink scribbles, knowing that it had been in Laing's possession for the entirety of his 1915 adventure. I admired its good condition, knowing that it would have been vulnerable, along with Laing, to all sorts of weather.

The act of riding a motorcycle requires making oneself vulnerable. There may be a price to pay for the ability to connect with the outside world. "The Winding Road" is a very exposed place. At the start of a long journey, many thoughts enter the head of the solo motorcyclist. There is plenty of the unknown ahead. Whether it is rain, mud or sand roads, or unforeseen obstacles that have to be dealt with in the moment, motorcycle travel commands the traveller to dig deep inside and sort out the challenges to be faced. It is a test. For Laing, having just finished several years of art studies at the Pratt Institute in Brooklyn, it was a test he welcomed. The unknown beckoned.

This Harley-Davidson 10-F at the Deeley Motorcycle Exhibition
in Vancouver is similar to Mack Laing's first motorcycle, passed down
to his brother Jim (Frat) and named Flying Maria.
(COURTESY: TREVOR MARC HUGHES)

met a lad who warned me.
and tried to persuade me to change
camp site *

waxwing, bluebird and chippy and robin were
in song, and then as dusk melted the whip-
poor-wills rose clear from the still
mountain side across the hazy
valley had been killed at Phone
pole beside where I had made comps. Perfect
day all through. 4 miles from Bedford

*— because last year a man on a H.D. too
into darkness

Meter — 323

June 25th Dawn songs noisy. Bluebird
in fine fettle early. Petit, Wren — a
corker, kingbird, goldfinch, killdeer,
chippy, Maryland yellowthroat (down
at brook). Downy W. pecker drumming,
no early slumber here below the locusts!
  Wonderful running to Stoyestown and
beyond — all the way to Pittsburg
barring town streets — no state aid.
Wonderful views and at 8 a.m. I was
on grandest view — indescribable,
impressive. — As I googled, 4 ravens
croaked overhead, — O for wings like
them to hover that valley! Many a tour-
eye had taken in this scene. Many a film
had been shot — the tabs and cases attested.
Today a touring couple had beaten me to it. Mr.
H. N. Baker and Mrs. B— were breaking out

(Least flycatcher)

and two swept down over scene

The June 25 entry from Laing's diary of his 1915 motorcycle journey.
(COURTESY: TREVOR MARC HUGHES)

It was that degree of the unknown that also fascinated me when I read his account. In the days before Google Street View preplanned our road trips, even before there were reliable maps describing road surfaces, there were motorcyclists who relished the unknown, were hungry for it. It was that need to take risks, and to step out into nature, after several relatively sedentary years at art school in Brooklyn, that compelled Laing to seek adventure.

—~~~—

Before discussing the cross-continent journey, however, it will be helpful to look at how, in the years before, Laing was on his way to becoming an illustrious writer-naturalist. In 1913, in his thirtieth year, his first book *Out with the Birds* was published through Outing Publishing Company. Each chapter featured his naturalist's observations of the birds he encountered while on a hike or camping expedition into the wilds of Manitoba where, exploring his home province's natural surroundings, he connected with the birds, sometimes giving them names such as "Madam Spoonbill." He described their lives and brought details of their activities to the reader, who no doubt lapped up his adventure tales, perhaps even living vicariously through the experiences.

On a break in studies from the Pratt Institute in 1914, Laing again returned to Manitoba, but this time on his first motorbike, the 1914 10-F. Using the material from this trip, he wrote the article "Gipsying on a Motorcycle: How a Greenhorn Rode From New York to Winnipeg and Enjoyed the Whole Way." In this *Outing* piece published in the summer of 1915, he furthered his argument for the role of the motorcycle in naturalist studies. The story focused on how he, a novice motorcyclist at the time, rode such a great distance on poor roads and connected with nature.

On one side, he saw the motorcycle as the ideal mode of transport for gathering new experiences where there were "genuine surprises" and "real thrillers." On the other, the motorcycle allowed for many chance encounters where the rider could "meet a dozen kinds of people in a day, travel a score of different varieties of road," and find himself a part of nature while on the open road. He described his getting the motorcycle bug as complementary to his ongoing wanderlust for the natural world: "Very long ago the hankering for the out-of-doors, the joy of the unknown road had possessed me," he wrote in *Outing*, "and now I felt that the motorcycle might be used in the indulgence of that weakness."

In this first long-distance motorcycle journey, which was a trial run for the transcontinental adventure of the summer of 1915, Laing soon learned that the benefits of finding an indoor bed for the night were often outweighed by the pleasures of camping next to his motorcycle, where he could listen to and observe his preferred travel companions: the birds. Tucked in a bed in Harrisburg, Pennsylvania, after a noisy night listening to the revels of an Independence Day party, he vowed never to occupy a "stuffy room" in a hostel again as "henceforth the open road was to be my night roost" — a term he used in reference to his avian friends.

What gave him solace after a day's riding was birdsong. "In the more rugged fastnesses," he wrote, "there were brooding valleys whose quietness was accentuated by the soft whistle of towhee or sparrow or thrush or the soft tapping of a red-headed woodpecker." Laing found success as a writer typing up and submitting articles like the *Outing* piece and that success put him in an enviable position in these early years. As a student at the Pratt Institute, the income he gathered as an established writer not only paid his tuition but it also allowed him to buy his own two-wheeled transportation.

———

Laing chose the 11-F to make his 1915 cross-country journey. It was the second of three Harley-Davidson motorcycles Laing would own, and it was paid for with earnings made from his freelance writing. A list price of $275 made it quite affordable. The 1915 Harley-Davidson 11-F was by the standards of its day a powerful machine. At 11 horsepower, yet boasting a 988cc engine and three-speed sliding gear transmission, the 11-F could propel the rider at a slow meander or push him to a top speed of 65 miles per hour. The joy of the Road inherent in his ability to get up to speed in third gear is illustrated most satisfyingly when Laing puts the poor roads in Nebraska behind him and accelerates on good Colorado roads: "We had been fighting so long on retarded spark," he wrote, "that to sit up loose and easy and open the throttle a little meant quite a new joy of the road."

The 11-F had a chain drive and weighed about 325 pounds, a substantial machine. It had a brake only on the rear wheel. This spelled trouble for Laing when trying to brake in mud. A rear wheel locked and sliding around behind the rider is no friend. Another feature of the bike was the "flat-style" gas tank, but this feature would be the last of its kind. The three-speed transmission, however, would continue to be in use until 1936. It may be hard to imagine today, but this was a state-of-the-art motorcycle in 1915. It was speedy, agile and Laing saw it as the kind of solo transportation that suited his needs as a naturalist.

———

When he came to give an account of his 1915 transcontinental motorcycle journey, Laing continued to combine his love of motorcycling with his love of the natural world, especially its birdlife. When travelling alone on Barking Betsy, many thoughts to do with birdlife entered his head. The naturalist was on display. He was in his element. "I had to halt to hear the birds," he wrote, describing how, while riding up Schooley's Mountain in New Jersey, he couldn't resist stopping and listening to the song of a field sparrow and a towhee, as well as the calls of kingbirds and warblers.

I greatly admire Laing in his ability to spot and identify a bird once he was settled in for the night after a tiring and muddy day. Bird songs were all that he required at the end of the day for solace. In fact, it was a large part of his criteria when choosing a place to camp for the night, such as in one spot near a telephone pole when he stated, "... but best of all, a red-headed woodpecker family lived in the pole and the old birds were almost completely in sight." Birds always competed for Laing's affections with the joys of the road, especially in the early parts of his manuscript.

Laing was happiest when he had pulled in to a spot just off the road where he could experience the "bird symphony," where "a chippy sparrow buzzed at regular intervals," where, spotting the character of a cheeky creature on another branch, "a selfish thrasher tuned his liquid instrument." As an especially avid lifelong naturalist, he was attuned to his environment like no other motorcycle travel writer I've read. Also extraordinary was that Laing allowed for the Road and nature to exist in such harmony. Laing would later on explain this close connection with the birds: "When I was young I had the ears of an owl. I built up in my head a dictionary of bird songs. Transcontinentalizing I could hear familiar birds in the woods even over the popping of my Harley."

———

While contemplating birdlife across the continental United States, Laing had few obligations in his itinerary. He knew he would meet up with his brother Jim (whom he affectionately refers to as "Frat" in his tale) in Nebraska. He had a destination in mind: the Golden Gate Bridge and the San Francisco World's Fair. After the fair, he and Jim planned to head north to Portland to stay with his parents, who had moved there from Manitoba years before. But other than these goals, and an interest in staying away from major cities, he looked forward to the open schedule and slow pace of a gentleman gypsy.

In this spirit was Laing's rejection of speedy travel. Early on in his journey, when settling in for a "night roost," he would chastise himself for his swiftness: ". . . for I had been nearly fifteen hours on the road; the meter said that I had travelled 176 miles — horrible, sacrilegious haste!" The initial pages of his manuscript also demonstrate his taking an as-it-comes approach to travel and his wish to take the road less travelled. "I was rather cutting across country here and not following the main highway of the state marked as preferable on my road map." Laing also felt reluctant to seek accommodation indoors. This "road gipsy" chose to track down a place to camp while it was still light out to find the connection with nature for which he yearned. "After a day on the road," he noted, "I abhor night quarters within doors. . . ."

The motorcycle is different from a car in that the traveller doesn't have to step out of one environment to be in another. The motorcyclist is already in the environment being travelled through, whereas the motorist riding within a contained frame that moves from one environment to another has to step outside to enter the world he or she is passing through. At no other time is this more apparent than when a significant vista appears, presenting the opportunity to apply the brakes and take it in. Laing had one of those moments while being guided by what he termed a "road-burner" fellow motorcyclist: "He could not understand why I could wish to stop on the long bridge and take off my dusty cap in silent homage to the great Mississippi, the Father of Waters."

Later on, in Nevada, while travelling with his brother Jim and Smith Johnson (affectionately known as "Tan" in the story), he found a lesson in simplicity that would serve him in good stead in his future endeavours. He encountered a young newlywed couple on "a walking tour" (Mr. and Mrs. B.) on their way to southern California. Laing described their homespun carrier: "They had loaded one hundred and fifty pounds of personal effects into a big, square box, mounted it on bicycle wheels and attached shafts and handles — a combination of a baby-carriage, dogcart and the doubtful vehicle-species of a Bowery huckster." Their St. Bernard was pulling, while Mr. B. was pushing, and it bothered Laing. To which he wrote: "When, O when will folks learn to go outdoors with just enough, learn to simplify life instead of complicate it, and leave the indoors behind where it belongs?"

———

An encounter in August 1915, following the end of the cross-country motorcycle trip when Mack and Jim arrived in Portland, would also influence his future endeavours. Laing's parents had retired to Portland after long years on a farm at Clearsprings, Manitoba, where Laing and his brother grew up. Laing's diary reveals that Barking

Betsy would get him just about to their home without incident. But it broke down just a few miles shy. Laing thought his motorcycle's troubles were serious: "Up at day peep to drain kerosene," he wrote in his diary on August 16th. Perhaps he had pumped some bad fuel as he had earlier on in his journey? It would turn out Laing was looking in the wrong place to cure Betsy. "But as I was to learn before many days, I was a rotten diagnostician," Laing lamented, "and was prescribing Epsom salts for a patient suffering lung trouble." In the end it was a quick fix, a simple readjustment of his carburetor's fuel to air ratio done with a twist of a knob.

After a couple of days' rest with his parents, he pressed on to visit his sister Jean and her husband Harry, who had an adopted baby son named John. When Laing came up to the house, he saw John in the arms of his nanny, nineteen-year-old Ethel May Hart. Ethel would prove to be the most influential of the figures Laing would meet during his motorcycle travels. She would become his wife.

—*~~*—

But before his wedding day, and his future illustrious expedition career as a naturalist, Laing had flourished as a writer. His motorcycle-naturalist articles continued to be published after his transcontinental journey was completed and as his experience as a motorcyclist developed. These years were still pioneering days for the writings of a motorcycle-naturalist. Laing was astute enough to seize upon the uniqueness of his perspective as a writer, choosing to exploit his niche in outdoor magazines. In "A 'Been-There' Motorcyclist's Touring Outfit," published in *Recreation* in July 1916, Laing described what goodies he packed in his panniers, no doubt to encourage other two-wheeled explorers. These panniers must be heavy canvas, he insisted. He recommended packing light in the categories of shelter, culinary items, clothes, and photographic equipment.

He described everything required by the discerning motorcycle-naturalist. When it came to his culinary kit, Laing insisted on packing "one knife, one fork, two spoons, a can opener, salt and pepper,

Laing with field glasses in his uniform as a gunnery instructor at Camp Beamsville, Ontario, during the Great War, c. 1918. (COURTESY: RICHARD MACKIE)

Mack Laing setting out for the Similkameen, on his 1917 Model J Harley-Davidson, the third and last motorcycle he owned, c. 1919.
(COURTESY: RICHARD MACKIE)

Ethel Hart, as Mack Laing would have first seen her, in Portland, Oregon, in 1920. (COURTESY: RICHARD MACKIE)

Laing takes a break from his prolific freelance writing career. Winnipeg, Manitoba, c. 1920. (COURTESY: RICHARD MACKIE)

National Museum expedition camp. Left to right: Hoyes Lloyd, Percy
Taverner, D. Alan Sampson and Mack Laing. Oak Lake, Manitoba, in 1921.
(COURTESY: RICHARD MACKIE)

At Vaseux Lake, with the National Museum's British Columbia field party.
Back row, left to right: Allan Brooks, P.A. Taverner, Frank Farley.
Front row, left to right: Mack Laing, George Gartrell, D. Alan Sampson,
May 31, 1922. (COURTESY: RICHARD MACKIE)

Mack Laing at the Chitina River, Alaska, during the
Mount Logan expedition. July 2, 1925.
(COURTESY: RICHARD MACKIE)

Mack Laing sitting in front of his fireplace for the first time at his new home, Baybrook. Comox, B.C., October 11, 1923. (COURTESY: RICHARD MACKIE)

Ethel Hart Laing writes in the doorway of a ramshackle cabin near Princeton, B.C., on their honeymoon, November 6, 1927. (COURTESY: RICHARD MACKIE)

The wedding photograph of Mack and Ethel Laing, January 19, 1927.
(COURTESY: RICHARD MACKIE)

Mack Laing with an impressive 44 lb. salmon on August 11, 1932,
Comox, B.C. (COURTESY: RICHARD MACKIE)

▲ Laing with some freshly caught
spring salmon near his Comox
home, April 26, 1929.
(COURTESY: RICHARD MACKIE)

◄ Ethel Laing, the day after her
wedding, January 20, 1927.
(COURTESY: RICHARD MACKIE)

▲ Mack Laing making salmon
spoons in Comox, B.C.,
August 11, 1934.
(COURTESY: RICHARD
MACKIE)

◀ Ethel Laing holds up a
healthy head of cauliflower
at Baybrook in Comox,
B.C., April 1934.
(COURTESY: RICHARD
MACKIE)

Mack Laing works in the Baybrook Nut Orchard in Comox, B.C., c. 1970.
(COURTESY: RICHARD MACKIE)

The sign for the Baybrook Nut Orchard, which Mack and Ethel would
develop in the 1930s and '40s into a large-scale producer of nuts that were
sold up and down the island. Comox, B.C., c. 1940.
(COURTESY: RICHARD MACKIE)

Mack Laing would invite prospective naturalists to Shakesides, c. 1980.
(COURTESY: RICHARD MACKIE)

salt and pepper dusters, a collapsible cup, a canteen (with screw-top, cork-lined) . . . a butter tin (also with a screw-top . . .), a tea tin similarly equipped, and a tea kettle (little pail with a handle to suspend it)." If he were wishing to extend his cooking abilities, perhaps on a longer trip, he would add "the small frying pan and a small cooker with a lid." A cornucopia of tinned goods from "pork and beans, spaghetti, soups . . ." might sound ordinary but could possibly tempt the palate of those enjoying the open road.

As for comfort when finding a bed for the night by the side of the open road, Laing's choice was military-issue. "I use the army rubber poncho, the army blanket, and have added an air pillow." Shelter from the elements came from "the tarpaulin tent, a flat, rectangular sheet about 8 by 12, and equipped with steel pegs . . ." and, of course, the tent would be of the "waterproof" variety.

What to pack to put on one's back? "One spare shirt, a heavy sweater, two changes of underclothing and three or four of socks is ample," he noted, with his caveat that "I plead guilty to the army shirts and riding trousers and leggings," noting that the "shirt and trousers ought to be of wool." The proviso here, however, is that Laing did not bring an extra pair of trousers; he simply mended his woolly trousers when torn. So, there needed to be a mending kit, as well as a shaving kit and eating kit.

This list was not yet complete. Hard to classify items included "the camera and films and folding metal tripod." There would also be a spare inner tube and tire, a lock for the motorcycle and spare straps should trouble strike and the bike have to be carted off by truck to the nearest mechanic. He concluded with the advice for new riders that motorcycle travel was "a rather new game" and that it included some risk. "Go light if you would go right," he affirmed.

———

Before leaving on his 1915 cross-country motorcycle adventure, Laing had met Dr. Francis Harper in Brooklyn. At this time Harper was already acquainted with Laing's writing for *Recreation* and *Outing*, and he admired Laing's abilities with a camera. Harper, who was an ornithologist who had worked for Percy Taverner on the Geodetic Survey of Canada as a naturalist in the Lake Athabasca-Slave Lake area, asked Laing to join him as "assistant bird man" on a return expedition to Lake Athabasca, where Harper would lead an ornithological expedition slated for 1916. The First World War would, however, put the expedition on hold when Laing and Harper enlisted in their respective country's armed forces. Laing would do his bit for King and Country, serving in the Royal Air Force as a gunnery instructor at Camp Beamsville in Ontario. He would receive his demobilization papers from the RAF in January 1919 after fourteen months' worth of service. But even before he received his papers, Laing's freelancer's brain was hard at work, and he continued to write for *Canadian Magazine*, *Sunset*, the Toronto *Globe* and the Manitoba *Free Press*.

The motorcycle would play an important role in gaining Laing his first post-war expedition. During his time in the RAF, Laing had become good friends with Gus Murchy of Princeton, British Columbia, and decided to join him on an expedition with Murchy's home community acting as their base. Laing had bought another Harley-Davidson, a J Model. He rode it from Vancouver to Hope, put the bike on a train to Princeton (as there was no Hope-Princeton Highway at this time), and disembarked, riding his motorcycle to join Murchy. Over a period of two weeks, Laing noted the bird and mammal life in and around the Similkameen Valley, submitting his observations to Francis Harper. Soon afterwards, Harper would let Laing know that the war-delayed Lake Athabasca expedition was going ahead and would happen in the summer of 1920 with a three-man team: Harper, Laing, and the English aristocrat ornithologist Lord William Percy.

The Lake Athabasca expedition, for the Smithsonian Institution, would depart with Harper, Laing, and a last-minute replacement for Percy, experienced bird specimen collector J. Alden "Pop" Loring.

Paddling two canoes north from Fort McMurray down the Athabasca River, the expedition would meet with some success although the report was never published. Laing wrote his own account of the expedition that he titled *Three Moniases Down North* (a "monias" was a Cree term meaning "Damned Fool White-Man"), followed by a strictly scientific account, co-authored with Harper, entitled *The Birds of Lake Athabasca*. Neither of these works was ever published. 1921 would prove to be a busy year, with Laing working for Percy Taverner in an assistant capacity in Saskatchewan on a National Museum expedition. He would work for Taverner for five more seasons.

Funded expeditions for museums were now becoming a big part of Laing's life. This provided a regular income, his travel expenses were paid for and he could accomplish his work as a museum naturalist during the summers while still maintaining his career as a writer during the winters. His days using the motorcycle, as a lone freelancer, had come to an end. Expedition travel would be done by Peterborough freight canoe instead of by Harley-Davidson motorcycle.

———

There is no doubt that Laing wrote his account of his 1915 cross-country journey to demonstrate his motorcyclist-naturalist's perspective in detail. But why, with all of Laing's savvy as a freelance writer, was the account he wrote over the winter of 1915–1916 never published? I would find the answer to this question in the Laing papers at the BC Archives when I lifted up the final page of Laing's manuscript. There I found two letters, replies to Laing from the Harley-Davidson Motor Company, sent to his parents' address at 1277 East 32nd Street, N., in Portland, Oregon, where Mack stayed for a time prior to his departure on a National Museum of Canada expedition to British Columbia.

The first letter, dated January 30, 1922, was sent from Los Angeles. It was from a Frank B. Rodger, who wrote in an apologetic tone. "You probably think me an awful duffer," he began, "not answering your letter of Nov. 21st sooner." After complimenting Laing on his adventures, he helpfully suggested that Laing forward his entire 148-page tome to a Walter E. Kleimenhagen, an advertising manager at Harley-Davidson. Rodger explained that "the expense of publishing your story probably was the deterrent," but he also very much encouraged Laing when he closed by saying that ". . . we wish to see your writings and in print too."

The second letter is the most kind, delicate and considerate rejection letter I have had cause to witness. It would seem Laing took Rodger's advice and wrote to Mr. Kleimenhagen, as the reply was from him and dated March 30th. "At the rate we have been replying to your recent communications," the advertising manager joked, "you must have concluded long ago you could cross the continent with old Betsy long before you heard from us." Once again, however, the response was negative. Kleimenhagen indicated that although the cross-country account was "a most interesting narrative," it was "too long for us to use in any of the literature we are getting out at this time." Ongoing cutbacks had reduced the size of their monthly *Enthusiast* magazine and had eliminated the possibility "to run your story in serial form." Then, writing much more like a salesman, he told Laing that he should not give up on Harley-Davidson: "We know you will have a pleasant surprise in store if you ever take a trip with one of our latest models."

Having to move on once he realized the account of his transcontinental motorcycle journey would not be published where he had hoped, Laing threw himself into the expedition season of 1922. It would be a memorable time for him. While taking on the duties of assistant ornithologist with the National Museum's British Columbia field party, he first met and worked with Allan Brooks. The meeting occurred during the first half of the expedition, which took place in the Okanagan Valley of British Columbia. Brooks was by then an influential ornithologist and famous bird painter. This meeting began a partnership between the two men that would last for decades. Laing held

Brooks in such high esteem that he would go on to write his biography during his retirement years: *Allan Brooks: Artist Naturalist*, published by the Provincial Museum of British Columbia in 1979.

The second half of the 1922 expedition would take place in Comox. The five-acre lot where Laing camped with Taverner and a summer student named Alan Sampson must have made a positive impression on Laing because he purchased it. In the meantime he continued to keep busy doing expedition work. In 1924, he accepted a job as naturalist on board the HMCS *Thiepval*, which was bound for Japan. His findings were published by the National Museum. He also signed on as naturalist with the Canadian Alpine Club's Mount Logan Expedition in 1925. Laing did not take part in the actual climb but stayed behind at the Chitina River in Alaska, collecting bird, mammal and plant specimens.

Amidst his expedition work, between the years of 1922 and 1927, he settled in Comox on the land he had purchased. Construction of his first Comox home was completed in 1923. Hamilton Mack Laing and Ethel Hart married on January 19, 1927. It was Ethel Laing who named their house and property "Baybrook," which was an amalgamation of the "Bay" of Comox Bay and the "brook" of Brooklyn Creek, which ran through the five-acre property Laing had bought.

After the end of the fieldwork season in October 1927, the newly married couple enjoyed a late honeymoon that would be the epitome of Laing's view on simplicity: they stayed for a week in a remote log cabin borrowed from a hunter and prospector at 12 Mile Creek near Princeton, British Columbia. Later settled in at Baybrook, the couple created a magnificent nut farm, grew vegetables and enjoyed the wonderful array of birdlife that also called Comox Bay home. Allan and Marjorie Brooks would be regular visitors to Baybrook. Mack and Ethel had a happy life for several years, fishing, hunting and developing their farm.

Laing's expedition career would be replaced by local specimen collection for various museums (including for the Canadian Museum of Nature, the Carnegie Museum of Natural History and the American

Museum of Natural History). At this time he was also writing a plethora of naturalist articles for newspapers and sporting magazines (including *Outdoor Life* and *Field & Stream*) and farming with his wife. He would also write several books, including *Baybrook: Life's Best Adventure, Rural Felicity and Romance of a Stump-Ranch*, to name a few that would describe his married life with Ethel on the farm in Comox. Unfortunately, their time together was not to last. Ethel Laing died in July 1944 after a battle with cancer.

Unable to live for long at Baybrook after his wife's death, Laing sold the house in 1949, then planned and built "Shakesides," named after the houses of John Burroughs and Ernest Thompson Seton in New York State, both of them called "Slabsides." In Comox he continued to write for a variety of magazines and eventually penned his biography of Brooks. Laing was mentor to many budding naturalists who travelled with him on local expeditions, and they later dropped by Shakesides to visit him and to see his meticulously kept collection of bird specimens.

—–∿∿–—

One of these budding naturalists was Gordon Olsen. Born in 1944, Olsen has lived in the town all his life. As a boy he noticed Laing strolling around town using a walking stick. Olsen remembers he would hear the clack-clack before he saw him, carrying a rucksack.

How Olsen met Laing would be especially apropos, given their mutual familiarity with motorcycles. At the age of fifteen, Olsen was riding a new Suzuki 80cc motorbike along the gravel road that was Comox Avenue. He next scooted alongside what is now known as Mack Laing Nature Park. Olsen was travelling close to Laing's land where Shakesides was built, but he was unsure where Laing's land began. Then he spotted Laing. Considering his proximity to Laing's property, Olsen thought he might be told he was trespassing. Olsen stopped his Suzuki motorcycle. Laing approached him, looked the machine over and told him he used to have a motorcycle, and began to tell him about his transcontinental journey.

Over the years, he and Laing developed a friendship, Laing inviting him to Shakesides "to see his collection of bird specimens kept meticulously in narrow drawers by species" as though catalogued in a museum's archives. Olsen especially remembers his many robins, all measured and tagged. He tells me of the approximately 650 articles Laing penned during his writing career. Regarding Laing's days as a motorcycle-naturalist, Olsen observes that the motorcycle "made it easy to get in to places." As a motorcyclist himself, Olsen tips his cap to Laing's adventurous spirit noting, that in the years he travelled on two wheels, today's road networks had yet to be built.

Loys Maingon, a long-time member of the Comox Valley Naturalists Society, has also been influenced by Laing. Maingon suggests that Laing began his career as a naturalist believing that the motorcycle would give him greater insights into the natural world, but once settled at Comox, Laing would become concerned over the long-term environmental effects of mechanization on a natural landscape he had grown to love. This life change would lead him to become British Columbia's first environmentalist.

There are hints in Laing's diaries and letters, not long after the time of his experience as a motorcyclist that would point to his eventual environmental concerns, which included the health of forest ecosystems and oceans. I can see that it really comes out full blown in his 1928 essay on marine pollution in the Strait of Georgia, and it is an issue that he will continue to write about throughout his life. Laing's growing need to help preserve the natural world also made him a welcome member of the Brotherhood of Venery. This was a group headed by Aldo Leopold, the influential American conservationist, environmentalist and author of *A Sand County Almanac*. The group included contemporaries of Laing, such as Percy Taverner and Hoyes Lloyd.

In the 1920s Laing also began to lament not just the savaging of the forests, but the impacts of fossil fuels on the environment. And he never drives again. He goes from being a great venison hunter to being a nut farmer, and ultimately a vegetarian.

In this sense, Laing's life, from his birth in rural Ontario to his upbringing in Manitoba, and ultimately, after much illustrious expedition travel, his settling down in Comox, is one of great catharsis and personal change. Maingon doesn't regard this as coincidental. He appreciates Laing as something of an innovator, "a man who sees the grandeur of the North American landscape from a Harley-Davidson and comes to experience the fullness of the tragic impact of the mechanized world on nature, long before the full blossoming of 1960's environmentalism."

―――

Hamilton Mack Laing died on February 15, 1982, at ninety-nine years of age, leaving both his land and Shakesides to the Town of Comox ". . . in trust, in perpetuity, for conservation and to encourage appreciation of nature." Instead, after Laing's death, the town of Comox rented out Shakesides for 32 years, putting the net proceeds into general revenue for the town when Laing had clearly willed his land and properties to Comox "for public enjoyment only." It now sits vacant, boarded up and covered in graffiti, in limbo, waiting for Laing's wishes to be fulfilled.

For the past four years, many of the citizens in the Comox Valley and from further afield have united to form the Mack Laing Heritage Society to foster Laing's wishes in his will to hold the property "in perpetuity for conservation." Although their project accords fully with Laing's wishes, they have had to fight against the town council of Comox whose mayor and councillors have strenuously worked to undermine the clear sense of Laing's will. In February 2015, the council voted unanimously to demolish both of Laing's homes, Baybrook and Shakesides.

Even when prestigious environmental organizations such as Heritage B.C., the National Trust of Canada and many others saw Mack Laing's first home of Baybrook as "irreplaceable," the town of Comox decided it wanted to have nothing to do with conserving the house for public use, and they had it demolished on August 6, 2015.

Laing's remaining home, Shakesides, was granted some more time when the Office of the Attorney General for British Columbia, as a "protector of trusts," intervened, and it was determined that Laing's remaining former home had clearly been willed to the people of Comox. Had it not been for that intervention, the town council would have demolished Shakesides along with Baybrook.

In July 2017, a legal battle ensued. The town council petitioned the Supreme Court of British Columbia, arguing for its right to tear down Shakesides. Whereas the town council has suggested the creation of a viewing platform on the property after Shakesides' demolition, the Mack Laing Heritage Society believes that preserving Shakesides and converting it into a nature house so that a new generation can gain the conservation values and love of nature Laing wished to pass along, would more honour Laing's wishes.

On October 16, 2018, the Mack Laing Heritage Society was for the first time given "intervenor status" by order of the Supreme Court of B.C. When the Society became represented by prestigious environmental lawyer Patrick Canning, it looked as though an expensive court battle was brewing. However, a new town council was elected soon after, which seemed better able to understand and agree with Laing's final wishes for Shakesides.

On February 6, 2019, all members of council, save Mayor Russ Arnott, voted in favour of giving out-of-court discussions a chance, postponing any court action for three months, allowing for all the interested parties to the Laing Trust, including the Mack Laing Heritage Society, to participate in face-to-face meetings so as to come to a compromise. The wind seems to have changed direction; perhaps Shakesides will be saved after all, due to the hard work of the Mack Laing Heritage Society, intent on honouring Laing's wishes.

When it comes to saving Shakesides, the Comox Valley Naturalists Society is clear about how Laing wanted his final standing home to be preserved, and to what end. The Society uses as a reference Laing's will: "Laing left over $65,000 in 1982, plus art and chattels, plus a house in excellent order." The Society points out that "$65,000 in 1982 is an equivalent of about $450,000 today. In 1982 you could buy a very nice house in Comox for $65,000. So the only question is: If one were to leave $450,000 today, plus a waterfront house and property, would it not be possible to run a community interpretive centre in it?" With such a Mack Laing nature house, Comox could become the envy of British Columbia.

—⁓—

My conversations with Laing's contemporary admirers are in the back of my mind as I stroll down the hill into Mack Laing Nature Park towards Laing's home, Shakesides, on a quiet day in January 2018. The carved wooden sign at the entrance displays a playful collage of a salmon leaping upstream, birds frolicking in the wind, and a stoic blue heron parked in the reeds, presumably waiting patiently for its next meal to swim by.

I encounter a few dog walkers on a narrow trail in this coniferous forest. A small wooden pedestrian bridge spans a trickling creek. I see several signs at this point. One denotes that this is a heritage walk, so identified by the Town of Comox. It is considered a "Comox Valley Heritage Experience." The next sign is much larger and further identifies the trail I'm about to walk as the Mack Laing Interpretive Trail.

"This park was donated to Comox by naturalist Hamilton Mack Laing," the sign begins. "Brooklyn Creek supports salmon and trout and the surrounding forest is home to many plants and animals." The sign further encourages walkers to stay on the trails, stay out of the creek, and "leave no waste (dog or other) in the park." A map shows a rectangular strip of land in beige, a squiggly trail line leading the eye to the baby blue of Comox Bay. At the trail's end is my destination: the last standing home of Hamilton Mack Laing.

Brooklyn Creek has a glassy appearance in the light of a dull, cloudy day, its waters meandering through the woods in the general direction of the houses of a quiet Comox neighbourhood visible through the thin collection of hemlock. The trail after the creek is rimmed with fern and sparse trees. It's a path similar to other paths

I've trodden in Vancouver Island regional parks: gravel, stones and drying mud well-tramped by local day-hikers. On either side of the narrow park are subdivisions, houses and parked vehicles, no doubt a different view from the time when Laing first started making a foundation for his second Comox home.

After a five-minute stroll it appears before me in a clearing: Shakesides. A cement foundation supports a shingled main floor where three windows, boarded up, appear. The shingled roof is heavily carpeted in moss. The building's foundation has been spray painted with graffiti. What I'm looking at is the rear of the house. But before I can walk around to the front of the house, facing what I can tell is a tantalizing unobstructed view of the bay, I'm distracted by a sign and a cairn to my right.

The sign explains who Mack Laing was. It mentions how, before he settled in Comox, Laing travelled across the United States on "a new-fangled infernal machine": a motorcycle. "Laing was a prolific writer and photographer," it goes on, describing his passion for natural history: "his articles appeared in almost every major North American outdoor nature magazine, and he contributed greatly to our understanding of bird species on the west coast of Canada." It mentions that Laing eventually sold the Baybrook Nut Orchard, "retaining four acres along Brooklyn Creek." This is where he built Shakesides, settling in on his own, in 1950.

Turning to the cairn, I see that it states that Laing, "was an ornithologist, artist and naturalist, whose life ended at Comox, on February 15, 1982. He remained independent and working to the last day of his ninety-nine years." There also appears a quote from Henry David Thoreau: "Simplify, don't waste the years struggling for things that are unimportant. Don't burden yourself with possessions. Keep your needs and wants simple, and enjoy what you have." It tellingly affirms how "he gave his home with this beautiful land to the Town of Comox, in trust, in perpetuity, for conservation and to encourage appreciation of nature."

As I make my way to a boardwalk at the front of the house, I gaze across the bay at the sumptuous view of the mountains of the Beaufort Range, blanketed in snow and low-lying cloud. In the bay, Goose Spit and the low-level structures of HMCS Quadra, a training facility of the Royal Canadian Navy, draw my eye next. Brambles and reeds cover the swampy expanse ahead, with large driftwood piles scattered throughout what would have been Laing's front yard.

To my left is the front of Laing's house, featuring a welcoming porch, despite its also being covered in layers of graffiti. I notice the main floor's boarded-up windows and front door, the two upper floor windows, also boarded up, looking out like sentries scanning the bay for possible predators.

Above me, three eagles play among the treetops. As I respectfully step up the eight stairs to Laing's porch, I notice the white banister looks freshly painted. I lean on the railing, look out at the bay and contemplate the view Laing enjoyed for decades. How often would he have reflected upon his adventures from this spot? Would he have remembered the rides he had with Barking Betsy and the birds he listened to when he turned off her barking and popping? What souvenirs of his expeditions would Laing have plucked from his memory and savoured in this glorious place of peace and solitude? I think of how I have held his diary from his transcontinental journey in my hand, and how it is I am now standing on his porch, admiring his long-held view of the world from his own vantage point.

When I return to the entrance of Mack Laing Nature Park, I straddle my BMW F 650 GS, pull on my gloves and strap on my helmet. As I pull away and ride along Comox Avenue, I hope that Shakesides will stand as a reminder of the importance of seeking out the unknown, enjoying the winding road and connecting with nature — more than a century after Laing's great transcontinental adventure.

Shakesides looks out at Comox Bay, June 11, 2019.
(COURTESY: TREVOR MARC HUGHES)

The carved wooden sign at the entrance to Mack Laing Nature Park,
Comox, B.C., June 11, 2019. (COURTESY: TREVOR MARC HUGHES)

A dedicated park bench next to a trail in Mack Laing Nature Park,
June 11, 2019. (COURTESY: TREVOR MARC HUGHES)

The mountains of the Beaufort Range and the structures
of HMCS Quadra are visible from Shakesides, June 11, 2019.
(COURTESY: TREVOR MARC HUGHES)

ACKNOWLEDGEMENTS

Marcia Turner at the Comox Archives & Museum Society was a great help in introducing me to photographs of Laing's journeys as well as some of his belongings in the archives held in Laing's hometown. Thank you also Gordon Olsen, Loys Maingon, Kris Neilsen and the Mack Laing Heritage Society for your insight into Laing's writings. Thanks also go to Frederike Verspoor and Diane Wardle at BC Archives. Frederike took it upon herself to find Laing's diaries, which was no easy feat. In fleshing out what model motorcycles Laing rode during his time as a motorcycle-naturalist, I'd like to thank motorcycle historian Terry Rea and Naomi Deildal, the manager of the Deeley Motorcycle Exhibition in Vancouver, in helping to identify the correct models and for answering my questions. Fellow motorcycle travel writer David G. Williams, someone who rides a Harley-Davidson motorcycle, helped me by lending a collection of books detailing the models created over the years. Thanks to my wife, Laura Sauve, for her support and patience as I revised, then revised again. Thanks also goes to Ronald Hatch of Ronsdale Press for agreeing to publish Laing's long-hidden story, and to Meagan Dyer for editing and organizing many files and Julie Cochrane for her wonderful layout and cover design. And last, but certainly not least, my thanks to Richard Mackie who, very kindly and generously, introduced me to Laing's writing.

NOTES

PAGES 7–8: "ABA cheques" — These were a type of traveller's cheque issued by the American Bankers Association. If stolen they would have been of no value without an endorsing signature from Laing.

PAGE 29: "Brother H.N. Baker and I exchanged stories of the road" — Laing would write in his 1915 nature diary about this traveller: "Brother of the Road leading a bicycle . . . also was headed for the Golden Gate. Mr. H.N. Baker and Mrs. B. were breaking out sandwiches and in the camaraderie of the road invite me to the party." H.M. Laing, "Nature Diary, 1914–1915," Meter 323, June 25, 1915 (original at BC Archives, file P2-DIA;1).

PAGE 41: "A 'stone' road here means macadam" — Of the variety of road surfaces Laing encountered, it would seem local description determined how he ultimately defined it. Here a road of macadam may mean one paved with broken stones or perhaps one that is gravel-paved.

PAGE 57: "King's jester of the Coleops" — No doubt this shortened reference to Coleoptera, the insect order to which beetles are part, was also made in jest.

PAGE 62: "Friend T. and H. had ridden from Milwaukee, Wisconsin. Friend G., a student at the University of Chicago was riding home to southern Oklahoma" — These riding companions were listed as follows: T. "Walter Tesch 3226 Highland Blvd, Milwaukee, Wis."; H. "Robert Hermann 778 27th St. Milwaukee"; G. "E.Z. Gregory, Lahoma, Oklahoma (new friend) a university student en route home." H.M Laing, "Nature Diary, 1914–1915," Meter 1394. July 2, 1915 (original at BC Archives, file P2-DIA;1).

PAGE 64: "At noon we parted: T. and H. were to take the road north of the Platte; G. and I were to follow the southern way." — At this point in Laing's manuscript an asterisk draws the eye to the bottom of the page where Laing has hand-written an addition to describe the fate of Tesch and Hermann: "We did not meet again. Next day after we parted T. was thrown in the ruts and his leg was broken. Thus H. was long delayed and reached Denver some time after we did." H.M Laing, "Nature Diary, 1914–1915," Meter 1489. July 3, 1915 (original at BC Archives, file P2-DIA;1).

PAGE 75: "Mr. S. . . . had been with Sherman on his devastating march to the sea in '64" — Laing had encountered a soldier present during General William Tecumseh Sherman's March to the Sea, a major 1864 military campaign where Union Army troops rose up and struck a decisive blow against the Confederacy.

PAGES 89–90: "blithe newcomer of the spring"; "blithe spirit"; and "light-winged dryad of the trees" — Laing offers this trio of quotes originating from poems of the ornithological variety to acknowledge, respectively, "To The Cuckoo" by William Wordsworth, "To a Skylark" by Percy Bysshe Shelley and "Ode to a Nightingale" by John Keats.

PAGE 101: "Still, as we were being escorted out over the Federal Boulevard by Mr. W." — Laing writes in his diary, "W.W. Whiling escorted us out to Federal Blvd. Speed (meter) 2200." H.M Laing, "Nature Diary, 1914–1915," Meter 2182. July 15, 1915 (original at BC Archives, file P2-DIA;1).

PAGE 119: "I had stumbled into the stamping ground of Mr. M., perhaps the pioneer of big game photographers in America." — Laing writes in his diary, "Met Monahan. He told of rattlers, elk, mule deer. I took pictures." H.M Laing, "Nature Diary, 1914–1915," Meter 2466. July 19, 1915 (original at BC Archives, file P2-DIA;1).

PAGE 130: "Mr. H. came along and made himself acquainted." — Laing writes of his alkali poisoning and Mr. H. in his diary, "J.T. Hayes of Vernal Commercial Club found me sitting on curb. . . . Hayes hauled me to doctor who gave me a lotion to cool down my crazy colon. Then Hayes took me to his home under poplars by a cool runnel and produced from an ice box a pint bottle of the finest milk I had tasted since I left the dairy farm on which I was raised in Manitoba!" H.M Laing, "Nature Diary, 1914–1915," Meter 2598. July 21, 1915 (original at BC Archives, file P2-DIA;1).

PAGE 147: "Today was noteworthy for the reason that we first met Tan. While we were occupying a goodly section of the outdoors roost provided by the House of H. for dust-begrimed itinerants of the road like ourselves" — At a Harley-Davidson dealership in Salt Lake City, Laing encountered Tan, "Smith M. Johnson of Middlefield, Ohio, a brother Harley rider. Just out of High School, he hankered for 2-wheeled adventure in a trip to the World's Fair in Frisco." H.M Laing, "Nature Diary, 1914–1915," Meter 2818. July 25, 1915 (original at BC Archives, file P2-DIA;1).

PAGE 185: "Mr. and Mrs. B. were on a walking tour; they had set out from Reno and intended to walk to southern California." — Laing writes in his diary of these newlyweds, "Shortly after we were halted, a half-ton dusted by. In the back was a big dog and a loaded dog-cart and we got a wave from our honey-mooning friends — now turned hitchhikers." H.M Laing, "Nature Diary, 1914–1915," Meter 3477. Aug. 4, 1915 (original at BC Archives, file P2-DIA;1).

PAGE 194: "I saw Tan and Frat turn into town . . . and spin off to westward." — Two days later, Laing would reunite with his brother Jim (Frat) and Smith Johnson (Tan), in San Francisco. In Laing's diary it reads: "At Harley Agency. Jim and Smith had beaten me in yesterday. Take glimpse at World's Fair in p.m. Wondrous illumination at night. Many visitors with light overcoats. Our army shirts felt thin." The entry for the next day, August 10th, has the three gathering again: "At Harley agency. See some city. Farewell to Smith. We will miss him." Laing and his brother would continue north to Oregon, departing August 11th. The diary entry for that day reads: "Off early on Lincoln Highway and ran fast. No punctures and made Sacramento at 11:30." H.M Laing, "Nature Diary, 1914–1915," Meter 3820. Aug. 9, 10, & 11, 1915 (original at BC Archives, file P2-DIA;1).

PAGE 206: "When I was young I had the ears of an owl." — Letter from Laing to Eileen Robertson, November 22, 1972, BC Archives.

PAGES 207–8: "An encounter in August 1915 . . ." — This information is found in Richard Mackie's biography, *Hamilton Mack Laing: Hunter-Naturalist* (Victoria, B.C., Sono Nis Press, 1985), pp. 61–62.

PAGES 209–10: "Laing had met Dr. Francis Harper in Brooklyn." — Mackie, pp. 59–62.

PAGE 211: "The first letter, dated January 30, 1922, was sent from Los Angeles." — Letter from Frank B. Rodger to Laing, January 30, 1922, B.C. Archives.

PAGE 212: "The second letter is the most kind, delicate and considerate rejection letter . . ." — Letter from Walter E. Kleimenhagen to Laing, March 30, 1922, B.C. Archives.

PAGE 213: For the naming of Laing's first home in Comox, "Baybrook," see Elizabeth Brooks, *The Pioneer Birdmen of Comox* (Comox, B.C., Comox Archives & Museum Society and Comox Valley Naturalists Society, 2006), pp. 12–15.

PAGE 213: "the newly married couple enjoyed a late honeymoon" — Mackie, p. 111.

FOR FURTHER READING

BOOKS

Brooks, Elizabeth. *The Pioneer Birdmen of Comox*. Comox, B.C.: Comox Archives & Museum Society; and Comox Valley Naturalists Society, 2006.

De Cet, Mirco. *Harley-Davidson: An Historical Snapshot*. Leicester, England: Abbeydale Press, 2007.

Laing, Hamilton M. *Allan Brooks: Artist Naturalist*. Victoria, B.C.: British Columbia Provincial Museum, 1979.

————. *Out with the Birds*. New York, N.Y.: Outing Publishing Company, 1913.

Mackie, Richard. *Hamilton Mack Laing: Hunter-Naturalist*. Victoria, B.C.: Sono Nis Press, 1985.

Middlehurst, Tony. *Harley-Davidson*. London, England: Bison Books Ltd., 1990.

Penn, Briony. *The Real Thing: The Natural History of Ian McTaggart Cowan*. Victoria, B.C.: Rocky Mountain Books, 2015.

Scott, Graham. *A Celebration of the Dream Machine: Graham Scott's Photo Essay about Harley-Davidson*. London, England: Hamlyn, 1991.

SELECTED MAGAZINE ARTICLES BY HAMILTON MACK LAING

Laing, Hamilton M. "A 'Been-There' Motorcyclists' Touring Outfit." *Recreation*, July 1916.

————. "Chugging about the Sound Country." *Sunset*, November 1916.

————. "Gipsying on a Motorcycle: How a Greenhorn Rode from New York to Winnipeg and Enjoyed the Whole Way." *Outing*, 1915.

————. "Human Touches of the Road." *Tall Timber*, June 1915.